Demon Barber

Lynn Barber

VIKING

VIKING

Published by the Penguin Group
Penguin Books Ltd, 27 Wrights Lane, London w 8 5 tz, England
Penguin Putnam Inc., 375 Hudson Street, New York, New York 10014, USA
Penguin Books Australia Ltd, Ringwood, Victoria, Australia
Penguin Books Canada Ltd, 10 Alcorn Avenue, Toronto, Ontario, Canada m 4 v 3 b 2
Penguin Books (NZ) Ltd, Private Bag 102902, NSMC, Auckland, New Zealand

Penguin Books Ltd, Registered Offices: Harmondsworth, Middlesex, England

First published 1998
10 9 8 7 6 5 4 3 2 1

Set in 11.75/14pt Monotype Garamond
Typeset by Rowland Phototypesetting Ltd, Bury St Edmunds, Suffolk
Printed in England by Clays Ltd, St Ives plc

A CIP catalogue record for this book is available from the British Library

ISBN 0-670-85354-2

For Rosie and Theo

Contents

Introduction

What is the *problem* with interviews? Why do people get so agitated about them? Why do they feel the need to buttonhole me at parties and blame me for the death of deference and the dumbing down of this Great Nation of Ours? I find that agreement followed by a swift admission that I also personally killed Princess Diana usually shuts them up, but what's it *about*? Of course it behoves journalists to be pariahs, but it is confusing to be pariah-fied for some crime you can't even identify.

I feel no guilt about being the sort of journalist I am because I feel no guilt about reading the sort of stuff I write. I don't just mean my stuff – I mean all celebrity interviews. I am not ashamed of being nosey and am rather suspicious of people who claim to have no curiosity about their fellow humans. When forced into a corner, I can make a quasi-serious case for the value of newspaper interviews as a way of celebrating the individual and discussing aspects of personal life that would otherwise be dumped in the ghetto of the women's pages. But actually the only good reason for reading celebrity interviews (or writing them) is for entertainment.

Is it fair that the entertainment sometimes entails duffing interviewees up? Nobody is forced to give an interview: I don't doorstep anyone or pester them; I put in a request and accept the answer, yes or no. Moreover, the people I interview are not novices. They know the media game and have usually benefited from it for most of their careers. They don't give interviews out of the kindness of their hearts – they are usually trying to plug whatever new film or book or record they are launching. The wisest among them count the column inches and recognize that four pages in a national newspaper is certainly big publicity, whether favourable or not.

And of course I don't always demonize them – in fact, as you'll see in this book, I very rarely do. My reputation as the Demon Barber is a mystery to me – I think I bend over backwards to be fair. It's true I ask very blunt questions, but that's really just in order to save time. Recently I noticed that Lesley White of the *Sunday Times* asked Harriet Harman, 'Would you call yourself an intellectual?' whereas I asked, 'Are you thick?' It comes to the same thing, though my question sounds ruder than hers. But often a rude question serves the interviewee well, by putting them on their mettle – too bad it didn't work in Harman's case. I always *aim* to be fair, and also accurate. No one has ever accused me of misquoting them and they wouldn't get very far if they tried – I keep the tapes. Also – though it's probably foolish to advertise this – I lay off anything that could damage anyone's marriage or children.

Everyone always tells me off for interviewing stars – why don't I interview 'real' people? They always know a fishmonger in Kensal Rise who is a million times more interesting than Rupert Everett. Well, fine – but who would *read* it? I once made the mistake, on the *Sunday Express* magazine, of including a 'real person' (a postman, and yes, he was fascinating) in the interminable series I did called 'Things I Wish I'd Known at 18'. All it produced was a lot of letters from readers saying they were far more interesting than this postman and why didn't I interview *them*? Of course it's possible to do good real-people interviews, but it's not my job, it's not my skill, and quite frankly I prefer stars.

Secretly, I admire stars, though I don't let it show much on the page. I like the fact that they are genuine meritocrats, they often come from disadvantaged or damaged backgrounds, they are frequently a bit weird and they have done something that makes them stand out from the crowd. I don't believe people become stars by accident – they must have some special drive that makes them try harder, take bigger risks, put up with more rejection. It is *difficult* to be a star; it is not an easy option in life to leave the safe haven of mediocrity, to be constantly observed, to know that you are envied, to know that there will be people rooting for your downfall, to know that you have to maintain the high or face public humiliation. It's a truism that Americans are much more kindly disposed towards success than we are, but the corollary is that they run a mile at the first whiff of failure. It must be really terrifying to be a star in the States.

Secondly, fame itself is interesting, both in its effect on the possessor and on other people. Famous people are forced to be self-conscious because they know they are observed all the time. The man in the newsagent will tell his wife, 'You'll never guess who was in the shop today,' and then he'll recount every detail of the famous one's appearance, speech and money-tendering technique. (Of course I am using fame rather loosely, in its crassest media sense – almost anyone who appears on television counts as 'famous', whereas some of our greatest living painters and authors can walk unnoticed down the street.) Most people go a bit crazy when they first become famous, especially if it happens suddenly, but even those who are used to fame still have the problem that their fame affects other people and makes *them* behave oddly.

Even me. I thought after fifteen years in this game I'd become completely inured to fame, but I recently had a *very* chastening experience with Jarvis Cocker. I'm always a bit fluttery with pop stars anyway – for me, they are the real stars, far more than film stars – and with Jarvis I went completely loopy. I think it was because he came to my house. Jarvis's PR wanted us to meet somewhere 'ordinary' – he suggested a greasy spoon caff in Islington – and I just couldn't face it. It might be ordinary for Jarvis, but it's certainly not for me. So after a lot of to-ing and fro-ing, I said, 'Well, if Jarvis won't let me come to his house, he'd better come to mine,' and, rather surprisingly, he agreed.

But it was a mistake. As I whirled around the sitting room, hiding the more embarrassing family photographs, wondering whether I should arrange the CDs in some faintly plausible order or remove the whole pathetic lot of them, I suddenly realized with a gasp of horror that I was behaving exactly like a *fan*. Of course I *am* a fan of Jarvis Cocker's – I do very much admire Pulp's lyrics – but it is totally incompatible with being an interviewer. You can't be both – you can't *afford* to be.

Here I was with my heart going pitter-pat, reliving some hideous fantasy from my teens whereby John Lennon would turn up at my house and recognize me immediately as the one woman who could understand him. Frankly, I was demented. And when Jarvis arrived, I did the naffest thing you can possibly do as a journalist which was to demand to have my photo taken with him.

But that experience made me think: why can't you be a fan? Why *not* be starstruck? I don't know – but you can't be if you want to be a good interviewer, because your job is to cut through all that dazzle and distance of stardom and meet as equals. Why? Is it just a reductionist motive – as stars often complain it is – to minimize their achievements, to 'cut them down to size'? I don't think so: I think it has something to do with not wanting to diminish the reader. Inevitably, the stance you adopt as a writer is the one you put your readers in, and if you grovel, then the reader is forced to grovel too.

An interview can be admiring but not adoring. It can be affectionate, but not infatuated. I'm quite pleased when people accuse me of contributing to the death of deference – who wants deference anyway? (Politicians, is the answer.) Deference is not the same as respect – respect is fine, although it's not particularly helpful in interviews. I've occasionally felt a twinge of 'Who am I to *dare* to ask these impertinent questions?' but I have banished it immediately because if you don't ask the questions, you don't get the answers.

Much has been written about the supposed ethical dilemma of the interview – the American journalist Janet Malcolm wrote a whole book about it called *The Journalist and the Murderer*. She sees interviewing as an intrinsically dishonest transaction, in which the interviewer falsely befriends the interviewee and then betrays them. I honestly don't even recognize what she's talking about. As long as interviewer and interviewee are both clear that this *is* an interview, conducted for the eventual benefit of readers, and that they are not meeting in order to forge a friendship, where is the betrayal? I'm quite shocked that so much attention should be focused on the interviewer–interviewee relationship as though it were of prime importance. What about the readers? Surely they matter more? It is betraying *them* if you omit certain facts, or fudge certain questions, in order to ingratiate yourself with the interviewee. And after all, the readers are the only reason you're there.

Janet Malcolm's book came about because she was accused – justifi-ably – of 'doctoring' quotes to the point where they meant something completely different to, even the opposite of, what was intended. Obviously that *does* create a moral dilemma, rather a serious one, and no amount of breast-beating after the event will solve it. But this problem could be avoided if both interviewers and interviewees used tape recorders. I wish this were standard practice – I'm fed up with interviewees telling me, 'Don't trust anything you read in the cuttings,' which is a terrible slur on my profession.

I don't believe there is any ethical problem about interviewing, but I think there can be a behavioural one for some beginner journalists (and presumably for Janet Malcolm), simply because they're confused about what they're doing. They want to be liked, they want to make an impression and find common ground with the interviewee. Which means they want the interview to be a conversation, a dialogue, the start of a beautiful friendship. But then the subject isn't quite as friendly as they hoped, so they go away and bitch about them. I was on the receiving end of some of these 'friendly' interviewers when my first book, *Mostly Men*, came out, and they gave me the creeps. They would babble away about their own tacky private lives, in the hope of eliciting some similar 'sisterly' confessions from me (they were always women), and I would find myself growing increasingly frosty and uttering amazing lies in Lady Bracknellish tones – 'I am glad to say that I have never even been *tempted* to get drunk at parties.' Ha!

The friendly approach might work with absolute beginners, but most famous people have enough experience of being interviewed to know not to fall for it. I always tell baby journalists: you don't have to make friends, you don't have to express opinions, you only have to ask questions. And yes, it does entail a suspension of ego, and sometimes the need to bite your tongue, but you can let your ego off the leash when you come to write the article. As long as you remember that you are there on behalf of the readers, then all these *soi-disant* dilemmas about your 'relationship' with the interviewee disappear.

I once made the huge mistake of comparing interviews to one-night stands. What I *meant* was that you meet as strangers, and hope to proceed to intimacy in an indecently short space of time – and then you revert to being strangers when you meet again. But of course I unwittingly contributed to the popular fantasy that there is some sort of sexual subtext. It used to be a rule in newspaper offices that you always sent the prettiest girl to do interviews because she could unleash the floodgates of confession merely by batting her eyelashes. Did it ever work? Maybe – interviews used to be such crap anyway. But I am walking disproof of the sexual chemistry idea because I was a lousy interviewer when I was young and pretty and became a good one only when I passed forty.

Anyway, you don't *need* sexual chemistry, when the chemistry of taking an intense, informed interest in someone is so potent. There are very few people in the world who can resist the opportunity to talk about themselves at length to someone who seems genuinely, deeply interested and who has obviously thought about (i.e., read up) their life beforehand. Even their friends and loved ones probably don't give them such a concentrated dose of attention, don't hang on their every word to the same extent. I often feel that I can 'will' people into being interesting, merely by being interested myself.

The interest doesn't have to be feigned either. Before an interview, I will have read lots of cuttings about the person, watched their films or read their books, studied their photograph, wondered what they were like as a child, what they had for breakfast, who has phoned them this morning. By the time I meet them, I will be almost throbbing with curiosity, and full of mad theories about what made them what they are (most of which will get shot down in flames in the course of the interview). I think I am quite unusually nosey anyway, but there is nothing like the knowledge that you have to write three and a half thousand words about this person to give you a burning determination to find them fascinating. That's really all I ask of interviewees – be as rude, difficult, vain, self-obsessed as you like, but please *please* don't be boring.

What is the point of interviews? Entertainment, first and last, so if you don't enjoy reading them, for heaven's sake don't bother. Journalists are always supposed to pretend their work contains some necessary information, but, honestly, there is nothing in these pages that you *need* to know. I hope the interviews I've chosen present a broad range of characters and careers, but mainly they're just the ones I enjoyed writing. Most of them come from the *Observer*, but there are a few older ones from the *Telegraph Magazine* and one from the *Independent on Sunday*. Consequently, I should like to thank the editors of those publications – Will Hutton, Emma Soames, Stephen Fay – for giving me permission to reproduce them. My warmest thanks go to my colleagues at the *Observer*, especially Jocelyn Targett, Justine Picardie and Stephanie Dennison, for putting up with my tantrums. Thanks too to Juliet Annan of Viking, to Gill Coleridge my agent, and to dear Mrs Tasiemka whose cuttings library is a constant joy. I often think I have one of the jammiest jobs in the world, and these are the people who make it so.

Eddie Izzard

5 October 1997

When I used to work for *Penthouse* magazine, one of my duties was 'researching the parameters of sexuality' which meant interviewing people with unusual sexual tastes. Most of them were fascinating but I always sighed when it was time for a transvestite, they were so preternaturally boring. Married, middle-aged, with tidy suburban homes and safe white-collar jobs, they would show me their drab array of frocks and aprons and tell me how thrilling it was to wear them. It seemed about as thrilling as ironing – and, indeed, they tended to enthuse about ironing, too.

So I have always had great difficulty getting my brain round the idea that Eddie Izzard can be so brilliantly funny and original, while being a transvestite. In fact, I thought maybe he was making it up – especially when I saw him on a flight to Edinburgh the other day, looking entirely masculine. This was also true when I met him this time, apart from his long, manicured (but unpainted) nails and some highlights in his hair. His manner is ultra-straight, too: there is absolutely nothing camp about him, though perhaps his honesty in discussing emotional subjects is unusual in a man. But anyway, he *is* a transvestite – though now I am totally confused about what that means.

We met in his office in Soho, which is packed with groovy je-suis-un-rock-star toys – inflatable furniture, revolving lamps, a lip-shaped telephone, arty porn books and a packet of giant Rizla papers posed carefully beside the silver ashtray. I bet he summoned a designer one day and said, 'Do it trendy.' When I asked what his house in Notting Hill Gate is like, he said he hadn't done it up yet (he bought it eighteen months ago) but he wanted it to be 'kind of cottagey but twisted, with lots of *trompe l'oeil*, reverse clocks, sort of Heath Robinson or *Alice Through the Looking Glass* effects.' Obviously, being a transvestite does not include the traditional feminine home-making skills.

He tells me he has done a lot of po-faced interviews lately because people tend to ask him serious questions and then he answers them seriously. (He recently gave an interview to the *Evening Standard* entirely about his pro-European political views.) So he says this time he should 'talk more rubbish'. Fine – I could listen to his rubbish all day. We both keep saying, 'This interview mustn't be all about transvestism,' 'Oh no, it mustn't be all about transvestism,' but neither of us can *wait* to get on to the subject, and in the end it is he who broaches it. But first we must do the statutory plug . . .

He is doing a new stand-up show called *Glorious*, starting in New York and Paris, coming to London in late October, then touring the regions. There will also be a video of the show released in time for Christmas. He describes the concept as 'kind of a Fall of the Roman Empire when the Huns were about to come in, or like *Ozymandias* (that poem by, is it Shelley?) like a dying planet type thing. And I'm talking about the creation of the world, and the Grim Reaper, but there's also stuff on toasters and lawnmowers and modern computer equipment.' In other words, the typical coherent Izzard mix.

Nothing is scripted, often a quarter of the show is improvised and it evolves night by night so that the end of a tour bears little relation to the beginning. He calls it 'molten material' and likes the adrenaline rush of walking on stage with no idea what he'll say. Audiences tend to assume that his bizarre mental jumps are drug-induced and he says he doesn't mind if they do assume that, but actually he can't perform on drugs and just gets terribly boring if he tries. He thinks, rather, that the mental leaps are connected with his dyslexia – he is a poor reader – and the sort of sideways logic that decrees that *obviously* elephants are good at skiing because they have more momentum. I can't begin to describe Izzard's humour and, since he refuses to do his stand-up act on television, you will either have to see him live or buy the video. (Good plug!)

He is thirty-five, but comparatively new to fame – it took him ages to arrive. A middle-class boy from a minor public school, he discovered his gift for stand-up while he was reading accountancy at Sheffield University and dropped out after one year to take his show to Edinburgh. 'In 1981 I was raring to go, I had the energy, I could work hard and I felt I could make people laugh. But nothing happened really till 1993, and it was a pain having to survive all that. I was always thinking, "Well, maybe next month . . .", but for years and years nothing happened. You just think you're mad, but you hold on to this idea in your head. Most people kill it and go and work for the council or something, but I didn't. But I was so long out in the cold.' He made a patchy living as a street entertainer, while taking any stand-up gigs he could get. The first glimmer of success came at the 1991 Edinburgh Festival when he was nominated for the Perrier Award. Then, in 1993, he brought his show to the West End, and won the British Comedy Award for Top Stand-up Comedian. (The video of that show, *Live at the Ambassadors*, reveals a strangely chubby, blokeish Izzard, dressed in sports jacket and Hush Puppies, though with a little flash of ruby varnish on his nails.) Since then, he has piled success on success, with a 'world tour' including New York, Paris and Amsterdam and two bestselling videos, *Unrepeatable* and *Definite Article*. Last year, he won another British Comedy Award and a New York Drama Desk Award for Best Solo Artist.

He has explained his urge to perform very simply: 'My mum died when I was six and she was a very affectionate mother. When that happens, an individual seeks to replace the affection that has been lost. The audience has become that for me . . . So I think it's quite a healthy way of dealing with an emotional problem.' It also accounts for the irresistible charm of his act. He *basks* in the audience, apparently totally secure in their love.

The trauma of his mother's death goes very deep – his video company is called Ella Communications after her. She knew she was dying (of bowel cancer), so Eddie and his older brother, Mark, were suddenly dispatched to boarding school when they were six and eight respectively – unfortunately, a Dickensian school which rang to the thwack of the cane – and it was there that they heard the news of their mother's death. Eddie claims he cried solidly for a year. His teacher once recalled,

'He was a very timid little boy and obviously completely lost without his mother. His brother was very protective of Eddie. They both just seemed very lonely.' The next year, their father (who worked as a top accountant, ultimately chief auditor, for BP) moved to Bexhill, where he had relatives, and switched them to a nicer boarding school nearby, but they were still a very shattered family. The boys said they wanted a stepmother and Mr Izzard tried hard to find one, putting out ads and going to dating agencies, but it was seven years before he remarried. When he finally introduced the boys to their prospective stepmother, they took her round the garden and told her all about their mother.

At the age of eleven, Eddie decided to stop crying. 'How to survive boarding school. Do not express emotion, do not feel emotion, do not have emotion. If someone hits you, hit them back; if someone argues with you, argue back – never give an inch, never look vulnerable and you will survive. I stopped crying after I lost this fight with another kid and I fell over and cried, and therefore I'd lost. And I thought, "Oo, mustn't do that, because it makes you a loser."' He almost deliberately started crying again at nineteen, when he saw a cat being run over and couldn't think how to react. Nowadays, he cries quite readily, especially at any mention of his mother's death. He says he must 'do analysis' on it one day, because he knows 'there's still a lot of emotion in there that's got nowhere to go. It doesn't really get better, you just don't think about it so much.'

He does not believe that his transvestism has anything to do with the loss of his mother. Her clothes disappeared from the house when she died, and he has no memory of them. He recalls that before she died, when he was about four, he heard of a boy dressing up as a girl and thought, 'Oo! That sounds nice!' He believes he was born a transvestite. 'It isn't a whim. It is a built-in urge.'

Many people assume that he's gay but he is perfectly clear that he's not. 'I'd be very happy to be, but I don't fancy men at all. I'd be up for it, but I haven't seen one I fancied.' And, in fact, he has had quite long relationships with women, one lasting four years, though he is unattached now. He says that, far from women being put off by his transvestism, they tend to say, 'Could you wear a skirt tomorrow?'

He claims he can't remember when he first dressed up (I bet he can really), but by his teens he was using his stepmother's make-up and also shoplifting make-up – once he was caught, but let off with a warning. He wore women's clothes when he could, but 'I didn't have much access to clothes. I tried to get girls' roles in plays . . . It's quite difficult to work out how to start, how to do it. And you're just trying to repress all that. It wasn't until I came out . . . And then I did and I bought some bad clothes – because you have to go through your frumpy transvestite stage, where you buy things out of a catalogue.' Was he fancying girls at the same time? 'Yes. All the time.' And wondering how to deal with it? 'Yes. I thought basically I'd just not have to tell anyone ever. It would just be some sort of big dark secret.'

As an accountancy student at Sheffield University, he was so worried that he went twice to his GP who promised to refer him to a psychiatrist, but the appointment never came. Then, when he was twenty-one, he thought, 'I've got to come out with it,' so he told an old girlfriend and she was fine. Then he told his brother a year or two later, and he was fine, too. And at twenty-three, he found a transvestite support group in London and was able to come out in public.

He also learned, early on, to face his attackers. Once he was followed down the street at night by a gang of kids asking, 'Hey, man – why are you dressed as a girl?' and instead of panicking, he turned round and said, 'All right – I'll tell you,' and they all ran away. 'Which just shows that, if you confront it, people will back off.' This has always been his way of dealing with 'remarks' ever since – though recently his opponent didn't back off but swung a punch and Izzard floored him and took him to court successfully.

He didn't bite the final bullet – telling his father – till he was twenty-nine. They had gone to a football match together, as they often do, and it was in a greasy spoon café afterwards that Eddie broke the news. John Izzard's reaction (as recounted to the *Daily Express*) was everything he must have hoped: 'I can't say I was best pleased. But then, what really was there to be displeased about? I looked at Eddie and realized, "He is my son, I love him, and this is who he is." There are so many worse things he could be.'

But what actually *is* a transvestite? It seems almost meaningless today, when most women wear trousers and many men dye their hair. Whatever taboo was meant to be broken barely exists any more. But Izzard explains that clothes are really a minor part of it – what it is really about is *identifying* with women, while also being attracted to them, and rejecting all the givens of masculinity. It sounds almost more like transsexism – would he really like to be a woman? 'I'd be quite happy to be a woman. But I seem to have this very blokey body. If I had more of a Sharon Stone body, then I wouldn't bother with clothes and make-up so much because they're more external things, and if I *was* a woman, then I wouldn't need to act like that in order to realign this very male exterior which means you get treated by society in a certain way. And the reason why people end up with these exterior interests in clothes and make-up is that that is all that's really *there* if you have that body – everyone is going to say you're a bloke, and everything you do is supposed to be in the confines of a bloke, and that's too constricting and really boring.'

The analogy he favours, and keeps coming back to, is that he is like a teenage tomboy – a girl who plays football and climbs trees but also likes wearing make-up – though I find this pretty unrealistic. But he has to somehow square his own love of football with his passion for dressing up, and he can only do this by comparing himself to *teenage* girls, presumably virgins. Because if he thought on, about what women of his age (thirty-five) are interested in, he would come to marriage and motherhood which would be difficult.

He says he's never read a book on transvestism, though he's often been given them. I told him I used to read them at *Penthouse*, but they were decades out of date. Still, he was interested, and asked what they said. I was a bit nervous of telling him – they bracketed transvestites with fetishists, as people who would find their greatest sexual fulfilment in masturbation. Izzard was obviously familiar with the theory but said, 'People get hung up on this idea of clothes and make-up and men getting turned on and the role of masturbation and lalala. But they've got to remember that these are male lesbians. And we know from gays and lesbians, especially gays, that men fancy men, but they also like their own bodies. They like their own look, and they like that look in other men, which is why there's a lot of very similar looks going round. So you have to understand that these male lesbians wear make-up and whatever, because they can create a look that they're actually attracted to. And therefore it can be an arousing thing.'

This seems to confirm the theory rather than deny it. But there are signs that he is moving on – he says his interest in dressing up has lessened over the years because now he can get any clothes he wants. 'It's much more humdrum. Like with teenage girls – when they can buy all the make-up they want to buy, and wear all the heels and skirts, they start saying, "Do I have to do this every day? What a shag!" So you can dress up and get sexy on occasions, but you're not going to do it every day.' And whereas in the past he used to feel different when he was wearing women's clothes, now, 'I'm trying to centre myself more and not have this difference between the way I talk, the way I behave. I don't change my voice. I don't become camp – there isn't a difference.'

He has described himself as 'a lesbian trapped in a man's body' and explains this is not a joke: 'That is the easiest way to look at it. I'm not really "trapped" in a man's body – I'm happily cohabiting, but I'm a male lesbian.' In other words, he feels like a woman, but a woman who is attracted to other women. I'd sort of taken this on board, or thought I had, when he explained that he meant not just any women – he was attracted to *lesbians*. Aagh! So now it becomes transcendentally complicated – he wants a relationship with someone who by definition doesn't want a relationship with him because he is a man. Perhaps he just wants a platonic relationship – when I asked what he and a lesbian would do in bed, he was uncharacteristically vague. 'Well, who knows? Who knows?'

Hadn't he ever tried it? 'Er . . . have I? No, I don't think I've ever had sex with anyone who is a decided lesbian and not bisexual at all. Yes, it is kind of confusing, but if you think about it, ordinary sex is quite confusing. I mean, all completely straight sex is horrendous and confusing to someone who is not into sex at all, who is totally blocked in that area . . .'

So when he says, as he often does, that he would like to marry and have children one day, there is something a bit never-never about it, as I might say I would like to climb Everest. I notice that his father, when interviewed by the *Daily Express*, said he wasn't the sort of father who longed for grandchildren – *he* seemed to assume that Eddie would remain childless. Eddie always responds to questions about parenthood with a stock joke, 'I'd be the ultimate one-parent family!' but when I ask why he couldn't be part of a two-parent family, he gets a bit flustered. 'Oh, I could be . . . Nothing stops me having kids and I think I probably will . . . I might adopt, though . . . but I'm not looking for kids at the moment. I've got my main drive. At the moment, I'm too busy trying to get America and trying to get Europe, and it would be a hellish life for a kid. I think my thirties are going to be very busy – they have been so far. I'm trying to make up for my twenties, which were just crap.'

He is a 'strategy nut' who plans his career carefully. He has always refused offers of his own television series, and he doesn't do the telly ads and conference gigs that provide most comedians' bread and butter. What he wants is to find new audiences in Europe and America. He is performing again in Paris (in French) this autumn and planning a six-month off-Broadway season next year – an enormous gamble, given that he won't break even for five months. He also wants to pursue a film career as a straight actor, and keeps going to auditions where inevitably someone says, 'But you're a comedian,' and he explains that, yes, but he wants to do straight roles. He believes he can play weirdos and 'shitheady parts' because there seems to be some sort of link between comedy and psychotics – he admires the way Woody Harrelson went from *Cheers* to *Natural Born Killers*. He has three films in the pipeline: Conrad's *The Secret Agent*, *The Velvet Goldmine* (with Ewan McGregor) and *The Avengers*, in which he plays Sean Connery's sidekick and gets to fight with Uma Thurman. (He wears gloves in the film, but one day he took them off and Connery noticed his nail varnish and did a double take. 'He was cool about it. But we didn't have big chats about sexuality!') He is working very hard indeed to make up for all the lost time in his twenties when he was 'ready' but nobody wanted him. Given the strength of his ambition, he is bound to succeed.

He is probably the weirdest person I have ever interviewed, but he doesn't *feel* weird at all, he feels eminently sane. He knows exactly who he is, what he wants: he is ambitious but realistic and very determined. But perhaps a little joyless, a little *too* controlled – he admits he is a control freak and deliberately keeps a rein on his emotions. 'I don't get very morose, but I also don't get very ecstatic. It's a sort of safety device, probably because I was so morose when I was a kid, I never want to go back there. Perhaps I should get more elated but I worry about it because I think it's all going to disappear, and I don't want to go too down because it's just so horrible to feel that. So I just put a compressor on my emotions. This is why I want to do more straight acting, because there's a lot of anger and a lot of sadness inside me that I'd like to bring out in roles.'

The anger, of course, dates from his mother's death: 'There is a distinct anger about that. Why the hell did my mother disappear when I was six? Why did Hitler stick around? Why did *he* live longer than my mother? But . . . shit happens, shit happens. There is no answer.'

He apologizes at the end for talking about his transvestism so much: 'But I only talk about it to journalists, actually, so I find myself banging on and on.' And although he doesn't want to proselytize, he thinks it might help other transvestites to come out. What he wants is a situation where men can go to work in skirt-suits and make-up if they want to – he realizes it's much easier for him, working in showbiz, than for someone in a conventional job – and not be marginalized. He is proud of the fact that he was invited to Tony Blair's first party at No. 10 and went wearing make-up. 'I am my own positive role model. I do this for me, and if anyone else gets anything positive out of it, that's great. I'm not flag-waving and trying to get transvestites marching down the street; that's not going to happen. But if you push through and you deal with your sexuality, and you come out and are open about it, you get this confidence from having done it, and it means you can *create* things. Because the people who have gone through it and come out, they *have* to have been brave to do it, so they will take more risks, creative risks, and people think, "Wow, that's great!"'

Reproduced by permission of *The Observer*.

Alan Clark

17 December 1994

It was flattering that Alan Clark said that he would enjoy being interviewed by me. But a couple of days later he rather spoiled the effect by asking, 'What's the fee?' I told him I was not a practitioner of chequebook journalism. 'Just a case of good wine then?' Certainly not – especially when he said in his *Diaries* that nowadays good claret costs £100 a bottle. 'There has to be something in it for me,' he said plaintively. This from a man who owns a £12 million art collection, a moated castle, a 27,000-acre estate in Scotland, a set in Albany, a chalet in Gstaad and whose worth was recently estimated by *Business Age* at £33 million.

In the end – it was like negotiating peace in Northern Ireland – we arrived at the formula that I should take him wine (Puligny-Montrachet, he suggested) to the value of the lunch I would have bought him (Claridge's, he suggested) if we'd done the interview in London. Having agreed all this he then explained blandly that in fact he wouldn't be giving me lunch because he didn't believe in lunch, but he would give me wine – though not the wine I brought down.

It is worth remembering that while he is an ex-Tory minister, Privy Councillor, and son of *Civilisation*, he also once worked in the used car trade. It was the used car dealer who conducted these negotiations. He admits to being mean enough to drive miles in search of cheap petrol and to send most of his mail second class. No wonder Josephine

Harkess (of 'Coven' fame) described him as 'one of the meanest men I have ever met'.

But once I was there it was fine – or fine*ish*, as he would say. He collected me from the station and drove me to his home, Saltwood Castle, an ugly Victorian filling in a decayed Norman tooth, poorly sited in Kent commuter country. His father bought it, and it slightly makes one question the taste of the man who made the classic television series, *Civilisation* – as do the countless dreadful portraits of Lord Clark scattered around the house. Mr Clark gave me a guided tour, then we went to the room he calls 'my father's study', where a chilled bottle of wine and a plate of assorted fancy biscuits constituted lunch. There was no sign of Mrs Clark, though she did appear just as I was leaving, looking girlish as always.

Alan Clark, as devotees of his *Diaries* will know, worries constantly about his appearance, in particular his jowls, so I had better say quickly that the jowls are bearing up well, and he still looks at least fifteen years younger than his real age, sixty-six. He kept standing sideways-on in front of the window so that I could admire his slim waist and boyish figure, though I could never take my eyes off his skull, which is *such* an extraordinary shape, going back for miles, like a slice of Cheddar; it almost makes you believe in phrenology: behold a totally weird man with a totally weird-shaped head.

I asked him what *exactly* was the problem with his jowls, and he explained that, 'They thicken up, you see. I suppose it's something to do with the lymphatic system.' He would have plastic surgery if he believed it would work but he doesn't and anyway, 'That's cheating, you see. The real point is to *keep* things, keep age at bay by your own genetic and hormonal strength.' I asked if he had tried slapping his chin like this (I demonstrated) to keep the jowls in order and he said he hadn't but, 'That's an interesting transitional phase. If there were anything you could do yourself that would help your own metabolism or whatever, then I think you should do it.' He has a great belief in the almost supernatural power of testosterone. At one point in the *Diaries* he muses about why he has been so foul to Jane, his wife, and concludes, 'Hormones, I suppose.'

I hoped to find him preparing the next volume of his diaries for publication, but he shocked me rigid by saying he was writing a history of the Conservative Party from 1922 to 1990. Oh come on, give us a break, who needs it? It would be absolutely tragic if our greatest living diarist got bogged down in some turgid tome. Luckily he is still keeping his diary, not every day but when something catches his attention, as he has done since 1955. He writes in a crabbed italic hand which, he says, gets noticeably smaller when he is embarrassed or ashamed, i.e. often.

His agent and publishers, not to mention his fans, are waiting breathlessly for the next volume but he says they will wait in vain. Why? 'Oh because everyone will say they're a disaster. There's a queue from here to Sandling of people who want to get even or to retract the praise they lavished on the first book – "Disappointing", "Can't keep it up", all that.' Poor sensitive flower. This is not the Alan Clark we know and love – why on earth should he care what a lot of lit crit whingers think? But he obviously *does* care – he is proud of the reviews he got for his first volume.

However, *nil desperandum*, because he then started asking which bit of the diaries he should publish next – whether a 'prequel' covering the years before the first volume, or a sequel, covering the years after Mrs Thatcher's departure. His publishers prefer the latter because it would include the Matrix Churchill trial, the Scott Inquiry, the fuss when the first volume was published and a brief marital crisis when Jane ran away. 'But that's almost *actualité*, you see, bringing you right up to the present time, and funnily enough, the exposure of a diary entry that is very recent is much more embarrassing than something historic.' I said he should run the full diaries from start to finish (the published version only represents about a fifth of the original), and he looked pleased. Would Jane be pleased though? He is known to have excised at least one major love affair in deference to her feelings.

He maintains – amazingly – that there is no sex in the *Diaries*, or at any rate no descriptions. No sex? But if you compared his memoirs with, say, Lord Howe's, you would notice a difference. Sex suffuses Clark's pages – he can't see a young woman without wondering what she'd be like in bed. He claims this is normal: 'I mean, sex is a part of life, isn't it? A very fulfilling and agreeable part of life. So if you describe your life and don't refer to sex you're excluding something.' I had vowed this interview would not be all about sex, but heigh, ho . . .

Alan Clark and sex – where does one begin? It isn't quite accurate to call him a Don Juan – he doesn't have that calculating coldness. He really adores women, and prefers their company to men's. And he doesn't seem to be the sort of bullying groper who goes in for sexual harassment – tiresome though it must have been for his secretaries to find him raving to his diary about their tightly controlled sexuality or whatever, I imagine they found his approaches quite easy to deflect. I wondered whether he had the sort of She Stoops to Conquer syndrome whereby he only fancied women of a lower social class but he said no, he fancied women of all classes. 'A lot of people of my class, if we must keep using that tiresome word, won't actually look at girls behind counters and things, because there's a sort of shut-off. That's not true of me. Anybody who sort of clicks, I don't mind what they are.'

When I referred to his 'peculiar' sexual orientation he got quite cross and said, 'My orientation *isn't* peculiar! It's perfectly natural. What's peculiar about it?' Well, what's peculiar is the way he flaunts it: he will keep talking about it. Take, for a mild example, the scene in the *Diaries* where, at a diplomatic dinner at which a bellydancer performs, he remarks to the French admiral next to him that nowadays he can only manage three orgasms a night. The French admiral is unfazed, but do you normally, I asked Mr Clark, go around telling people you can 'only' do it three times a night? Would you say that to John Major, for instance? 'Yes – why not?' Well, I suggested, because Englishmen generally are rather nervous of sexagenarians who boast about their sex lives. 'It wasn't boasting, it was a melancholy admission.' Oh come *on*!

A general rule of life is that people who talk about sex an awful lot don't like doing it, but Clark seems to disprove the rule: he likes doing it and he likes talking about it, particularly to other men – he thinks it's what chaps do. When I told him that some men never talk about sex at all he said, 'No! How can you say that? You're an absolute baby!' I suspect Clark is completely clueless about what goes on in other men's heads.

It is as if, as a teenager, he adopted some gruesome old buffer's view of what being 'a man of the world' entailed and has persisted in it ever since. He is like a little boy trying to pass for a grown-up but eternally getting it wrong. He seems to have missed out on peer group pressure;

it is hard to place him in any 'set' or even any class. When the *Diaries* came out, he was attacked as a snob because he talked of the 'lower classes' and joked that Michael Heseltine was not a proper gent because he bought his own furniture, but in fact Clark belongs to the furniture-buying classes himself – he bought his own Scottish estate, and his father bought Saltwood Castle. The family's money was made by his great-grandfather (from sewing cotton) in the late nineteenth century. And as he says, 'I don't give a sod about how rich someone is or whether he's the Duke of Bananas. The point is: is he entertaining and fun and intelligent and can enhance one's life, and has she got, er, the qualities that one looks for? What is true is that the females in the lower class (so-called) can stride from one category to another without any problem if they've got enough confidence. With the male it may take a generation or so.'

I asked him how, class-wise, he'd describe himself? Aristocrat? 'No, of course not. I'm not in the Debrett class and don't pretend to be.' Well bred? 'You'd have to ask people who are "bred", whose lineage can be traced. I mean, my arms were matriculated by Lyon in 1872. My grand-father was offered a title by Lloyd George's fundraisers and refused – sometimes I regret that, sometimes I don't.' Gentleman? 'I don't think I could be considered a gentleman, do you?' No, I agreed, absolutely not – he looked a bit upset. What about grandee? 'That is not a title you can arrogate to yourself – some might regard me as one and some not. Some grandees might want to keep me out, and others might accept the fact that in a curious kind of way I was one, or was becoming one. But I can't say – it's too close.' So, to summarize, he is not a gentleman, not an aristocrat, not well bred and only hopefully a grandee. Obviously he is not 'lower class', and nor is he a self-made gent in the Archer, Parkinson or Heseltine mould, because he inherited his money. What is he then? I suggested a toff, and he seemed happy with that.

But why isn't he Lord Toff or Sir Toff? Was he hurt that he hadn't got his K? He found the question almost more offensive than any I asked. 'A *knighthood*! [uttered *à la* Lady Bracknell]. What would I want a knighthood for?' Possibly because he said in the *Diaries* that he would like Jane to be a Lady, though obviously he would prefer a peerage. He turned suddenly pompous: 'Actually I think it's improper to discuss titles, because they're in the gift of the sovereign.'

It was Jane, not him, who made the memorably snobbish remark in the middle of the Harkess affair that, 'Quite frankly, if you bed people that I call "below-stairs class" they go to the papers, don't they?' Was she, I wondered, perhaps more of a snob than him? There was a long silence before he replied, 'I don't think so.' The silence might have meant that he was considering it, or that he was wondering how to react to the subject of the Harkesses.

For anyone who was on a desert island at the time: Mr and Mrs Harkess and their daughter Josephine came over to England from South Africa to sell their story to the newspapers – the story being that Clark had bedded the mother and her two daughters. Clark tries to brush it off as a 'wonderful great furore, romp, episode' but there is a slight gulp before discussing it. He claims that it was the journalists who made Jane sound like a snob. 'In fact Jane – as so often – sort of bailed me out, because when the dust began to settle, a mate of mine rang and said, "You conducted yourself very well." And I said, "Yes, but of course Jane's been marvellous too." "Jane!" he said. "Listen, Al, if it weren't for Jane, you'd be the most hated man in England." And I suddenly realized what he meant. She just . . . she's very clever.'

Afterwards, he said, he felt remorse but the remorse, it turns out, was more for the Harkesses than for his wife, 'Because I liked all those girls. It was horrid to see them doing that, to have got into the clutches of Max Clifford, it was awful. I wish it hadn't happened but I don't bear them any ill will for it at all.' Crikey, I told him, I'd bear them ill will in spades: they went to Max Clifford, he didn't come to them. 'Well, maybe . . . but I didn't, because I was . . . fond of all three of them. You can't change your feelings just because people commit some kind of *faux pas*.'

At the time, he said he was suing the *News of the World*, which effectively brought the story to an end. But no writ ever materialized. He said he was reluctant to sue because it would mean putting 'the girls' in court. He didn't object to the original episode, which said he had affairs with all three Harkess women, but to the second episode which claimed he told Mrs Harkess he had an illegitimate son, Billy. The same episode claimed that he exposed himself at gay parties and quoted a witness saying, 'He'd hold it up for everyone to see. He was very proud of it.' Clark says this is 'utter tripe'.

However, I pointed out, the really serious allegation was Josephine Harkess's claim in the *Sun* and on Sky TV that he exposed himself to her when she was in her early teens. His response was bizarre: 'Is that really serious? Yeah. Well, of course I've denied it – that's exactly the sort of thing I don't think you should put women in court on. I don't think, if you've had relations with someone, that you should query their testimony or try and disparage them. I mean I just shrug my shoulders and walk away.'

Funny. Funny that he doesn't seem to see that in most people's eyes the allegation of flashing at a schoolgirl is a different order of misbehaviour from having extramarital affairs. But then he really is not like most people. The word that springs to mind for him is 'spoiled' – it's as though he is used to having his whims indulged and has never had to worry about anyone else. But in fact he wasn't spoiled – he was, if anything, neglected as a child, ignored by his parents and very lonely. Most of the time he was left in the care of servants who laughed at him. 'I have memories of defiantly making remarks when pretty young, six or seven, and people going [putting on a horrible affected voice], "Oh hahaha, you don't understand." ' Why on earth didn't he complain to his parents? '*God* no! Staff rank *far* higher than children! *They* can complain about you being horrid to them, and then you get slapped, but you can't complain about them – staff are sacrosanct. You might as well complain about the police in a totalitarian society.'

The staff might have been unusually uppity because his mother was an alcoholic, getting progressively worse through the fifties and sixties. It all started, Clark believes, when she fell in with a fashionable doctor who treated society ladies, ascribing their symptoms to blocked sinuses, which he treated with cocaine. 'He was a quack really, and naturally he got a *big* following. There was quite a lot of doping anyway at that time, and my mother was into that *heavily*. And then a terrible thing happened. The doctor was arrested, so my mother took to the bottle as second best.'

In consequence, she was an alarming mother. 'Not peculiar. Just . . . volatile. She had bouts of ill temper. Not physical, not blows. But verbal violence, which is just as frightening in some ways . . . The power of speech is not to be lightly discounted, when you are aware that there is a great ferment of rage behind the speech.' His mother sometimes seemed to find his presence, even his existence, enraging and he learned to guess her mood from her clothes – 'I used to dread certain suits she put on.' He and his father would keep out of the way, but separately, there was no sense of shared suffering. She is strikingly absent from the *Diaries* – her name does not even appear in the index, though she is referred to in passing as B'Mama or Bonny Mama. When I mentioned this omission, Clark was shocked and rushed to the book to check: 'This is terrible. How awful! She's not in the book at all. I got very fond of her towards the end, too.'

She died in 1976 and his father married his stepmother, Nolwen, the next year. Clark firmly believes that he saw his stepmother killing his father with poison mushrooms – though Peregrine Worsthorne, who knew Nolwen, says she adored her husband. Clark obviously has very mixed feelings about his father. The *Diaries* contain a touching account of his death, and many affectionate tributes; Saltwood Castle is almost a shrine to his memory. Yet when Ginny Dougary interviewed Alan Clark she saw him make a rude V-sign at one of his father's portraits. His life seems to have been shaped by a desire to keep out of his father's shadow. He suppressed his natural interest in art because Lord Clark's expertise was so colossal that 'even the tiniest comment might have irritated him, as exposing ignorance'. Instead, he became action man, soldier and politician, conquering fields where there was no contest with his father. 'That was the form that my reaction took – and probably the root of some of my problems.'

It is quite rare for him to admit that he *has* any problems. He got annoyed when I kept asking if he had ever consulted a psychiatrist and said he couldn't see why he should need to. But he admits that he gets 'moods' that he doesn't understand. From the *Diaries* it's obvious that he gets very strong impulses, almost compulsions, to upset applecarts. He talks of longing to stand on his ministerial balcony and pee on the crowds below – though, to be fair, he did manage to resist this one.

But he didn't manage to resist the girl on the train. The incident is recorded in his diary entry for 18 February 1984 when he was a minister at the Department of Employment: 'Yesterday I travelled down by train, and a plump young lady came into my compartment at Waterloo. She was not wearing a bra, and her delightful globes bounced promi-nently . . . I gave her a huge grin, couldn't help it. After a bit I moved over and sat beside her. She was adorable. Am I crazy? Death wish? Above us in the luggage rack the red box gleamed like a beacon. She works as a shop assistant in Folkestone.'

Wouldn't it have been simpler just to take her phone number? '*No!* I'm amazed you say that! You've missed the whole code of the thing which is that when I say, "Above our heads the red box gleamed like a beacon," it was because we were *lying* on the seat. It was the immediacy of the thing – that's what was so delicious.' But supposing he was caught? Imagine the headlines! 'Bonking on a train? I honestly don't think the public would mind. I don't see how it could.'

There is something quite dazzling about his naivety – has he never read the tabloids? But what he betrays, apart from naivety, is an extraordinary solipsism – *he* doesn't mind being caught bonking on a train (probably, given his exhibitionism, he'd quite like it) but how would his party, how would his adored Leaderene have felt? It might have caused a tiny stutter next time she wanted to bang on about Victorian values. Didn't *any* of those thoughts occur to him when he gave his 'huge grin'? No, he admits complacently: 'I have always been culpably weak and to some extent impetuous in that kind of situation and I behave in a manner that is not calculating. And if that is a sign of political infirmity, then you're right.'

Well, it *is* a sign of political infirmity and it's a mark of the weakness of Mrs Thatcher's judgement that she ever made him a minister – first at Employment, then at Defence. However good he was at the job, and that's debatable, his potential for scandal, his courting of scandal, should have disbarred him from office. Beside Clark, a Cecil Parkinson quietly bonking his secretary looks like a paragon of virtue. Clark thinks we're hypocritical about this – that the British public's capacity to seem outraged by sexual misdemeanours is much exaggerated by the newspapers. And as he says hotly, *he* never took a bribe or accepted freebies – though as he is a rich man, the temptation was less. He also argues that the very fact that he didn't care who knew about his sexual peccadilloes proves that he was not blackmailable and therefore not a security risk. This is quite a strong argument – though if I were prime minister I'd still prefer not to waste my time dealing with the potential media fallout of ministers who bonked on trains.

In any case, there is something almost subversive about his desire to risk that. It is not just that he fancies the girl – perhaps he wouldn't even fancy her at all if she were in her shop – he fancies the frisson of risking exposure. Matthew Parris wrote at the time of the Stephen Milligan débâcle about the personality of politicians. He said they were by definition risk takers. So when they get bored (as they are bound to do after years in power) they go looking for new risks, be they sexual or financial. But with Clark you feel there is something else again – a cackle of glee at the risk of exposure which seems to be connected with sexual arousal. He is almost like a transvestite or a closet gay in the way he gets off on his own naughtiness. I asked why he didn't simply go to prostitutes, but he said that was *'disgusting!'* He regards all his sexual adventures as romantic interludes, even when conducted on the grimy banquettes of Southern Region.

He says he *has* reformed a bit now. There was a showdown with Jane two years ago when he saw how hurt she was by his philandering. Previously she'd always reacted by being angry or contemptuous (she referred to his mistresses as 'the bluebottles') but this time she was hurt, and even walked out on him for a couple of days. And whereas her anger might have been rather titillating, her sorrow moved him. At all events, he says they have a more equal relationship now 'though equal is a funny word, she's certainly my superior in many respects. But yes, paradoxically, our relationship gets better and better.'

His one huge, lasting regret is that he left Parliament in spring 1992, simply walked away, which he regards as 'a *colossal* and self-indulgent error of judgement'. He was disheartened by the loss of Mrs Thatcher, wearied by the thought of fighting another election, and there was also a personal reason (another woman, inevitably) which made him feel it was a choice between politics and Jane. 'I had to choose, and I made what I suppose in human terms was the right decision, but on a broader canvas I think it was the wrong decision. I regret it very much.' Later he thought of standing for the Newbury by-election but was not even considered by the selection committee – he believes he could have won it even without (or perhaps especially without) any front-bench support.

He has still not entirely given up hope of getting back into Parliament. 'While I'm not a buffer, I still want to do things. I like public life. I am a historian by training but I've tasted the delights of participating in it as well as recording it, and it's highly addictive.' But even if he were elected, could he still be a player? 'Oh yes. Well look at them – total nonentities, just sort of Rotarians, so dreary and dull.' Rather surprisingly, the one politician he says is *not* dull is John Major, who is 'really quite compelling company'. He hopes he remains as leader for many years but if he ever does go, he says, again surprisingly, that he would favour Gillian Shephard to succeed him.

As the epilogue to his *Diaries*, Clark prints the Keith Douglas lines,

> And all my endeavours are unlucky explorers
> come back, abandoning the expedition;
> the specimens, the lilies of ambition
> still spring in their climate, still unpicked;
> to find them, as the great collectors before me.

By any common-sense judgement, Alan Clark's political career was a waste of time. He failed to achieve the two great reforms he put his heart into – reorganizing the Ministry of Defence and preventing the killing of rare animals for their pelts – and added no lustre to Mrs Thatcher's premiership. And yet, ironically, he has succeeded in another field which he discounts as unimportant. As a diarist, I believe he will live as long as diaries are read. And it is precisely the qualities – recklessness, outrageousness, frankness – that made him so 'unsound' as a minister that make him incomparable as a diarist. I asked what his answer would have been if someone had promised him he could end up prime minister provided he behaved himself. 'A sort of Faustian deal you mean? Mm . . . Given the assurance, yes. Given the mere likelihood, Be a good boy and maybe . . . I fear not.'

Reproduced by permission of the *Telegraph Magazine*.

Damien Hirst

17 February 1996

It was a lovely television moment – scruffy old Damien Hirst, wild-eyed, greasy-haired, clutching his baby, Connor, with Mum and girlfriend Maia in the background, saying thank you for the £20,000 Turner Prize. Perhaps he will look back on that night – 28 November 1995 – as a kind of turning point, the end of Hirst's First Period. Many art critics thought he should have won the prize three years earlier for his pickled shark, *The Physical Impossibility of Death in the Mind of Someone Living* (now owned by Charles Saatchi). Damien thought so, too: 'I did more for British art in 1992 than I did last year.' And he had got so excited the first time he was nominated, and then so disappointed when he lost, that he couldn't allow himself to care so much the second time. Besides, there was a niggling worry in the background, provoked by a story in that morning's *Daily Mail*. He must have worried that his life was going to be disrupted again, just as it had been when he was twelve and first discovered the truth about his parentage. So while he stood grinning on the podium, accepting the applause, he must have felt even more acutely than he always does – this could all end tomorrow.

His winning the Turner Prize, of course, was the cue for everyone to start slagging him off – not only the philistines who never saw the point of pickled sharks anyway, but also the trendies who grumble that he hasn't had a new idea for years. The *Daily Telegraph* duly obliged the next day with a furious leader about the wickedness of rewarding artists who, by their own admission, couldn't draw or paint. Damien is always happy to add to this line of attack by reminding everyone that he got an E in art A-level and was turned down by two art schools. He is more worried by the other accusation – that he has been repeating himself for too long. He thinks now that he's working in a new medium – film – he'll tap new well-springs of inspiration. We shall see.

Despite the haunting melancholy of his work, he comes over as a cheerful soul. It's not difficult to understand why he has so many friends – he is fun to be with. The crew who worked on his film début, *The Hanged Man*, voted it the most enjoyable shoot they'd ever been on. His generosity to young artists is legendary: he has twice put on exhibitions to promote their work, the first while he was still a student himself. Gordon Burn, one of his many writer friends, says, 'He's by far the most exhilarating person I've met in England in the last ten years, and some kind of genius as a person – fantastically generous with his money, time, views and humour.'

We met in the Groucho Club, where he practically lives in the evenings, if he's not at the Colony or Green Street – he likes the Groucho because the staff are very good at scooping him up and putting him in a taxi home when he's drunk. Drinking figures large in his life, though *he* says journalists exaggerate it and that he often spends a quiet evening at home. I tried this idea out on some of his friends and they all collapsed with laughter – they reckon it must be at least six years since Damien spent a quiet evening at home. However, I must record, sadly, that he only shared a genteel bottle of white wine with me and the wickedest thing he did all evening was to throw his cigarette butts out of the window. Someone must have warned him to be on his best behaviour.

Damien says he used to feel guilty that he wasn't suffering enough – he believed that artists were meant to be 'pained'. But then he decided, 'We're all pained in our own way' – and anyway it was just another crummy old art cliché, ripe for overturning, so now he makes no secret of his happiness. He is *thrilled* with his nine-month-old baby, Connor, and even enjoys changing nappies. He loves his glamorous Californian girlfriend, Maia, who is 'pure *Baywatch*' according to their friends – keen on surfing and health food and having a good time, with no interest at all in the art world.

They flit together between their homes in Devon and London, often with Damien's mother, Mary Brennan, in tow – he feels that if you can't share your success with your family then it can't be worth having. He is friends with David Bowie and Dave Stewart and Jarvis Cocker and Blur (he directed their *Country House* video) and last summer took Maia and Mum and the baby to the Glastonbury festival in a big Winnebago camper. But he turned down an invitation to meet the Princess of Wales at the Serpentine Gallery because, 'It was one of those things where you had to stand by your work and shake hands and say Hi, and I thought I'd rather go and have a pint in the pub.'

He claims not to know what he is worth because it takes so long to do the sums – his dealer, Jay Jopling, takes half of everything, but also pays half the fabrication costs – but he doesn't seem fazed when I suggest he's a millionaire. His major sculptures sell for £100,000 upwards and he does a steady trade in smaller works, especially his ubiquitous spot paintings, at about £7,500 each. He employs two full-time fabricators, one in his Berlin studio, one in London, and hires other assistants as needed. His work *is* costly to produce – imagine buying a 14ft Tiger shark (he specified the size as 'big enough to eat you') and shipping it from Australia – but he makes enough, anyway, to have recently bought a £162,000 five-bedroom farmhouse in Devon with twenty-four acres of forest, as well as a new flat off the Strand in London, which is pretty good going for a thirty-year-old.

This is all very apoplexy-inducing for people who believe that artists should draw and paint, preferably every blade of grass, and feel cheated if they don't. Damien says he *can* draw, but these days he doesn't bother. He creates art by phone, and does most of his planning in taxis. When he gets an idea he explains it to one of his fabricators and they start making it. His spot paintings are drawn with compasses; his spin paintings produced on a potter's wheel. He lets friends, assistants, even journalists, help with them – there is no Damien Hirst 'handiwork'. When the owners of one of his spot paintings called to say their child had crayoned all over the painting and could he come and retouch it, his immediate reaction was to say that the crayoning improved the painting. (Though later, being the obliging fellow that he is, he repainted it.) But to all the many people who look at his work and say, 'I could have done that,' Damien has an unanswerable answer: 'But you didn't, did you?'

We want our artists not only to draw immaculately but to be innocent, unworldly naifs, surprised by fame. Damien is not innocent and not surprised. He chose to go to Goldsmiths because he knew they had courses in marketing. He knows about hype and publicity and how one person's fame can feed off another's. While he gravitates to Blur and Pulp, older rock stars like David Bowie and Dave Stewart gravitate to him. Of course there is mutual massage – that is what the fame game is all about. But you would have to be pretty thick not to recognize it, and Damien Hirst is by no means thick. He says soberly, 'Once the hype overtakes the art work, then you're fucked. But I think there's no point in shying away from it, if we're living in this world. It's like if you try to have integrity you're invariably not going to have any, whereas if you try not to have integrity, you're going to find out where your integrity lies.'

Anyway, he has plenty of contact with 'real people', to whom pickled sharks and bisected cows are just a joke – his family, for a start. His aunt, Barbara Brennan, told the press, 'I think Damien must be a good conman.' Even Damien's dad confided, 'I am in awe of the lad and I love him dearly, but I can't for the life of me see the art in his work.' Damien's mum, not surprisingly, admires his work, but she 'nearly had a heart attack' when he paid $500 in New York for a sculpture consisting of eight pieces of Lego hung on nails.

'It's quite difficult to get your mind round it, isn't it, that something could cost somebody nothing and then cost me $500?' Er, yes, Damien . . . but then that's exactly what people say about *your* work. I think he probably thinks that the prices are a joke, but the work itself is serious. One of his oft-repeated axioms is: 'Art is about life; the art world is about money.'

The Natural History series, which he has been working on for about six years, and which includes the shark (£50,000) and the divided cow and calf (£140,000) that won the Turner Prize, is now coming to an end. He still has one or two outstanding commitments, and wants to do a pig in a sort of bacon slicer, but 'In my mind the series is finished.'

His thoughts are turning to new impossible ideas – notably a real rainbow in a gallery – and he plans a *jeu d'esprit* called *The Pram in the Hall* (one of Cyril Connolly's *Enemies of Promise*), in which a baby in a pram will be connected by a Mothercare walkie-talkie to a skull. And, he adds, the skull will have ping-pong eyes suspended on jets of air so they roll about. He has already done one good baby joke – he got so fed up with friends saying, when Maia was pregnant, 'What'll you do with the baby – put it in formaldehyde?' that he had himself, Maia and Connor photographed for *Esquire* floating naked in tanks.

But what he is *really* into now is film. He has just finished a 25-minute short, *Hanging Around*, for the Hayward Gallery's 'Spellbound' exhibition. He wants to follow this with a full-length feature film to be called *God Games*, about a future world in which rich people have servants but ordinary people have clones of themselves to do the chores. He has already written the script and will use the same actor, Keith Allen, and the same producer, Nira Park, as he used for the Hayward film: he is very attached to his team. The attraction of film, he explains, is that, 'As a sculptor you get really inhibited by things like gravity. Like, if I say I want a rainbow in a room, it's a massive problem, whereas in a film you can have it immediately.' And he grew up watching television, so he believes he ought to understand film.

The trouble is – sorry, Damien – his film is just not as original as his sculpture. He showed me an early rough cut of *Hanging Around* and I thought it was *quite* interesting, with good performances from Keith Allen (of *Martin Chuzzlewit* fame) and Eddie Izzard and brilliant music from Blur and Pulp and the Pogues, but it didn't feel like a whole new vision. Brian Sewell was of the same opinion: 'Hirst's intellectual force in this new field is negligible, for he takes as his model the most vulgar of television's opiates.'

But it is useful as a footnote to his sculpture, because it confirms again his choice of subject matter: death. The film's protagonist, Marcus, goes round visiting people who die soon afterwards and Marcus eventually realizes that he is working for 'the Reaper' – death. It was originally meant to be called *Is Mr Death In?*, which is an anagram of Damien Hirst. When I exclaimed over this coincidence, Damien quickly added that alternative anagrams are A Denim Shirt or Ten Mad Irish. Aha, I said, but then isn't it significant that he chose to make a film about Mr Death and not about the ten mad Irish or the denim shirt? It's an art critic's cliché to say that each of his works is really a *memento mori*. And of course – because, as I've said already, he is not an innocent – he *knows* this and perhaps plays up to it in interviews. Perhaps. But it is

really striking how often he mentions death in conversation – he's
always saying 'If I'm still alive' or 'If I don't get hit by a truck' and he
talks familiarly about 'the Reaper' as if this were an expression in
everyday use.

Damien says he's surprised that all the critics bang on about death
in his work because 'They're more about life. I mean, *The Physical
Impossibility of Death in the Mind of Someone Living* [the Saatchi shark] is
not about death but about the lack of it, or the lack of understanding
of it. I'm obsessed with life. It seems to me that life is so rich and full
and wonderful and fantastic that the fact that it ends seems . . . rude.'
He doesn't see his work as melancholy: he sees it as optimistic. He
thinks that when he uses dead carcasses he celebrates their beauty and
that, 'If you lost that, then there'd be no point in carrying on. Once
you take the smell away, it becomes visually attractive. The colours –
I mean, if you just look at it, the red of meat is really a fabulous red. I
remember seeing a cow slaughtered in Turkey in the sunlight and it
just looked like the colour of fire engines, you know? If you saw it on
a film you just wouldn't believe it was blood.' Of course he's not the
first artist to have recognized this – Soutine, whom he much admires,
also conveyed the beauty of dead flesh, but Soutine went mad.

The normal reaction to violence, to death, to decay, is to turn one's
eyes away. Damien's has always been to stare, to drink it in. Even as a
child: 'I went to a Catholic school and I remember the thing I liked
the most was the gruesome pictures in the illustrated Bible, of Christ
being nailed to the cross and heads being cut off, all that stuff. I
remember loving them and just thinking, "Oh wow, look at that!"
There was never any kind of horror. But then they're beautifully painted
images of unacceptable things, really, aren't they?'

Why this apparent obsession with death? Why did someone who
grew up in very ordinary circumstances, the son of a used-car salesman
in a semi in Leeds, develop this ever-present, urgent, awareness of
mortality? Most people brood about death when they first grasp the
concept, usually at about seven – and then decide it's not worth worrying
about. Damien seems to have retained that seven-year-old's sense of
outrage.

His first close exposure to death was his grandmother's, when he
was about fifteen. She fell asleep smoking in a chair. He had been very

close to her indeed; she was his confidante, his truth-teller, the person who told him about sex and that Father Christmas didn't exist. 'She was like cows, you know? Completely real.' He once had a conversation with her about death. 'I was saying, "So if you get hit by a car, then you die, and if you fall off a block of flats, then you die, and if you get shot, you die" . . . And I remember listing all these and then saying, "So what happens if you *don't* get hit by a truck or . . ." – I was trying to work out this way to avoid everything – and she said, "Well then, you die of old age." And I remember thinking, "Oh, that's a cheat."' And when, at fifteen, he saw his grandmother in her coffin, he simply rejected the idea: 'It's like – my granny died, but where did she go? I mean the corpse is there, and you look at it, touch it, and then you go, "That's not her." You just *cannot* accept it.'

Damien always says in interviews that he had a very happy childhood, at least until he was twelve. That was when his parents split up, and his contact with his father diminished. Damien had always been 'naughty', but in his early teens he took to shoplifting and playing truant. What made the divorce more complicated for him was that his mother simultaneously broke the news that his dad wasn't really his dad. Damien was a love child, born the year before she met her husband. William Hirst formally adopted him and changed his name when he was two. His brother and sister were really his half-siblings.

Damien says that the news didn't make much impact at the time. 'I mean, the worst thing was my mum and dad getting divorced. That was a lot worse than finding out that my father wasn't my father. I felt special for a week or something and then forgot all about it. I thought, "Well, hang on, even if that's true, what have I missed? I haven't missed out on anything," I had a perfectly normal childhood with my father till I was twelve. So I thought, "Well, that doesn't make any difference," quite quickly. And I still feel like that – does that seem weird? In a way it's probably like death, it's probably like thinking, "No, that's not it." It meant I'd have to change the way I looked at my dad, and I didn't want to, and the best way to not change it was to treat it as if I hadn't been told.'

So he continued to think of his 'dad' as his dad, and his half-siblings as his brother and sister, and indeed he still thinks of them that way. But the question was unpleasantly reopened the day he won the Turner

Prize, when the *Daily Mail* excavated all this family history. The danger then was that his real father would step forward. Damien has no desire to meet his real father. 'It would be just a nightmare for me to meet some guy who goes, "Hi, forgive me, son." And it would also cause problems with my brother and sister, who *are* my brother and sister, to say to them, "Oh, this is my real dad," and bring someone else into the situation when there's nothing wrong with it. I had everything I ever wanted as a family so . . . I hope nobody turns up. I'll just say, "Thanks but no thanks."' He claims to know almost nothing about his real father, beyond that he was a photographer. Damien's aunt Barbara Brennan was reported as saying, 'His mother went to work in Jersey for a short time and when she came back she was pregnant.' Damien jokes rather bitterly, 'He probably just had a shag!' But then he says that no, he thinks his parents lived together for a bit, until Mary got pregnant.

'She was in love with him.' He adds, worriedly, 'I think Mum would quite like to find him. I don't know.' Why hasn't he asked her? 'Because . . . because I'm not sure what my mum's feelings are. I don't want her to get hurt. I mean *she* might want to find him, and if she does, I don't want to get involved. She obviously liked him then, on some level. But it's not been said, so I don't really know. To be honest, I don't really think about it.'

To be honest, I find it hard to believe that he doesn't think about it. He has recently become a father himself and there is nothing like having a baby to make one conscious of heredity. When I said that his father being a photographer meant that he had artistic genes on both sides he said dismissively, 'If you believe in all that stuff.' Can he really *not* believe it? 'Once you've had a father who's given you everything you've needed when you were young, then that makes anything heredi-tary insignificant.'

So it seems as if he practises denial – dealing with unpleasant facts by ignoring them. The trouble with denial is that it's rather a precarious way of coping. Damien's teachers at Goldsmith's were always telling him to go to a psychoanalyst and he was quite attracted to the idea but, 'I haven't had time. If I'm not working, I'm too drunk.' He uses drinking as a kind of sedative and admits, 'I think if I didn't drink I probably would have had a nervous breakdown by now. It's like there's a whole load of ideas that come together in your head and when it gets too much, you get drunk. But I drink less now than I used to.' Marcus, the hero of his Hayward film, seems to be on the verge of a crack-up: he keeps telling people he can't sleep, his life is 'disjointed', he feels a deep sadness, an unbearable sense of boredom. Damien says that far from Marcus cracking up, 'He's the only one in control at the end.' But, you think, for how long?

Everything about Damien Hirst provokes the feeling, But for how long? How long can he go on drinking so much? How long can he go on working so hard? He knows that the media will soon tire of him and that the art world is fickle. He badly needs the next big idea. 'I mean a lot of people say, "Oh, you haven't gone anywhere since you did the shark to the lamb." But that series was bound to take a lot of time and now it's almost finished. I could carry on with it and make a lot of money, but I wouldn't be happy, so to suddenly do this film thing . . . In the end all I want is a house in Devon, a baby, I just want to be able to enjoy myself. I don't have to sell work for millions of pounds in order to afford that.'

But there is always that sense of urgency, the immanence of death, driving him on: 'But at my back I always hear/Time's wingèd chariot hurrying near.' He has to produce works quickly, perhaps too quickly, because his oeuvre might be finished tomorrow. 'You have to carry on as though each day is your last. There's lots of artists, like Géricault, who did fantastic works but died when he was twenty-eight or some-thing. [Actually, thirty-three.] So it depends how long . . . If I died tomorrow, then that's it.' But why *should* he die tomorrow? 'I could get hit by a truck. People do. It's not that normal to die when you're ninety-five, is it?'

Reproduced by permission of the *Telegraph Magazine*.

Julie Burchill

18 January 1998

My relationship with Julie Burchill is one of wary mutual respect. We admire each other's work and exchange queenly greetings across parties. I am the older, but she is the longer established, and the higher paid. To lesser fry who try to stir up rivalry between us, we explain severely that column writing and interviewing are different arts, so there is no competition. Privately, though, I bow the knee. I love the rough-hewn vigour of her style (no matter if it doesn't always make sense) and I thought her television screenplay *Prince* was pretty near a masterpiece. I am also intrigued by the fact that she, like me, has an incongruously weak speaking voice – hers with the addition of a quaint Somerset accent – and I treasure her remark that when she discovered writing it was as if she'd found her mother tongue.

Still, she is a difficult so-and-so, what might be called a proper little madam were she not such an improper and enormous madam. She refused to let me come to her house in Brighton because, 'If you saw my pink mansion with leopardskin furniture and a swimming-pool in the garden, I know you'd make fun of me!' Now she is a *Guardian* columnist she wants to be taken seriously, as an intellectual. So we meet at the Sussex Arts Club, her Groucho from home, where she lived when she first moved to Brighton. The people in the club fuss over her – she has the knack of acquiring slaves wherever she goes – and maintain the drip-feed of dry sherries that sustains her through the afternoon. She says she is off drugs these days (she was a great consumer of speed in the 1970s, cocaine in the 1980s), and she certainly looks much healthier than when I last saw her two years ago. She was terribly fat and pasty then, but now she is buxom and glossy, with nice clean hair to toss. She has an acolyte in tow, Emma Forrest, former Generation X columnist now about-to-be novelist, who stays with her in Brighton two days a week 'to keep me on the straight and narrow'. Julie says she regards Emma as a daughter, though, given her record of motherhood, that's no big deal.

The story so far: Julie Burchill was born in Bristol thirty-eight years ago, the only child of two factory workers, her father a keen Stalinist trades union agitator, her mother a 'diva' (her word) who would climb over fences to attack the neighbours. Julie – bookish, bright, mildly delinquent – ran away to London aged seventeen to answer an *NME* advertisement for a 'hip, young gunslinger' and almost immediately became a star of the rock press, writing about punk. Married her fellow gunslinger Tony Parsons, aged eighteen, and had a son, Bobby. Abandoned both in 1984, to run off with Cosmo Landesman, another journalist, by whom she had a son, Jack, in 1986. Moved from rock journalism via the *Face* into mainstream journalism, writing brilliant columns for the *Sunday Times*, the *Mail on Sunday* and the *Sunday Express*. Also turned out a couple of forgettable blockbuster novels, *Ambition* and *No Exit*, and the superb television screenplay *Prince*, as well as co-founding the *Modern Review* with the journalist Toby Young.

In the early 1990s, she was much in evidence at the Groucho Club, holding court with Toby Young and her husband Cosmo and a host of hangers-on. She earned £130,000 a year, but managed to spend it easily, by dint of always picking up the Groucho tab, and shelling out £50 notes to almost every beggar she passed in the street. But in 1995, she disappeared from the Groucho, and from London. She made her exit in a delicious blaze of tabloid glory, when the *Daily Mail* revealed that she had deserted her husband and child to run off to Brighton with a girlfriend, Charlotte Raven. Raven was then twenty-five, the daughter of a Brighton millionaire, and working as an assistant on the *Modern Review*. Just to make matters even juicier, Raven had previously had an affair with Toby Young. Anyway, she and Julie posed happily for the *Daily Mail*'s doorstepping cameraman – though he had fallen asleep in his car and they had to wake him up – and told the world they were in love. Toby Young responded by closing the *Modern Review* and flouncing off to New York. (Incidentally, Young used to claim he helped write Burchill's articles but when I asked her, she snapped, 'In his dreams!')

After this enjoyable brouhaha, Burchill fell most uncharacteristically silent. She remained in Brighton, separated from her husband and son, whereas Charlotte Raven soon surfaced in London, with a boyfriend. She wrote for the *Guardian* and is now editor of the recently relaunched *Modern Review*. Burchill still writes for the *Modern Review* but no longer has money in it. The mystery of her disappearance is explained by the fact that she has three books coming out this year – obviously she has been working like a fiend. There is a novel called *Married Alive*, which she describes, apparently without irony, as 'a bittersweet comedy of manners'; a book on Princess Diana, her heroine; and an autobiography, *I Knew I was Right*, published this week by Heinemann. The latter is, of course, brilliant 'vintage Burchill', and seems shockingly frank, though as we shall see, it is only frank as far as it goes.

The jacket of *I Knew I was Right* has the usual old photograph of Burchill at eighteen, very thin, with a cloud of dark hair. She says she wanted a more recent photograph but the publishers insisted. She claims she has *no* hang-ups about ageing and, 'The reason I've got no fear of getting older is, when I was seventeen I was the sweetest chick in London. I had a 38in bust, and a waist like that [handspan] and what did it get me? Tony Parsons. So I've got no affection for my good looks. I'm happy to lose them, in fact. Now I'm ageing, I've got a 25-year-old boyfriend, and I'm getting it five times a night.'

This is accompanied by much hair-tossing and the famous when-in-doubt pout, which means it is not necessarily true. But I believe her when she says, more soberly, that she was happy to lose her looks because 'I always wanted so much to be taken seriously. Nobody took me seriously for years, because I was so pretty. It was nothing but a burden to me, frankly, from the time I was twelve when I first grew my chest, it was just something I hated. I'd leave home half an hour earlier to go to school so I could avoid every building site or anywhere where there might be men yelling at you. To be shy, to be intelligent and to be beautiful was the most *awful* combination of stuff, and I do blame it for starting me off on the wrong foot. If I'd been an ugly kid, I'd have been a lot happier.'

She warned me at the beginning, 'I won't tell you *all* the truth, Lynn, but I won't tell you no lies.' Specifically, she said she would not talk about her second husband, Cosmo Landesman, 'because Cosmo has respected my privacy and he's never talked about me.' Anyway, it was a stormy interview, with her in tears within about five minutes – but she cries very easily – and me choking at some of her casual revelations. She enjoyed shocking me and I was happy to oblige, but also I was sometimes *really* shocked to the point where I couldn't look her in the eyes. She sees it as her mission to *épater les bourgeois*, and I was well and truly *épater*-ed.

She cried as soon as I asked her about her parents. She is besotted with her father, the Stalinist, whom she describes as 'the apex of any woman's ambition'. After she ran off with Charlotte Raven, she assumed her parents would never speak to her again, and was hugely relieved when they did. 'You must remember what a conventional home I come from,' she explains as the tears start. 'I always knew they were good parents, and I always loved them, but I never thought they were that nice. When I ran away with Cosmo, they forgave me for that, but I thought a girl was beyond the pale – because they came from such narrow-minded back-grounds, they'd had horrible lives. And to see the full splendour of their forgiveness, it just makes me sentimental . . .' She is splashing tears by now but quite unembarrassed – 'I always cry when I talk about my parents. I must say I cry quite easily – psychopaths do.'

She is very keen on this idea that she is a psychopath. She likes to come across as a callous heartbreaker, a goddess Kali of emotional destruction, though those who knew her in her *NME* days claim that, on the contrary, she was much victimized by men. But, anyway, she insists she behaved as an absolute monster in the Charlotte Raven affair: 'Charlotte is the most honourable, decent person I've ever known, and were it known by the world what I'd done, I was the one who behaved dreadfully. They've all finally forgiven me now but there was a period of a year when I was just a pariah, and Susan [Charlotte's mother], my best friend, wouldn't talk to me, which hurt me more than anything. But I've been welcomed back into the bosom of the family now.'

This is all a bit obscure until she explains that she is now going out with Charlotte's younger brother, Daniel. 'Her *brother*!' I screech, losing all pretence at cool, while Julie laughs her head off. 'Well, they're both Ravens. I've got to tell you, Lynn, frankly, the whole family are bloody adorable, they're the sexiest family I've ever seen in my life, even the grandmother. I don't mean I'm sexually attracted to her, but she's eighty and she looks about thirty-nine and she's like a flapper from the 1920s. People always try and make out it's kinky if you go out with one person then with their brother, but you see they've got the same DNA!' Did she actually leave Charlotte for her brother? 'Not really – in fact, it was worse than that – they were overlapping!' (She says this with such theatrical delight I am not sure I believe her.) But why? 'Because I liked them both so much. And it's the DNA, innit? Oh, I'm enjoying this!'

At the time of the elopement, many of Burchill's friends said they always thought she was a lesbian *really*, but she says no, she wasn't. 'Charlotte's the only girl I've slept with properly. I sometimes fancied other girls, but when push came to shove I couldn't be bothered. I tell you what it is about me and women: I like women much more than men. I know my own character, and I know that I'm a bitch and I know that when I'm in love, I'm treacherous, and no matter how much I love somebody, at some point I'm going to do something bad to them. When I did that thing to Charlotte, I couldn't stand it, because I was hurting a woman, and so I think now – if I'm going to hurt people, I'd rather hurt men than women. So I'm going to keep away from women in future, completely.'

Apparently, it is better to hurt men than women because: 'You know, politically one doesn't feel so bad because it's like black feeling about white, frankly – they've always had the upper hand and they deserve what they get. It doesn't stop them, though. They like a challenge. It's like moths to a flame. Men want to be punished because *they know they've done wrong*. When they meet a good woman who's nice to them, they despise her because she isn't punishing them.'

She is not yet divorced from Cosmo, but says she could no more go back to him than she could fly out of the window. But she raves about him as if she were still in love, saying that she couldn't leave him for another man because he was the best of men, so it had to be a girl.

And now it is a boy – 'I must say I like boys.' Daniel is twenty-five, and works as a carer for senile ex-servicemen. They see each other most days but he doesn't live with her. I asked what would happen if he started wanting children, and she said, 'He won't. Because he's not wet like that. The Ravens brought their children up not to want them. Susan's a very unconventional woman, she's my best friend, Susan.'

Perhaps she should have an affair with Susan, I suggested, and for once it was Julie's turn to screech. 'That's *disgusting*! Because I just love her like a friend. Charlotte is my soulmate, and of course I love her in that way now, but obviously when I met her – have you seen her? It was like having a loaded gun put in your mouth. She's just so forceful and gorgeous, she just swept me off my feet. We were madly in love, even though it only lasted a few weeks. But I just couldn't live with her. I couldn't live with anybody – I just don't want to do it again. It comes back to the same thing – I don't want to break a girl's heart.'

But *did* she break Charlotte Raven's heart? A cynic might say that, career-wise, Charlotte Raven did rather well out of her brief fling with Julie Burchill – she jumped from being a virtually unknown journalist to being a columnist on the *Guardian* and editor of the *Modern Review*. But Julie insists that this is quite wrong, and that Charlotte 'did everything for me'. Nevertheless, when I ask if she taught Charlotte Raven to write, she laughs: 'If you look at her writing, I say good luck to the girl – I do love her. She can't communicate to save her life. If I'd taught her, she'd be funnier than that.'

But Charlotte's humourlessness, she claims, was one of her attractions. 'Because she's so different from me. I have a terrible gift for levity, which, while it goes to make me very happy, on the other hand, I'm not as brainy as I could be, because I just find things so amusing. Charlotte couldn't crack a joke to save her life, but she can really think. Someone said she was like a polytechnic lecturer – it's my dream to be like that. She is *so* academic, but I left school at sixteen. You know, when we ran off together people said it was this Svengali relationship and it was – but what they don't realize is that I was Trilby. She taught me so many things.'

Above all, she claims, Charlotte rescued her from her coke-fuelled life in the Groucho Club, which she now looks back on with disgust. She says she 'partied ferociously' for six years and doesn't know how she lived through it. 'I was brought up as a very pure Stalinist and to find myself sitting in the Groucho pouring booze down my throat – I was sickened with self-disgust and loathing.' But was she really so wet that she couldn't have left the Groucho without Charlotte's influence? 'It's a terrible thing to say – yes, totally, totally.'

But of course, in running away, she also lost her child, Jack, who she says was the only person she ever loved more than her parents. 'And that really changed me, I just adore him.' She couldn't take him with her, she insists, because Charlotte's flat was far too small and anyway she assumed she could get him back later. But then – and this is the nearest she will ever get to expressing regret – she found she couldn't. 'I did fight a vicious custody case to get him. I never *dreamed* I wouldn't. He and I had been everything to each other. I never had a nanny, never had an au pair. Whatever I'd been doing the night before, every morning of his life I got up to make him breakfast. I'd been *everything* to him – it never occurred to me I wouldn't get custody of him, because he was my pride and joy. If I'd sucked off twenty men I could have got away with it – go down on one girl and they take your child away from you. I spent £50,000 fighting the custody case and I can honestly say that losing custody was the worst day of my life.'

At least she still sees Jack (she took him to spend Christmas with her parents and has him to stay at weekends); when she abandoned her first son, she didn't see him for years, though they are on good terms now he is seventeen. I can't even begin to imagine what it feels like to abandon a child but then, as Julie helpfully explains, I am bourgeois and she is not. 'We're different characters, Lynn. I'm not conventional in any single way. Having been brought up as a communist, we don't make any fuss about unimportant bourgeois conventions.'

Motherhood as an unimportant bourgeois convention – gulp. Before I met Julie this time, I'd always assumed she was a wickedly brilliant columnist who said outrageous things just to provoke the readers. Now, I wonder if she is actually wicked. She sometimes wonders it, too. She says, with an air of puzzlement: 'I'm not psychopathic enough that I don't understand what I've done. I do. But – I just don't *feel* it properly. And I can't feel sorry. You know what, Lynn? – it's so bad of me – but whenever people say they feel guilt, I think they're lying! I know I have hurt people. I don't understand it myself. My parents brought me up nicely. I don't want anyone to think that they neglected me, or made me bad. But as I say, I don't understand it – I hope one day I will.'

'Why not go to a shrink?'

'You're joking! I'm English!'

But for all her exhilarating public bravura – and she does it so heartbreakingly well I kept wanting to applaud – she is quite a timorous soul, really. She told me that she 'started life as a shy person, and still am quite a shy person', hence her need for acolytes to cushion her from the outside world. She can't hail a taxi by herself; she used to get Cosmo to escort her to the loo in restaurants. She avoids unfamiliar milieux – she has only been abroad once – and is happiest in places she knows, surrounded by people she knows. She has her strategies for emotional self-protection – notably the habit of dumping people before they dump her – but you feel they are getting a bit feeble.

At one point in the book, she says that she has written 18,000 words so far and each one is a cry for help. When I quote this she screams with laughter, and says, 'Did I say that?' and pretends she meant it as a joke. I'm sure she didn't. Her autobiography often has a desperate whistle-in-the-dark feel to it, and moments when the braggadocio slips and she reveals the confused child within. (I can imagine her hoot of derisive laughter at the above sentence, but too bad – suddenly, with her, the expression 'inner child' seems meaningful. She is thirty-eight, but she is not quite adult.)

I told her, tactfully, I found a discordance in the autobiography between her 'real' emotional voice and her witty, aphoristic columnist's voice, and she agreed immediately. 'I think you're right. It's like I was being debriefed and it's come out a bit patchy.' Couldn't she have written it all in the same quieter style she used for *Prince*? 'That's what I want to get to – but Lynn, it's like banging a walnut with a hammer. And don't forget I've been writing since I was seventeen. I've been in this racket longer than anyone my age. I am literally the oldest juvenile lead in the business. And – I'm not putting myself down – but sometimes I read my stuff and I want to scream. God help me. If you can find a way for me to get out of this bloody aphoristic bloody voice, I'll get out of it. There's an absolute brittleness to me that is like a Russian doll and God knows, I hope and pray I'll get away from it, but I don't know if I ever will. I don't know what it is – I've been doing it so long – they say people become their masks.'

She seemed so disconsolate for a moment that I found myself comforting her: 'I think you're incredibly talented.'

'I don't know, Lynn, to tell you the truth. I think a lifetime in hacking has drained a lot of the initial talent away.'

'Perhaps if you spent a long time just reading, like when you were a kid?'

'It sounds like a beautiful dream, Lynn, but I don't think it's me. It's nice of you to say it, but I've had *such* a good deal – for a girl who was meant to go into a biscuit factory. I often do feel like Dame Edna when she says "Welcome to my gorgeous life". I feel I've been so lucky, and that's why I'm invariably chirpy. People have said, "Why are you so happy all the time?" And it's because I escaped from the biscuit factory. Nobody else did, they've all been made into biscuits!'

Reproduced by permission of *The Observer*.

Jarvis Cocker

5 April 1998

Of course, it is chic nowadays to pretend that one loved Pulp from their first album *It* in 1980 but, like half the nation, I only became aware of them with 'Common People' in the summer of 1995 and only fell in love with Jarvis in February, 1996, watching the Brit Awards on television. Just as the gorge was rising unbearably at the sight of Michael Jackson pretending to be the Messiah, salvation arrived in the unlikely shape of Jarvis, stumbling around the stage and mooning ineptly. Thus a national institution was born. If the Queen had given him a knighthood the next day, she would have done herself a lot of good.

And now he is coming to breakfast. This is a sort of fugue experience because I spent an embarrassingly large part of my teens and twenties fantasizing that a pop star was coming to breakfast. In those days it was John Lennon but Jarvis is a not entirely unworthy substitute – as a lyricist I'd almost give him the edge. Quite why Jarvis is coming to breakfast remains a mystery – his PR minders wanted us to meet in a caff but I refused (risk of being mobbed by fans) – so Monday morning finds me whirling round the house in a complete tizz, hiding the potpourri (he told the *Face* that potpourri, along with Belgian chocolates, counted as his 'worst fear') and double-checking that I haven't suddenly acquired a copy of *A Year in Provence*.

On time to the minute, a gleaming antique Porsche draws up to the kerb and a very glamorous pop person in heavy slap and earrings steps out. It is the PR. Jarvis, in thick specs and belted granny cardie, unravels from the passenger seat. I find it quite confusing trying to combine the roles of interviewer and hostess, but he makes it easy – he is *so* likeable. All he wants for breakfast is old-fashioned tea and toast. He comes into the kitchen and rabbits on while I make it. He goes into a great long rap about *The Graduate*, which he had watched on telly the night before, or rather 'I didn't really watch it because I've seen it so many times but I had a record on and I just had the picture on because you know, I'm postmodern – that's what we're all supposed to do, now we're living in a fragmented, almost millennial society – do five things at once and only pay attention to little bits of them.'

He keeps asking whether I think the closing shot of *The Graduate* is meant to be a happy ending. He seems really to care about my answer. But I, trying to make his breakfast and do five things at once, am not really paying attention. Only afterwards do I realize he was talking about his own situation, post-fame: 'I always thought it was a happy ending, but having seen it again, the way that shot lingers at the end, it was like, Well what next then? The event's happened and now it's actually the reality of living the rest of your life.'

After a while I start panicking – is he going to talk about *The Graduate* all morning? He avoids questions by swerving past them and talking about something else – mainly film and telly trivia. He says he's trying to wean himself off watching telly, but he obviously watches it a lot. He told me the entire career of John Nettles, ex-*Bergerac*, ex-World of Leather, before admitting, 'That's a bit of a digression. But that's the trouble, you see – my mind is littered with all that kind of stuff, which takes up the room that important, proper memories should be in.'

Or maybe he's just tired of talking about himself. 'Being the singer, it's always me me me, I, I, I – I think this, I do that, this is *my* insight into the world. It's a very self-obsessed thing.' And talking about himself only adds to the self-loathing that seems to be an ineradicable part of his character. He doesn't like his own company, he gets sick of hearing himself, that's why he always has flatmates. He formed a pop group originally, aged fifteen, because he wanted to be in a gang. And Pulp *is* a gang – they share the money equally, they make decisions democratically – but he always ends up doing the talking. And so he has created this sort of monster, the public Jarvis, who *is* Jarvis, but perhaps a slightly cute and cuddly version of the real thing.

It's important to remember that Jarvis has been Jarvis for an awfully long time. He *seems* new, in that he only 'arrived' in 1995, but he had thirty-two years of being Jarvis before most of us were aware of him. And by all accounts he was always the *same* Jarvis – he hasn't been styled up for stardom. There are plenty of sightings from Sheffield in the early 1980s or from St Martin's College in the late 1980s that describe essentially the same man. He always dressed like he does, he was always thin and nerdy and low-key, he was always a misfit. Lotte Heath, who went out with him at art school, describes him as 'like an old man – he always wanted to go home and have his cup of tea'. But also, she remembers, 'He was so weird and different and unique I always knew he would be famous.'

He was an 'accident', born in 1963, when his mother, Christine, was an art student and his father, Mack Cocker, was a local jazz musician and occasional actor who was apt to claim to be Joe Cocker's brother (one of life's little ironies – he would have been better off staying as Jarvis Cocker's father). Mack and Christine married, settled down next to her parents, and had a daughter, Saskia, two years later. Note the names – there might be a Jarvis and a Saskia (Rembrandt's wife) in every playgroup now, but I bet they were the only ones in Sheffield in the early 1960s.

Jarvis describes his mother as being 'as close to a Bohemian as it's possible to get in Sheffield'. The two big events of Jarvis's young life were that at five he developed meningitis, and was left with permanently damaged eyesight, and then at seven, his father left home, emigrated to Australia, and disappeared – no letters, no Christmas cards, nothing. Christine got a job emptying fruit machines to support the family.

Henceforth, Jarvis was entirely surrounded by women – his mother, his sister, his grandmother, his aunt, his great-aunt. As he remembers it, all his friends' fathers also disappeared in 1970. Two years ago, an Australian tabloid tracked down Jarvis's father in Darwin. It said he had been an alcoholic, but had now reformed; and had worked as a radio DJ, claiming to be Joe Cocker's brother. The *Sun* of course offered to fly Jarvis to Australia for a big reunion but Jarvis refused – 'I can't imagine anything worse.' But in fact he did go privately to meet his father, which was probably the inspiration for 'Help the Aged' and, more specifically, 'A Little Soul' on *Hardcore*, in which a father tells his son: 'You see your mother and me, we never got along that well you see. I'd love to help you but everybody's telling me you look like me but please don't turn out like me . . . I've only got a little soul.'

So he doesn't feel bitter? 'No, I don't feel bitter at all. I understand it totally. If you think about that time, the 1960s, and I know that I wasn't a planned pregnancy so, for a start, he probably didn't want to get married. Then, I know he had aspirations to be a musician and to be an actor, which probably had to be put on hold. And also he ended up living next door to my mother's parents – and they're nice people but, you know, it probably made him feel just a bit under pressure. So I don't feel any bitterness towards him at all. I feel *sorry* for him.' How does his mother feel about it? 'My mother's all right, you know, she's sensible.'

When Jarvis talks about his childhood now, he always plays it for laughs, but it can't have been much fun at the time. Fatherless, brotherless, pathetically thin and weedy, bespectacled, useless at games, and called Jarvis, he was exactly the sort of boy other boys pick on. But he was bright; he learned to use wit as a weapon.

At fifteen, he formed a band because, 'I couldn't play football so it was an alternative way to hang around in a gang. Also, because I was a sad teenager, I thought being in a band would solve all my problems. I thought I'd be able to get girls.' In fact he didn't get a girl – or not enough to lose his virginity – till he was almost twenty, but his attempts to do so provided some of his best lyrics.

When he was seventeen, he had the first of many false dawns – recorded a session for John Peel, released his first album – but it didn't lead anywhere. This was the beginning of the 1980s, his dismal decade. The original members of Pulp went off to university, but he hung around in Sheffield for six years, drawing the dole, living in squats. He got a new band together and released a second Pulp album, *Freaks (Ten Songs about Power, Claustrophobia, Suffocation and Holding Hands)*, which was inspired by 'me thinking we were turning into freaks living on the margins of society which I've never wanted to do. I've always wanted to fit in, really.'

In 1985, he was trying to be Spiderman to impress a girl when he fell off a window ledge and ended up in hospital with a broken pelvis, wrist and foot, and spent two months in a wheelchair. It seems to have had a galvanizing effect. Up till then, 'I'd done nothing but live in the future' but suddenly he decided to apply for a film course at St Martin's in London. It was here, of course, that he encountered the class system and met the girl who inspired 'Common People'. He also discovered Acid House raves and the joys of being Sorted for Es and Wizz. He made a third album, *Separations*, but it wasn't released for three years. In 1990, a Pulp single, 'My Legendary Girlfriend', was chosen as *NME*'s single of the week, and suddenly labels were vying to sign them. Pulp actually signed with Island and went through the whole champagne celebration party knowing that the contract wasn't worth the paper it was written on because they were already signed with someone else. It took a couple of years to sort out their legal entanglements, but finally they released *His n Hers* with Island in 1994 and got shortlisted for the Mercury Music Prize.

And then in 1995 they released 'Common People', the first single from their new album *Different Class*. Incredibly, it was never number one, it was beaten by two blokes from *Soldier, Soldier.* But Pulp were called in to replace the injured Stone Roses as the headline act at that summer's Glastonbury Festival, and when Jarvis started 'She came from Greece, she had a thirst for knowledge, she studied sculpture at St Martin's College', the whole 100,000-strong crowd sang along, word perfect. Jarvis was too nervous to enjoy it then, but he said afterwards: 'It makes you feel you haven't wasted the last fifteen years of your life, that you were right to have carried on. It makes you feel you weren't mentally ill all that time.' The album went triple platinum and won the Mercury Music Prize.

But of course – and this is where *The Graduate* comes in – his problem was what happens next? He'd spent more than half his life being an *unsuccessful* pop star – he was so used to it that he was completely unprepared for success. For the first year, he went to every party he was invited to and got very drunk. He'd stopped drinking beer because he didn't want to get fat, so he was drinking whisky and brandy instead. Would it be true to say he was drunk for the whole of 1996?

'Could be. It's a nice thought. You know, it was quite an exciting time. I'd been going along, being in a band, since I was seventeen and so obviously, by the time we actually achieved that ambition, I was a completely different person. So then there's a sort of examination of motives, because instead of it just being a fantasy, now you've got the reality, and you think, "Well hold on, why did I want to do this? Is it because I want to be successful and show off and go to places? Or is it a pure and noble artistic intention to create something?" And after having been a marginal character, on the fringes of things, suddenly being in the centre, the eye of the storm – you are kind of cut-off from your former life, because you can't really just do normal things. And so you think, "Well, do you just have to hang around with famous people now because they're not going to hassle you so much?" The thing is, I always worry about things, all the time – but if you get pissed, then you stop worrying, you kind of go on to autopilot. So, it's not like I turned into Oliver Reed or something, but I have to admit there were some hairy moments. But luckily, through a combination of still knowing people I'd known for a long time, from before getting famous, and maybe having a bit of common sense, in the end you realize you're going to have to stop, otherwise you're going to be a kind of laughing stock.'

There were darker rumours about heroin, not exactly discouraged by a recent interview in *Select* in which he seemed to admit he'd experimented (though he told me that he was misquoted). I would have bet he was too sensible to get into hard drugs, but he seems keen to prevaricate. 'Well, you know, I've had 'em. But if you talk about them then it's like as if you're showing off, like there's something really great about the fact that you've had them. And there isn't. And it's not even like a big deal because there's lots of people in the world who've had lots more than me, or who are much more experienced at taking drugs.'

Anyway, whether he was drunk or drugged, 1996 and 1997 were virtually missing years. Pulp were supposed to start recording their new album in autumn 1996 when they came back from their world tour, but they had only written one song, 'Help the Aged'. And when they *did* assemble in the studio in November, Jarvis suddenly pissed off to New York for three weeks on some unexplained mission to 'find himself'. Meanwhile, Russell Senior, Jarvis's oldest, most loyal lieuten-ant, decided to leave the band because he found 'it wasn't creatively rewarding to be in Pulp any more'. Pulp managed the split amicably, agreeing a financial settlement between themselves without lawyers, but obviously it took a while to adjust. Jarvis still sounds a bit cool towards Russell: 'He'd been with me for thirteen years. But I wouldn't say we were close like confiding things in each other. There was always quite a bit of friction between us.' Russell told Radio One that Jarvis slept in brown pyjamas and had halitosis.

The new album was due in 1997 but in the end Pulp released just one single, 'Help the Aged', which only got to number eight in the charts. There were obviously disagreements within the band about what to put on the album – guitarist Mark Webber told *NME* that there are two tracks ('TV Movie' and 'A Little Soul') he can't bear to listen to but 'recently it has been a case of Jarvis's will overriding everyone else's common sense'. This sounds bad – but one of the many attractive features of Pulp is that they all feel free to slag Jarvis off, and often do. Steve Mackay, the bassist, says the band pick on Jarvis because 'He's got to have something to write about, hasn't he? Paranoia, psychosis, lack of self-confidence, those are the kind of things that lead to fairly reasonable songs.'

All the group seem quite resigned to the idea that *This is Hardcore* won't do as well as *Different Class* – it's a very dark album. The title track entered the charts last week at number twelve, which is not promising, and there are no immediate plans for a tour. Instead, Jarvis is going off to make three programmes for Channel 4 about 'Outsider Artists'. He thinks film-making is what he'll do when his pop career is finished – 'It could save me from the trout farm.'

And what of his long-term plans? He turns thirty-five this year, so in theory the pram in the hall beckons, but he still feels he wants a refund on his adolescence. 'I've always been a bit immature, you know, in that I never saw much attraction in becoming an adult.' He thinks he *might* buy a house (at present he shares a rented flat with friends) but 'I don't want to get too settled. Because being a pop star, or any kind of artist – they're not like real people you know – it's always a balancing act that you play. Because you have to write about things that real people are interested in, because they're the people that buy your records, but you don't really live your life like a normal person because in a way you *invite* disasters, because it gives you material. I hate that aspect of it because it's like you're something less than a real human being and I think it's more important to be a human being than to be an artist.'

'Really?'

'Well, *yes*! Because otherwise you're some kind of unnatural monster. It's like that song "Dishes" [I am not Jesus though I have the same initials – I am the man who stays home and does the dishes] and this aspiration towards doing the pots – which will never be more than an aspiration I'm afraid – I don't know if I'm just being some kind of sentimental prat really. I probably couldn't hack it, if I tried to live a domestic life. I'd like to be able to do it, you know – most of the rest of the stuff is just a load of shit really – but I think it's much more difficult nowadays because there's so many distractions and so many options. I don't *like* choice. I'd rather be in a kind of Soviet discipline where you just had one thing and it might not be very good quality, but at least you didn't have to go to the supermarket and choose from ten varieties of it. You watch the telly, and there's so many lifestyle choices, so many things that will make you feel dissatisfied with what you've got in your life. And so, for two people to stay together and be happy and not resent each other, it's very difficult. But that's the thing to aspire to. Because the other things are just illusions, really.'

He has been with the same girlfriend, Sarah, a psychiatric nurse, for several years. There is no question of marriage because he doesn't believe in marriage, but he is obviously thinking in terms of commitment, possibly even children eventually, though he doesn't think he can combine being a father with being a pop star. Though even that . . . He used to make all these rules for himself but now he's loosening up. He wouldn't *necessarily* retire if his girlfriend got pregnant. A couple of the band have become fathers recently and they seem to have survived. And what does Sarah feel? Jarvis won't talk about her because 'I've come to realize – having had certain intrusions into my private life – that it's quite important to keep it private.'

One of the intrusions was a make-up girl he had a fling with in early 1996, who kissed and told to the *News of the World*. (She gave him a good write-up – she said: 'In bed, he satisfied my every need' – though he never took his shirt off.) It sounded such an obvious tabloid trap I wondered if he was set up – did he feel like an innocent dupe in that entanglement? 'Oh no no no. I'm not innocent at all. I probably even knew that kind of thing was going to happen. I didn't *know* that but a lot of people had told me from the outset that I would find myself in trouble if I got involved. But sometimes – well, that's how it happens, isn't it? It's not a logical thing, sexual attraction. And sometimes the fact that you can see this car crash about to occur, in a way it's a kind of a turn-on, you know?'

I wondered if the fling with the make-up girl was perhaps intended to provoke a crisis with Sarah? He gives me a nasty look and says, 'I don't know. That would be something for me to go and talk to a psychiatrist about, wouldn't it?' Might he do that? 'No. I believe in DIY therapy – you write songs about it – that kind of works things out. Because a lot of times, the things you end up writing songs about, like "Help the Aged", is something that is preying on your mind, and somehow using it and facing it somehow defuses it.'

If *This is Hardcore* is DIY therapy, he's been grappling with some horrendous problems – panic attacks, self-loathing, disgust, drugs and (on 'The Professional', the B-side of the single) sexual exhaustion – 'I'm rapidly losing interest in sex, I can't even hold myself erect.' Only one song, 'Dishes', holds out a slender hope of redemption – and he says that if the Jarvis of six or seven years ago had heard that song, he would have said, 'What a load of sentimental twaddle!' Now he thinks it's borderline sentimental. But he is still, he believes, emotionally cold. 'This is something that's always worried me, really – I can get involved and affected by programmes and stuff that I watch on the telly, and even books you know' – he stops and shakes his head reproachfully, '*Even* books!' before continuing – 'But when it comes to emotional or supposedly emotional events in my life, I have difficulty summoning up the kind of requisite feelings. You kind of know what kind of response you're *supposed* to have but . . . Someone can be crying and I'll be just sat there stony-faced, saying, "Can you keep it down please, I'm trying to watch the telly."'

He always comes across in interviews as sensitive and caring. But if you listen to the lyrics, a quite different Jarvis emerges, a cold-eyed stalker lurking in the shadows, a class-war guerrilla raiding the bourgeoisie, preying on its women. 'I Spy', on *Different Class*, is the clearest exposition: 'You see you should take me seriously, very seriously indeed.

'Cos I've been sleeping with your wife for the past sixteen weeks. Smoking your cigarettes, drinking your brandy, messing up the bed that you chose together. And in all that time I just wanted you to come home unexpectedly one afternoon and catch us at it in the front room . . . Take your year in Provence and shove it up your ass.'

Russell Senior said he always felt Jarvis was a hypocrite when he sang about the Common People, because by the time he sang it, he was a celeb. But that is why it is important to remember that successful Jarvis is a very new phenomenon. *Now* he has fans throwing their knickers on stage and passing him their phone numbers, but for most of his life he belonged to the ranks of the sexually deprived and envious – 'You were the first girl at school to get breasts. Martyn said that you were the best. The boys all loved you but I was a mess. I had to watch them try and get you undressed.' He can't suddenly forget all those years. And so I think he finds himself now in the position of a voyeur who has spent every evening watching a girl undress, and then one night she opens the door and says, 'Hi! Do you wanna shag?' The reaction is a mixture of shock and glee – but also disappointment at losing his reliable fantasy. The reality is never so good. I think that's what his whole problem with success is about – it was more fun dreaming about it. And now he is too old, and too aware, to enjoy it shamelessly, as he should.

Reproduced by permission of *The Observer*.

Lord Rees-Mogg

3 August 1997

There is nothing like a walk round St James's, I find, to get the bile flowing before an interview. Lord Rees-Mogg has an address in Pall Mall above a bookshop he used to own, but I arrived early, so I took the opportunity to stroll around the Buffer Zone, admiring those fine gentlemen's clubs towering like cliffs, the gunsmiths, the hatters, the wine merchants, the bootmakers, the shops selling unbelievably small, expensive fiddly bits connected with fly-fishing. It is an area designed exclusively for the elderly pinstriped male – one expects female pigeons to tumble out of the sky as they hit Pall Mall airspace – and therefore an ideal setting for this pillar of the Establishment.

Rees-Mogg upholds established wealth, established privilege, established mores. He is of the dare-to-be-dull school of journalism, never afraid to urge acceptance of the accepted, or to iterate the obvious. The only unusual feature of his writing is its strong streak of self-advertisement: he once began a column, 'Of the five prime ministers I have known . . .' Wherever the great and good are assembled at some self-congratulatory solemn seminar, Lord Gravitas will be there, delivering a paper on this or that, and then writing a *Times* column about it to display his hobnobbing status at the tables of the great. Many people seem to take him at his own evaluation as an important political pundit and expert economist. This belief is easier to sustain if one doesn't read his *Times* columns.

It isn't *quite* true to say that Rees-Mogg is always wrong – he was right about the recession and right about the French election – but let's just say that when Mystic Mogg predicts the coming of the ice age, you can safely put away your winter clothes. He said that Watergate was all a leftie plot against Nixon. He said that Clinton could never be re-elected, that Colin Powell would be the next American president; that Heseltine would be the next prime minister and Berlusconi would be the Mrs Thatcher of Italy. He said when the Pan Am flight came down over Lockerbie that it would prove to be metal fatigue: he knew because he'd flown Pan Am a few weeks earlier and noticed that the plane had rattled. Best of all – a moment treasured by Mogg-watchers – on 18 September 1995, he said that a new set of OECD figures proved that Britain was the most economically successful of the G7 countries. Several top economists then pointed out that the figures proved no such thing, rather the reverse, and that they illustrated a quite different subject. Rees-Mogg in his next column offered not an apology – heaven forfend! – but an admission that he had 'misconceived' the figures.

He seems to welcome these howlers. On 20 November 1990, when the first ballot for the Tory leadership was being held, he wrote in his *Independent* column: 'Thatcher has won – the victory was clearly a decisive one.' Later in the day, when it became apparent that Thatcher's decisive victory was no such thing, a sub-editor rang to suggest he change the sentence before it went to press. He declined.

As chairman of the Broadcasting Standards Council, he blithely confessed he rarely watched television, and when he did, his favourite programme was *'Inspector Thaw'*. As chairman of the Arts Council, he admitted he had not read any English fiction after Trollope, though he told me he had rectified that since, because he had read 'that book about the First World War, *you* know, oh what's its name?' I suggested he meant *Birdsong* and he agreed, but I have a sneaking suspicion he thinks *Birdsong* is the *only* novel about the First World War. Maliciously, I told him that if he liked *Birdsong*, he would *love Trainspotting*, and he promised to read it. But, actually, it is a well-known fact that people who say they read Trollope never read fiction.

How can someone be so frequently wrong and still be so complacent? No prob for the Mogg. I asked whether the teeniest shadow of a blush ever crossed his cheeks after, say, Clinton's re-election. 'Not at all. If you're a columnist, you have to remember that you're not the Pope and that what people want is a clear expression of what you *think*, on the basis of imperfect knowledge – writing much too early in the process – is going to happen next. It's one of the functions of a columnist to do that; it starts the discussion going. But if you're going to do that you're going to get a lot of things wrong; it's inevitable. A columnist, therefore, who doesn't ever get things wrong is, in my view, a columnist who is not doing his job properly. And I think that my sort of batting average, of getting forecasts right to getting them wrong, is a perfectly respectable one.'

The fine grammatical sentences roll on and on, not as a torrent but as a smooth-flowing mature river. The effect is weirdly impersonal. At one point, talking about television censorship, he gives me a lecture about 'what mothers want' without apparently ever asking himself whether I might be a mother. It is as if he is talking about the Ancient Egyptians or the Kalahari Bushmen. I keep wondering, Am I here? But then I remember: as editor of *The Times*, he was famous for dictating his leaders straight off the top of his head to a secretary. I am now that secretary.

He is, with one exception, as we shall see, unflustered by awkward questions. He is courteous, and gives an impression of diffidence, though that is misleading. He has an engaging lisp and a rather wild schoolboyish giggle. At sixty-nine, he seems ageless. (There are no recorded sightings of Rees-Mogg as a young man: he always wanted to be middle-aged and achieved it soon after he left school.) He is tall and elegant and beaky, perfectly tailored, though with suede shoes. His top-floor flat is as impersonal as a Harley Street waiting room. Later, I get overexcited when a trip to the loo reveals a blouson jacket and some rather trendy boxer shorts hanging on an airer. Good Lord, I fantasize, does he doff his pinstripe and don a blouson and cruise the Coleherne of an evening? Alas, no. He tells me that although he owns the flat, he rents it to a young Tory, who lets him use it in the daytime when he is out.

Most of Rees-Mogg's credibility derives from the fact that from 1967 to 1981 he edited *The Times* – in those days probably still the most prestigious newspaper in the world. He had previously worked at the

Sunday Times and the *Financial Times*, but it is not clear that he was a good editor. He first tried to make *The Times* more popular but retreated when existing readers complained. He seldom stayed late in the office and would hand over to a night editor, even when a front-page story was breaking, to attend important dinner parties. Once, he removed a news story (about Rhodesia) because it didn't fit his editorial 'line'. But at least on that occasion he had read the paper; there was one memorable Monday conference when he suggested it was time for a leader on Beirut, and his colleagues had to point out that the paper had run a leader on Beirut that very morning. In 1979, when *The Times* was facing closure, he descended to the newsroom, apparently for the first time, to meet the reporters. Some members of staff never encountered him in his fourteen years as editor. And although his Tuesday general policy conferences (known as Moggologues) were much enjoyed by the leader-writers, it is difficult to find any journalist who claims to have been inspired by him in the way that you often find journalists saying they 'owe everything' to Harold Evans or David English or Kelvin MacKenzie.

In 1981, Rupert Murdoch bought *The Times* and Rees-Mogg made a quick departure. He accepted a directorship with GEC and took up a string of predictable Establishment jobs – vice-chairman of the BBC Board of Governors, chairman of the Arts Council, chairman of the Broadcasting Standards Council. In 1988, he was made a life peer, though he has never made much impact in the House of Lords. He started writing columns for the *Independent*, then switched to *The Times*.

One of his more quixotic gestures was to buy the antiquarian bookshop Pickering and Chatto, but he sold it in 1992 because it was losing money (though he retains its more profitable publishing imprint). He has always been quite beady about money. He inherited £3,000 from an aunt and played the stock market while still at school. At Oxford, he read the *FT* in bed every morning – a fact that appeared in an undergraduate profile of him and led to his being offered his first job on the paper. (His son, Jacob Rees-Mogg, was an even more precocious investor and offered share tips as a schoolboy.) The family fortune derives from Mogg's great-grandfather who was a north Somerset solicitor when north Somerset had a thriving coalfield. Anyway,

Rees-Mogg is well off, and owns a nice rectory in Somerset as well as his digs in Pall Mall.

He has various directorships – the most surprising is one with John Latsis's company, the Private Bank & Trust Co Ltd. Potential depositors who might have qualms about investing their money with the mysterious and controversial Latsis are reassured by an invitation to lunch to meet Lord Rees-Mogg. They might be less reassured if they knew how incurious Rees-Mogg is. He told me he really only knew Latsis's son, Spiro, and 'I don't know much about the history of the family. I believe they have been major Greek shipowners of the Onassis/Niarchos kind from the 1930s and now have a connection with the Middle East.' Anyway Latsis's respectability is vouched for by the fact that the Princess of Wales has holidayed on his yacht and, of course, that he was a major donor to the Tory Party, as revealed by Lord McAlpine.

So much for Mogg's public career. Now what of the private man? He is a practising Catholic and has been happily married to his former secretary for thirty-five years. They have five children, all clever. He has never attracted a whiff of scandal; he has never been seen drunk or misbehaving or even in a temper. He admits that any passions are well repressed: 'I've got a tremendously strong feeling that I want to be in control of myself, and a dislike of being out of control.' Edward Mortimer, who worked for him on *The Times*, recalls once being told that Rees-Mogg was 'furious' about a news story he'd written on Rhodesia. Puzzled, Mortimer rang him at home and Rees-Mogg told him: 'I am at this moment furious. I shall no doubt in due course cease to be furious.'

But, despite his air of cool, impersonal cerebration, there is also a wildly irrational side to him. He is moved to tears by sentimental films; he believes in banshees and has seen them on three occasions; he believes in time travel and once found himself attending an eighteenth-century funeral. Far from being embarrassed by these psychic adventures, he loves talking about them – the green greatcoat of the man in front of him at the funeral, the feeling of straw underfoot – and says, 'I have no doubt that there is another world. And also that time doesn't really work. The idea that there is an arrow of time which allows time only to point in one direction I think is a mistake.'

At this point one wonders: is he really a great brain? The evidence is inconclusive. He won a scholarship to Charterhouse and a (highly prestigious) Brackenbury scholarship to Balliol, but then he only got a second. As a writer, he is a master of the higher intellectual fudge, using qualifiers like 'to some degree' and 'on the balance of probabilities' to suggest that he has armies of facts at his disposal which he won't trouble you with right now but that you can trust him to summarize. Though after those 'misconceived' OECD figures, one might have one's doubts. Anyway, when I put it to him that he wasn't really a first-class brain, he agreed readily enough: 'I think that's absolutely true. What I was very good at was showing promise. But then there comes a moment when . . .' And he gave one of his strange high-pitched giggles.

The Rees-Mogg giggle is really disconcerting, like a glimpse into a completely different character. Harold Evans noticed it and commented in *Good Times, Bad Times*: 'There is an emotional and showy side to Rees-Mogg which is disguised by his solemn demeanour and revealed only occasionally by an impulsive command or a schoolboy giggle.' Most people who have worked with him attest to this quality of showmanship, which was most glaringly apparent in 1967, when he wrote a *Times* leader ('Who Breaks a Butterfly Upon a Wheel?') defending Mick Jagger from a drugs charge while it was still *sub judice*. He then appeared in a silly television 'debate' with Jagger after his release from prison. A similar desire to jump into the limelight seemed to inspire the curious case he brought in 1993, applying for a judicial review of the Maastricht Treaty. His image as the fearless crusader was only slightly weakened by the revelation that Sir James Goldsmith was paying.

One does not expect such a quintessential Englishman to be a showman. But Rees-Mogg is only half an Englishman. His father's family, to which he often refers, was Somerset gentry, but his mother was a) American and b) an actress, which, I believe, accounts for a) his worship of Mammon and b) his somewhat fake, show-off side. He says of the former, 'Being half American . . . I have always been unsympathetic with the British distaste for thinking about money.' On the latter, he concedes: 'I think one of the influences my mother had on me was that she saw English life as romantic. She was fascinated by how they did it, and played the role herself to some degree as a role.'

Casually, thinking of them both having American mothers, I asked if I would be way off beam if I compared him to Harold Macmillan. The question had a quite astonishing effect, not unlike the moment in a whodunnit when the detective says, 'I put it to you, Colonel Carruthers, that it was you who fired the poisoned dart into the locked library.' The normally unstoppable flow of his speech was cut off at the mains and only a trickle of gulps and sputters got through. His first reaction was a glum-sounding 'Yup' followed by a long, nervous, whinnying laugh. This seemed to be all he was offering by way of answer, so I asked again if I would be wrong to make the comparison. 'Er . . . not entirely, not entirely. And, er . . . yes . . . I had quite a sort of fascinating relationship with him because we got on very well together without ever wholly . . .' He pauses again and sighs. Then the nub. 'There was an element of seeing through each other.'

Was he ever aware of himself hamming up the old-fashioned English gentleman persona? 'Not to the Harold Macmillan degree, I'm glad to say. But yes . . . I'm not theatrical in the professional sense that my mother was, but yes, there's an element of seeing that there is quite often a role to be played. And I enjoy public speaking, I enjoy the business of how you sort of start a speech rather slowly, sort of slightly fiddling around, to get people wondering when it's really going to start, and building a bit of the momentum and so on. All of that I do take pleasure in.'

Once he has admitted this much, he suddenly becomes almost confiding. 'As a schoolboy I was certainly fascinated by intrigue. I remember one particular intrigue which indicates the sort of schoolboy I was. There was a nice boy called, I think, Tony Rimell, who was captain of the eleven and a possible candidate to be head of the school. And there was another very able boy called George Engel, who was the other candidate. And George was editor of the *Carthusian* and I was deputy editor. So if George became head of the school, I was going to become editor of the school magazine. And another boy called Peter Newton came to me and said "I think we ought to abolish Corps" – this was in 1944, rather an inappropriate moment at which to abolish Corps. And I got Tony Rimell to sign a letter to the *Carthusian* saying that we ought to abolish the school corps. And George Engel refused to publish it. And Rimell said, "Do you think I should go to the headmaster, and tell him that it's an outrage against freedom of speech that this letter is not being published?" And I, without blinking an eye, but seeing all the obvious consequences, said, "Yes, I think that's a good idea." And he went off to the headmaster and Tony Rimell did not become head of the school, George Engel did become head of the school, and I did become editor of the *Carthusian*. So that is the kind of schoolboy I was!'

Actually, we know quite a lot about the kind of schoolboy he was from Simon Raven, who was his contemporary at Charterhouse, and portrayed him both in his autobiography, *Shadows in the Grass*, and in his *Arms for Oblivion* novels. The portrait that emerges is not very likeable. Raven claims that Rees-Mogg deliberately put a rumour round the school that masturbation gave you syphilis, and, when accosted, explained: 'My motive is twofold: first to see how many people are stupid enough to believe it, and secondly to discourage shagging, since my church holds solitary vice to be a mortal sin.'

Rees-Mogg denies the story and says that, anyway, his character has changed since school. He was unhappy as a teenager, because he suffered from jaundice, which left him depressed for several years. He *could* have become the cold-hearted schemer portrayed by Raven, but he grew out of his taste for intrigue, and no longer practises it. But it left him with a useful understanding of what sort of intrigues people *might* be getting up to, so that he can still count heads at a committee and know where he stands. 'I've always had a good sort of defensive capacity. If people were laying traps for me, on the whole I've seen through them, and I've got enough of a residue of that kind of temperament not to be often taken in. But I don't *do* it. And I don't do it because I have no feeling that that's a sensible way to organize life, or enjoyable or worthwhile.'

But despite this renunciation – and despite his Catholicism, his blameless private life, his air of Establishment rectitude – one still feels there is something terribly cold-hearted about him. It is difficult to see what he deeply cares about, apart from money. He supported Nixon throughout Watergate, right to the bitter end, because, he argues, Nixon was never guilty of *financial* impropriety, as his predecessor LBJ certainly was. And on recent Conservative sleaze, he says: 'I mind about money and don't mind about sex.' But why? Presumably because he thinks people's private lives are of piffling importance. The only principle he consistently and vehemently upholds is the need to increase wealth and to preserve the status of the 'cerebral élite' (Moggspeak for clever clogs) to which he belongs.

Perhaps I have been ruder about Rees-Mogg than I need have been. Who breaks a butterfly upon a wheel? All his chums kept telling me: don't get so *cross* with him, Lynn, don't take him so *seriously*. They regard him as a bit of a fraud, but an amusing and likeable one. The fact that he has never quite lived up to his 'promise' doesn't seem to matter. He has the pinstripe, the accent, the background, the manners, the appearance of gravitas, so naturally he deserves his peerage, his directorships, his space in *The Times*. I suppose what I'm really complaining about – boringly – is the persistence of the class system and the fact that we are all such suckers for pomposity. So I'd better stop being chippy and hand over to one of his fans, Andreas Whittam Smith, who launched Rees-Mogg's career as a columnist on the *Independent*. He says of Mogg: 'He has tried many things – politics, economics, investment, bookshop, Arts Council – he's now in the House of Lords but has made no impact there. Finally, what we have is a very civilized, well-read eccentric columnist who writes beautifully, and that is the beginning and end of William Rees-Mogg. He tried to be more – he tried to be a politician, he claims to know prime ministers – but finally he's just a highly informed columnist. Which is something we need more of, and if there's ever a collection to put up a statue to him, I'll put in £5.'

David Hockney

15 March 1998

Why is there this far-flung bit of Yorkshire stuck in the Holly-wood Hills? Why isn't David Hockney in England, where he is needed? Even if he isn't our greatest living painter, he is certainly our most popular one, and heaven knows we don't have many of those to spare. He doesn't even *like* Los Angeles any more, now the anti-smoking health Nazis and his increasing deafness make it impossible for him to socialize. These days, he barely leaves his studio; the American art world passes him by. He was lured to Hollywood in the 1960s by sun and fun and boys, but the fun and boys have been culled by Aids and the friends who were meant to comfort his old age are all dead. Meanwhile, his 97-year-old mother lives on in Bridlington, his sister is there, his brother is up the coast at Flamborough and Bradford is hatching a whole clutch of baby Hockneys. His roots are in Yorkshire, and it's also the inspiration for his recent paintings.

But to interview Hockney about Yorkshire, I had to go to Los Angeles. When I first met him in the 1960s, he looked totally Californian, with his dyed blond hair, outrageous clothes, big coloured spectacles. But now, at sixty, he has reverted to pure Yorkshireman – the jutting jaw, the pursed mouth, the Alan Bennett haircut. Like Bennett, he manages to look both boyish and elderly. He had a minor heart attack in 1990 and now pounds a treadmill every day, but he still smokes heroically. Sadly, his deafness has advanced to the point where he can no longer enjoy music, so he will not do opera designs any more.

He is friendly, approachable, a joy to meet. I can't imagine anyone in the world ever disliking Hockney, but they might say nowadays he's becoming a bit of a monologist. It's the fault of his deafness, of course – he does the usual deaf person's trick of talking non-stop and throwing in a lot of fillers – 'frankly', 'I must say', 'I would point out' – to cover pauses. It gives him a slightly hectoring, soapbox tone. But – more – you get the sense that he has talked too much to himself. It seems absurd to call him a recluse when he is surrounded by more gofers than most film stars, but there is a touch of the Ancient Mariner about him. His theories, ideas, opinions come tumbling out as if he has been hoarding them through months of solitude.

His studio is a former indoor tennis court, though with one corner lopped off so it is slightly funnel-shaped. It contains tables and tables of huge fat tubes of paint, and racks and pots of brushes, an elephantine easel and a beautiful life-size wooden articulated horse. There are several recent and current paintings on the walls, the latest a sketch – but a sketch comprising sixteen separate canvases – of the Grand Canyon. On the opposite wall, for reference, he has one of his old 'joiners' – photocollages – of the Grand Canyon. Unfortunately, he has grown keen on these photocollages again (a few years ago, he said he was done with them) because the new Getty Center has bought an important one, *Pearblossom Highway*, and it has been much admired. Although he talks dismissively of art critics (and they of him), he is not entirely immune to their opinions.

The studio is full of good jokes – a headline from the *New York Times* saying, 'Science confronts the unknowable – less is known than people think' and a sign saying, 'Thank you for Pot Smoking'. Hockney is quite keen on pot smoking but he is positively fanatical about ordinary smoking: he smokes at parties, premières and exhibitions, which in Los Angeles makes him a crazed and dangerous sociopath. His personal assistant, Jimmy, mentioned he had heard an item on the news saying that city officials were urging people not to call 911 to report people smoking in bars, because they were jamming the emergency lines. Hockney immediately responded,

'*We* should do that – jam it up, Jimmy, jam it up!'

Jimmy is one of Hockney's many assistants: his job seemed to be answering the telephone, pouring tea (from a 'A Present from Lowestoft' teapot) and fetching bones for the dogs. There is also Richard, his studio assistant, and Maurice, in charge of etchings, and Gregory (former model and boyfriend, now employee), who turned up to report on the state of Hockney's house at Malibu after a week of El Niño storms (water damage but not serious) – but, anyway, Hockney rarely goes there these days. Offstage, there is a housekeeper, and an office manager to run his office downtown. So, quite a little court, for a Bradford socialist's son.

And still no boyfriend, two years after his last boyfriend left. They had been together seven years, so it still leaves a gap. Hockney's friends reassure him that he will fall in love again but he says he barely leaves the house now and never goes to parties, so how can he meet anyone? 'But I always assume things will turn up – they always do, frankly, in my life. Somehow I manage.' His loneliness is exacerbated by the loss of friends to Aids. 'I've lost *too many* friends. And it's odd, for someone my age, to have lost so many; I thought I would grow old with them. For instance, when I lived in Paris, I had four close friends – none of them alive now. New York, far more. I'm really a bit of a loner now.' But he has his much loved dachshunds, Stanley and Boodgie, stars of the exhibition *Dog Days*, who loll around the studio in odalisque poses.

Hockney has been an exile for most of his adult life, and yet, as he says, 'I never turned my back on Bradford.' Once, when his friend R. B. Kitaj was bemoaning his own rootlessness, Hockney responded: 'I've got Bradford; they'll never take that away from me.' Bradford, of course, means more than just the place – he means his family, his childhood, his solid early training at the Bradford School of Art, but also the Yorkshire grit, the doggedness, the work ethic that has allowed him to live in the lotus land of LA all these years without being softened or corrupted. Even in the 1960s, when he seemed to be at parties everywhere you looked, he still maintained his usual Stakhanovite working pace.

He always went back to Yorkshire to see his mother at least once a year, and says rather grimly, 'I'm sixty years old, and I've spent fifty-eight Christmases with my mother. And she's ninety-seven so I can't stop now, can I?' But in recent years, he's gone more often, usually staying just a week at a time. Last summer, however, he stayed in Bridlington much longer than usual and started painting the countryside, something he had never done before. 'I realized,' he said, 'I wanted to paint the landscape I'd known since my childhood, but in a new way, different from all those watercolours.'

Different indeed – the resulting canvases are recognizably Yorkshire yet unlike any English landscapes. They make the wolds seem glamorous and exotic, hot, unfamiliar, unpeopled, painted in blazing Californian desert colours. And the treatment of space is extraordinary, too – these are moving landscapes, or rather the eye seems to be moving, swinging fast through the countryside and villages in an open car. And besides the strange colours, the strange perspectives, there is something else again – a great freight of emotion, making these ecstatic, ideal landscapes as visionary in their way as Samuel Palmer's.

He painted them for his friend Jonathan Silver, who was dying. Silver was a Bradford businessman who made a fortune from property and clothing shops, and then travelled the world for two years with his wife and daughters. But in 1987, he heard that Salts Mill, Saltaire, one of the great old Bradford textile mills, was for sale and he dashed home, bought it and restored it. He turned one wing into an art gallery, the 1853 Gallery, and, as a friend and fan of Hockney's, held many Hockney exhibitions – *Tennis*, one of his fax works; the *Very New Paintings of 1992–1993* (which attracted 100,000 visitors); and then the riotous dog show two years ago when Hockney's portraits of Stanley and Boodgie were reviewed in *Dog World* and about 500 dachshunds dragged their owners to see it. The paintings were roped off with dog leads. That event was typical of Saltaire – it's a completely unpretentious gallery where local housewives pop in on their way to buy carpets.

Hockney describes Silver as, 'really the first thing in Bradford, outside my family, that was exciting and interesting. I didn't know many people in Bradford other than my relatives, I'd been away too long, and my old friends, like me, had left. But Jonathan went back to Bradford and did this thing [restored Salts Mill] so of course I was very impressed. I'd known the mill since childhood, I was brought up three miles away. We met because he was keen on pictures – not art necessarily, but painted pictures – that's what he liked and that's what I liked. He had a very sophisticated eye, and he could talk about pictures in an interesting way, he really *looked* at them.'

Was Hockney in love with him? 'Not sexually, but yes, in a way. He was an amazing person – dynamic, intelligent. You did grow to love him, he was a very special, unique kind of person, there are not many people with that kind of energy. And the fact that he did it in the provinces, I'm deeply aware of it. Most people in the south of England have never been further north than Oxford, have they?'

Hockney was at home for Christmas with his mother in December 1996 when Jonathan was first diagnosed with cancer of the pancreas. He stayed on, through January and February, painting portraits of Jonathan, himself, his mother, his brother, trying to hold on to the familiar faces. These are as different as possible from the pretty, pastel portraits he used to do in the 1960s. Gauche, charmless, almost repellent, with sci-fi turquoise eyes staring out of meaty faces, these are portraits of pain. The two self-portraits, in particular, are harrowing, and look nothing like Hockney. But how do I know, Hockney asks, what he looked like when he heard that Jonathan was dying? 'I had a sense of what was torturing me. For others I would cover it up a bit, but for myself I wouldn't.'

Hockney returned to Yorkshire in the summer, when Jonathan was near the end, and painted the Yorkshire landscapes for him. Every other day he would drive over the wolds from his mother's house in Bridlington to Jonathan's house in Wetherby and, 'I realized I had fallen in love with the landscape – the landscape's beautiful there, it's a very unspoiled bit of England, east Yorkshire. I've known it for fifty years and it's hardly changed. I found out why in the end – it's grade-one agricultural land, so the villages aren't extended, there's nothing for tourists, no tearooms, just these beautiful undulating hills. I worked on it when I was at school, harvesting corn for a summer job. So, looking at the landscape again, especially from an open car, and driving rather slowly because there's no one else on the roads, and going to see my ailing friend made me see the *living* aspect of the landscape. I must admit it was a glorious summer, it was incredibly fine. I was there just as they were beginning to cut the corn so you'd get these golden fields and then these great big machines, like insects laying eggs, leaving these big bales. Some days were just glorious, the colour was *fantastic*. I can see colour, I mean other people don't see it like me obviously.'

He painted against the clock, working very long hours, with no interruptions, no 'nattering', so he could finish the paintings before Jonathan died. He even painted Saltaire mill, though he wasn't keen on doing 'all that architecture', because he knew it would please Jonathan. 'Someone asked me, "Are they sad, these paintings?" and I said, "Well, I keep taking them over to show him" – meaning why on earth would I be showing him sad things? He's *dying*, frankly, and I'm showing him how beautiful the world is and he thinks so as well.' Silver died on 24 September 1997, aged forty-seven. Hockney returned to Los Angeles and there, from memory, painted another two astonishing Yorkshire landscapes, which are even brighter and more hallucinatory than the others.

Suddenly, Hockney hands me a scrap of paper and says: 'I was going to do this.' It is a tiny thumbnail sketch of his mother (staring straight ahead as she always does in his portraits of her), Jonathan Silver in profile, and himself, curled into a foetal ball. Although it is only a few lines, it carries an enormous emotional charge, recording the psychological tensions of last summer, when, for once, Hockney was in Bridlington not to see his mother but to see his friend. Mrs Hockney, though fond of Jonathan herself, was slightly disapproving; in the sketch she offers no comfort and seems to ignore her son's distress. Hockney explains that at this stage the drawing is just a note of an idea, but he will blow it up on the photocopier and pin it on the wall, and think about it for a few months and then maybe make a painting. I hope he does.

Of course, he always expected Jonathan Silver to be there to comfort him when his mother died. But at ninety-seven, she shows no intention of dying; and keeps a beady competitive eye on the Queen Mother and Barbara Cartland, her contemporaries. Hockney describes her as 'a very very strong-willed woman. Tough as old boots, frankly. I remember when Diana died, saying to my mother, "That's very sad, isn't it?" and she said, "Oh yes, very sad. Is there any more tea in that pot?" And I assume if you're ninety-seven you take a different view of death. Must do.'

His mother was and is very religious, and reads the Bible every day. I wondered whether she was upset by his homosexuality which he was always quite open about, even when it was still illegal. 'No, I think my mother is very tolerant, she's concerned with tolerance of human frailty, she knows we're all frail. Probably more than my father, who was more puritanical.' But does she worry that he won't go to heaven? 'I don't know now. She's not an utterly orthodox Christian. I think essentially she thinks I'm a good person. I might not be that respectable but I think kindness is a virtue.'

As the fourth of five, he didn't feel he was his mother's favourite while he was growing up, but he thinks he has become so, simply because he is her only unmarried son. 'My mother knows she's the most important woman in my life. Whereas my brother can't quite say that – he's got a wife, children. I suppose that has an effect – well, I know it does, of course it does. It has a powerful effect on *me*, really.'

But actually, he says, he takes after his father more. Kenneth Hockney was a well-known local character, often to be seen on the streets of Bradford selling *Peace News*. He died in 1978 but there are still people in Bradford who think of David Hockney as Kenneth Hockney's son, rather than vice versa. He was a political activist, always going on demonstrations, mainly CND, but also anti-smoking (all his children smoke). He was a member of the Methodist Peace Fellowship but not averse to working with the British Peace Committee, a Communist front organization. Hockney describes him as like the Peter Sellers character Mr Kite, the trades union agitator in *I'm All Right Jack*. 'Do you remember when he's asked, "Have you ever been to Russia, Mr Kite?" and he says, "No I haven't but it must be very nice – all those cornfields and ballet in the evenings." My father was like that – unrealistic but *idealistic* essentially. He was always involved in some kind of left-wing politics, but mostly for peace, it was *peace* he was on about.' Hockney himself, of course, was a conscientious objector when it came to national service – he worked as a hospital orderly.

Hockney gave me an article about his father from a book on Old Bradford. It described Kenneth Hockney as 'a small man with a strong, rather nasal voice, earnest, insistent. I believe he spoke rather loudly because he was slightly deaf . . . Mr Hockney was a model of a respectable citizen and dressed as such, polite and well-spoken with a mere touch of the North in his speech . . . He was constantly bombarding the CND Committee with offers, ideas, suggestions and producing ever more banners large and small . . . The Committee was sometimes embarrassed, a little overwhelmed by his suggestions.'

Hockney has painted his mother far more often than his father, but the first painting he ever sold – for £10 – was a portrait of his father, painted when he was still at Bradford Art School. Then there are two famous 1970s portraits of his parents together. In both, the mother gazes out lovingly at her son, while the father sits sideways on. But in the better, later, one, painted shortly before his father died, Kenneth Hockney has obviously got bored with posing and has buried his head in an art book. He studies the book very intently, hunched over the page, with his heels drawn up off the floor in excitement, shut off in a private deaf world, much like his son.

Given two such strong-willed parents, I asked Hockney if he was ever intimidated by them, or if he'd ever not done something for fear of upsetting them. 'No, I wouldn't let them govern my life. No, I wanted life my way. And for the last thirty-eight years [since he left the Royal College of Art] most days I've done what I wanted to do, and I intend to carry on that way.' As a teenager, he was quite ruthless in getting himself to art school against the wishes of his parents who wanted him to stay at grammar school. He mentions in his 1976 auto-biography that his eldest brother had wanted to go to art school but wasn't allowed to – 'I was obviously more devious and keener on art than he was.' And yet he wasn't a total rebel. He espoused his mother's vegetarianism and his father's pacifism. But it is significant that in his early work *Myself and My Heroes* (1961), his heroes are Gandhi (vegetarian and pacifist), but also Walt Whitman – poet, homosexual, American.

His three brothers and sister have led more conventional lives. The sister, who never married, lives with their mother in Bridlington. The eldest brother, Paul, was an accountant (and mayor of Bradford) but has now retired to the coast, to Flamborough. He acts as Hockney's business manager. The other two brothers live in Australia, but they visit their mother, and Hockney visits them. I asked if they were artistic and Hockney said not particularly – once, when he was staying with his brother Philip in Australia, Philip asked what he thought of the painting over the mantelpiece. 'It was just some piece of junk, and I said, "I don't think much of it." Then he said, "What do you think of the *frame*?" and I said, "Well, what do you mean? It's OK." He said, "Do you know what it is?" and he puts on some music and the sound comes out of the frame – it's a speaker!'

All the brothers have children, so Hockney is an uncle many times over and now a great-uncle as well (two new Hockneys were born in Bradford last year). He enjoys being 'Rich Uncle David' to the clan, often having a dozen or more to stay in Los Angeles or hosting great parties for them at Saltaire. Some of the new generation seem to be keen on drawing. Or maybe, he adds with Yorkshire canniness, that's just what their parents tell him because then he sends them lavish boxes of crayons and paints. Anyway, he will still have plenty of connections in Yorkshire even when his mother dies. But then, he says, he'll probably only go back in the summer, because in winter there just isn't enough daylight painting time. This is the answer, sadly, to my nagging question about why he doesn't move back to England permanently. He can't while his dogs are alive because he wouldn't put them in quarantine, but actually he can't anyway – he needs all those hours of Californian light.

The light was fading as we sat in his studio, talking about Yorkshire, and when it had gone completely, we walked down to the house. It is magical, like one of Hockney's stage sets, painted in rich blues and greens and purples, with a funny painted fireplace with *trompe l'oeil* ornaments on the mantelpiece. Outside the window there is a giant fake aquarium, with rainbow-painted fish hanging on strings above luminous seaweed.

There is a huge sitting-room-cum-dining-room-cum-kitchen, with a grand piano and framed photos of Hockney with Hillary Clinton, with Alfred Brendel, with Pierre Boulez – an oddly Hollywood touch, proving he is not as immune to celebrity status as he likes to pretend. He also has a beautiful den with a giant television screen (not that he ever watches it) and many of his flower paintings with big brass lights over them. There are books everywhere – he is a great reader, and even more now he can't listen to music. The phone rings incessantly – each time, he has to take out his earpiece and use some other device. He tells all the callers that he has A Journalist With Him and to phone again later – for someone who claims never to go out he seems to have an awful lot of callers.

The *Daily Express* got very excited recently and outed him as a one-time heterosexual. Apparently, the late Ossie Clark's diaries reveal that Hockney had an affair with Ossie's wife, Celia Birtwell, in about

1970. That is why, of course, the great Tate portrait, *Mr and Mrs Clark and Percy* (Percy being the cat), has such a strange atmosphere – as Hockney says, 'Well, he's sitting down, isn't he? She's stood up. That's the way it was, it seemed to me. I was there when they got married, and I saw it disintegrate really.' But he says his affair with Celia was never very serious – she comforted him when his first great love, Peter Schlesinger, left him, and 'She was a pal, a very close pal who listened to all my mumblings and moanings – everybody needs somebody to lean on and she was great.' But it wasn't love? 'No. And Ossie knew. Celia's a bit upset about the diaries, but frankly I don't care. Ossie called me Mr Magoo but I just laughed.'

I remind him that I interviewed him around that time for an article in *Queen* called 'Where does £10,000 a year get you these days?' (£10,000 a year, believe it or not, seemed a fabulous income then, and there was much discussion at *Queen* about whether he was *really* earning that much. He was.) He was a very fashionable artist about town in those days, much like Damien Hirst today, a star straight from art school, and you couldn't go to a party without bumping into him. Apparently, Hamish Bowles of *American Vogue* is playing the 1960s Hockney in a forthcoming John Maybury film about Francis Bacon, and it will be interesting to see whether he can capture Hockney's unique mixture of earthiness and glamour. It seems unlikely.

The fear then was that Hockney was so successful so young that he would burn himself out. Some critics maintain he has done precisely that – that his work since the 1960s is all downhill. But then there are people who say Picasso was never any good after his Blue Period. Hockney's present relations with the art world are sniffy on both sides.

'I don't take art critics that seriously,' he says. 'I mean, I'm very aware, I know what the art world is like, and I know they'd love to dismiss me totally but, of course, they don't, really.' I think it puzzles him, though, having been so fashionable once, that he can be so completely ignored by art pundits now. But he is in the familiar career doldrums between brilliant *enfant terrible* and grand old man with, in his case, the added encumbrance of being hugely popular with 'ordinary' people who like a nice Hockney print to go with the new Ikea rug. It will be many years, probably after his death, before we can get a clear-eyed take on just how good he is.

Part of the difficulty in evaluating Hockney's work is that it changes so much, both in subject matter and technique, and often seems to change quite arbitrarily. I think it is because he is driven by the flight from facility. He recognized early on, probably while he was still at the RCA, that he was almost *too* good at drawing – everyone loved his drawings and they came very easily, but there was always a danger of becoming slick. So his path through art has been a constant attempt to duff himself up, to make life difficult, to attempt something he *couldn't* do rather than repeat something he could.

Consequently, almost every new development has been greeted with dismay by the public – why is Hockney doing this, when he could be doing more of that? – and appreciation usually lags a decade or so behind the work. English critics spent most of the 1980s lamenting the fact that he was doing photocollages and saying Why couldn't he go back to painting? Then when he *did* go back, with the flower paintings and portraits and dogs, they said Ugh, why was he being so conventional? I reacted the same way when I saw his new work in progress, the painting of the Grand Canyon. Why was he doing *that*, when he could be doing more Yorkshire? But it is the way he works and there is no point lamenting it – Picasso, his idol, was exactly the same. And when one looks back at the late 1960s paintings, one can see he *was* getting slick, he *was* right to change. Moreover, although his phases seem discrete to the outsider, he sees them as a continuous process of learning, each feeding into the next. The portrayal of space in the Yorkshire landscapes, for instance, owes a great deal to his photocollages, while the colour seems to derive from the *Very New Paintings* which in turn grew out of his opera designs.

He is currently the most highly valued living British artist in saleroom terms (a painting of his went for £1.2 million at auction in 1989), though there is an important Lucien Freud, *Large Interior, W11 (After Watteau)*, 1981–3, coming up for auction that will probably displace him. Hockney disclaims all knowledge of saleroom prices – 'I must admit I don't follow them myself' – and of commercial considerations generally. He can afford to be aloof because his brother Paul, the former mayor of Bradford, handles his financial affairs very astutely. Hockney's attitude is that he's always had sufficient money, ever since, at art school, he started selling his work. 'The moment you can sell the work, you're rich. You're doing what you want to do, you can make a living at it somehow, and that's all I was concerned about.'

Hockney used to give paintings to friends but he doesn't any more because too many of his gifts subsequently turned up at auction. 'I thought, "Oh well, if you want the money, I'll give you some money," but I assume that if I give you a little picture you would keep it, really. But I suppose some of the people I gave them to, the money was just too tempting. So I don't do that any more.' Nowadays he is cautious about selling, too. 'I don't let everything go. I'm a bit careful what I let out. When I want to sell them, we sell them. Frankly, we've never had any trouble. Sometimes I'd spend a year on an opera and there's nothing you can sell from that. Meaning I am subsidizing a whole year of work. But that was my choice – I do what I want to do.'

Has he made a will? I imagine that Saltaire, for instance, must be rather anxious to know, given that the gallery has a lot of Hockneys on loan. Hockney says he will leave them there as long as Jonathan Silver's widow and brother are in charge, but he is evasive about what will happen after his death. 'Oh, I think about it sometimes. I mean, if I didn't make a will, everything would go to my mother! But you know, Lynn, I simply want my creative life going on. I certainly don't want to be meeting with lawyers and accountants every week. I'd rather have less, I'd rather have my time really.'

This is a theme he often reverts to – so much to do, so little time. At sixty, he wants to work, work, work, and if that means cutting out his social life completely, he won't mind. He knows he will probably be totally deaf eventually: 'It'll get worse. They've told me. So, what does it matter? I don't need to listen to paint. But even if I wasn't deaf, I would probably still isolate myself a little, simply because I want the time for me. I've something to do.'

Increasingly, he is obsessed with space, which he believes has something to do with his deafness. 'You know, I used to say I came to LA because it was sexy and warm. But I also now think there was another reason I wouldn't have known then, but that I'm more aware of now. And that is, as I get older, I'm aware that I'm getting a bit more claustrophobic, or certainly its opposite, agoraphilic – I *love* big wide open spaces, I find them exciting, I find the desert exciting. The city I don't care about any more, you can't smoke in it, but it's a very spatial city and I've now realized that was the attraction.'

But the awful thing is, he seems so unhappy these days and surely that can't be good for his painting? But yes, he says, it can. 'It's a mistake to think that people who paint happy pictures are happy. Do not assume that. A lot of Van Gogh's great pictures are happy pictures – but of course *he* wasn't happy. This summer I found myself in a situation – I knew what it was going to be like because I've watched a few friends die – but because of Jonathan it was important to paint with joy, and that meant a lot to me, for him, you see. I agree with Jonathan. He told me ten days before he died, "Life is a celebration." So – make it the best you can. Enjoy every day, if you can. Sometimes it's hard. But the world *is* beautiful – anywhere you look, actually, looking is thrilling. Sometimes I go out in the desert, look at it, and think: "Well, it's marvellous."'

Reproduced by permission of *The Observer.*

Julian Clary

30 November 1997

Such a nice man – and so filthy! I am still completely gobsmacked after seeing his show. I saw it at High Wycombe but apparently it's the same anywhere – nice, straight, middle-of-the-road mums and dads and grannies, laughing their heads off at jokes about penis rings and muscle relaxants and hamsters up the bottom. I was shocked they even *understood* the jokes, let alone laughed at them. It was like seeing the Diana flowers outside Kensington Palace – is this Britain? The only time the audience failed to laugh was when he dropped his stage baby and made a joke about Louise Woodward, but then he quickly added, 'I'm sorry – was that tasteless?' and, of course, it brought the house down. *Everything* was tasteless. Not cosy, smutty, trad-camp humour, but unadulterated filth.

At least at High Wycombe his audience were all adults. On his current BBC2 show, *All Rise for Julian Clary*, he has children. Last week, he made a joke about a penis ring in front of a twelve-year-old boy and his parents. Of course the child didn't get the joke, but you could be damn sure there'd be some embarrassing conversations back home in front of the video. I felt – oh God, I sound like Mary Whitehouse! – that a child's innocence was being corrupted in front of my eyes. And what did the *parents* think they were doing? I can't remember when I've felt so hot and bothered by a television programme. But then you look at the audience and they're lapping it up, KY jelly and all. *What is happening to this great nation of ours?* I suppose my attack of the Mary Whitehouses is a sign that Julian Clary has the true comedian's power to disconcert.

And, of course, it's a million times more disconcerting when you meet him and discover that this Corrupter Of Our Nation's Morals is just about the most charming man you've met. He welcomes me to his flat in Camden Town, in London, and shows me his dearest love, his cat – he explains that Fanny the Wonder Dog has been pensioned off to his parents'. The flat is prettily furnished but with disturbing touches – a framed photograph of Tammy Wynette, a large picture over the mantelpiece of a man's bottom with ivy growing up it. While making tea, he chatters about his current *Special Delivery* stage show which he describes as 'a *new* set of buggery jokes, not the same buggery jokes'. He enjoys touring, he says. More than that – 'I think it's the meaning of life!'

At home, he doesn't seem remotely showbizzy – he is quiet, serious, self-contained. If you asked me to guess his profession, I'd say probably a New Age healer of some sort – there is something wonderfully serene, restful, benign about his presence. You feel the better for being in his company, even if he doesn't speak. But therein lies the rub: he *doesn't* speak, he just smiles encouragingly, which is rather my own technique, and so, being good listeners together, we spend a lot of time smiling and nodding. He thinks deeply before he speaks, chooses his words carefully and often seems to find that one-word answers will suffice. He explained – and I could hardly disagree – 'An interview is not an ordinary conversation. I have to think, don't I? What am I going to say and how will my mother react, and will I upset my father?'

This is a pity because I am quite obsessed with how a policeman father and probation officer mother can produce a Julian Clary. Both those jobs, I would have thought, demanded a pragmatic, no-nonsense, down-to-earth personality, whereas Julian is so many miles off the earth he might be a Martian. And how did Teddington produce such cool sophistication? A school report when he was fifteen said 'Julian is always either languid or superior' – I would not quite say superior, but there is something remote, patrician, almost paternalistic about his kindly concern for your welfare. He addresses his audience as 'you bog-standard people' – it is a joke, of course, but it reflects a reality – the tone is definitely *de haut en bas*.

He was born in 1959, the youngest child, with two older sisters. He had what he describes as 'a very liberal upbringing' but with emphasis on good manners and speaking properly. He was very much his mother's boy: 'I remember as a child I would do anything to please my mother, all my focus was on my mother.' She encouraged him to be 'sensitive' – gave him the works of D. H. Lawrence, all of which he read by the time he was twelve, took him to the ballet and to concerts.

His father was less of an influence – he was 'certainly around', but he often worked nights and was asleep during the day. Julian describes him as 'a very placid man and a very kind man – not a particularly butch man, not what you imagine when you think of a policeman! He never shouted at me even. My mother was always the more dominant of the two.' Perhaps an uninvolved father? 'Yes. I'm not trying to soften it or counteract it, but we've made up for lost time, my father and I, we understand each other quite well now. And as he's got older, he's mellowed.' Would he, during Julian's childhood, have been the sort of man who would make remarks about poofs? 'Yes, probably. I think I've educated my father. That's one of the things that makes me happy – that he understands more than he would have done ten years ago. Prejudice is ignorance, isn't it, and he probably never knew a gay man. Well he knows me now, so it's been demystified for him.' Perhaps that's what his stage act is about – demystifying gay sex, but also de-cosying it – his act is definitely about gay *sex* rather than gay love.

Julian claims he knew he was gay from about the age of eight. Most gays claim they were born gay, so eight is odd – it suggests that something happened to him. 'It does, doesn't it?' he says with an ambiguous smile, lapsing into one of his easy silences. Eventually he adds, with a tinge of sarcasm, 'I was very close to my mother – that makes you gay, doesn't it?' Does it? 'No, that's not fair. There are all kinds of theories . . . I think I probably was gay at the age of eight, if not before.'

His mother is a Catholic and brought him up as one – he was an altar-boy, and won a scholarship to a good Catholic public day school, St Benedict's in Ealing. At school, he was known as Clary the Fairy, for obvious reasons. 'I had quite an effeminate walk – probably still have. I tend to walk on my toes. Then voice, mannerisms, flapping hands – things that I went through a period of thinking I ought to suppress. My friend Nick and I talk in a very similar way, we both talk on the breath, you know. It's now my perfectly natural way to speak, but I think it's slightly affected – when I sing, my voice is actually quite deep. As an adolescent, I knew it would be provocative to walk in a certain way and to cross my legs all the time. I remember parading down the school corridor being very camp and wearing too much cologne.'

He and his friend Nick enjoyed their celebrity status as 'the school poofs', though they were not practising poofs. 'I was in complete denial then. But we looked like we were – and as it turned out, we were.' They were both very keen on *The Prime of Miss Jean Brodie* and thought of themselves as the *crème de la crème*, lone individualists in a sea of conformity. Nick had a Polaroid camera and they would spend hours posing for photographs. 'It was a strange mixture of narcissism and terrible adolescent insecurity. We *did* think we were better than anyone else, and we must have been terribly irritating to a lot of people at school. But they were horrible to *us*, so I think the whole thing aggravated itself.' His comedy, he thinks, derived from what went on in the playground. 'I am very placid but my way of dealing with anger is to diffuse it through comedy.'

He and Nick were big David Bowie fans and planned to be pop stars. They wrote songs and advertised for backing singers in *Melody Maker* and got two black girls who could really sing. They called themselves The Mind and Body Floorshow and practised in Nick's living room, but their pop ambitions never materialized. Instead, they switched to wanting to be actors. 'Nick had the nerve to say he wanted to go to drama school – I couldn't bring myself to say that. If I'd said I wanted to go to drama school, that would have been like saying I wanted to be an actor, and it was a *secret*.' So he told his parents he wanted to do English and drama at university, and went to Goldsmiths'.

He loved university and was terribly happy there, acquiring women friends for the first time and joining in endless student productions. Many of his friends were radical feminists and members of the Socialist Workers' Party, so he became interested in left-wing politics and went on pro-abortion marches. 'It was a lovely time, it was all kinds of revelations to me – one of which was sex.' He slept with a girl before he ever slept with a man, and it was a serious love affair, but she dumped him in the end. 'It was quite traumatic, the parting of the ways. But I think if I'd married her I would have been one of those men who hang around public toilets. Once I'd had a gay relationship, I felt that's what's right.'

Another traumatic change at this age was leaving the Catholic Church. For a while, he continued going to Mass with his mother when he was at home, but he started to get panic attacks every time he went in a church. At first he would be all right if he stood at the back, 'But then I still had them and it was as if some terrible inner turmoil was being stirred up, and so I just couldn't go any more.' Was it a fear that God would denounce him as a poof? 'Not God. But as I became well known, I imagined people would say, "What are you doing here?" Not only as a practising homosexual but because of my views on abortion and other things that I felt very strongly about. And I didn't want people's disapproval, really.' Nowadays, he says he is a pagan and attends a witches' coven – 'Tell me what you want, Lynn, and we'll have a ceremony at the next full moon and get it for you.' When I go pooh-pooh, don't talk nonsense, he says, again with a little flicker of sarcasm, 'The *News of the World* really loved that story!'

At college, he enjoyed performing, but his mother was worried; she thought he'd be happier backstage. 'I think she couldn't think how it would work, if I wanted to be an actor. And I wasn't any good as an actor, so she was right there. Being overtly gay was not done in her generation – you'd just be a confirmed bachelor and that was fine – but you weren't meant to go on about it, which of course I do. I think she found that a little bit alarming – not because she found it distasteful but she thought it would get in the way of my career. She wasn't to know there would be this little niche of camp comedy.'

But, in fact, he found his little niche while he was still at college, doing a drag act called Glad and May with another student. Then, when Glad left, he became Gillian Pyeface, and also a Tarzanagram around Chalfont St Giles, apparently a hotbed of Tarzanagrams. He remembers his days on the comedy circuit with great nostalgia, getting £50 a show and doing three shows a week at places like the Comedy Store. 'I had my suitcase and my dog and it was all so self-sufficient, I loved it. It was not leading to anything else, it was not like, "One day I'll get on telly." It was *Friday Night Live* that changed everything – the producers would come round on the circuit and we'd all hear, "Oh, they're in tonight," and eventually they asked me to go on – and there we are.' He sounds rather wistful for the days before television discovered him.

In 1988, he gave up drag and became the Joan Collins Fan Club, with Fanny the Wonder Dog. His friend Paul Merton started writing for him and in 1990 he had a hit on television with a spoof game show called *Sticky Moments*. His career was all going swimmingly until December 1993, when – a great honour – he was asked to present the British Comedy Awards live on LWT. He spotted Norman Lamont in the audience and made an off-the-cuff remark about 'fisting' him on Hampstead Heath. The tabloids went berserk and Garry Bushell, Lynda Lee-Potter, Bernard Ingham, and Bernard Manning (crikey!) pronounced themselves shocked. According to the next day's papers, the LWT phonelines were 'jammed' with complaints – actually there were twelve complaints from an audience of 13 million viewers. But obviously the television bigwigs were rattled and Clary has not been invited to an awards ceremony since.

'You don't really know what goes on on the seventeenth floor of LWT,' he muses, 'but I think they may have been horrified. I quite like all that – I mean, I like it and I hate it at the same time. I like being a bit dangerous and a bit infamous and rocking the boat. Part of me does, and part of me is the same as when I was at school – likes upsetting everyone really, that kind of vengeful part of me. But then I honestly didn't know that joke was going to cause such a fuss.' Has it damaged his career? 'It has affected it. But I think it's one of those things that happens for a reason and perhaps I wanted a bit of a break. I just wanted a quiet time, and I had a quiet time.'

In fact, he seemed to vanish completely in 1994 – he worked in Australia for several months. It was the culmination of a long, unhappy period in his private life and he thinks that the Lamont remark might have been symptomatic of a general mood of self-destruction. In 1991, he lost his lover, Christopher, to Aids. They'd met in 1988, fallen in love, had an affair, then Christopher disappeared. When they met by chance six months later, Julian said, 'Where have *you* been?' and Christopher said he'd been in hospital, where he was diagnosed HIV-positive. They lived together for the last three years of Christopher's life. When he died, Julian scattered his ashes on a beach in Portugal where they'd spent a happy holiday.

Was that the most important relationship he's had? 'Mmm . . . oh, I don't know. It was a very important relationship. He was lovely. I mean, there was an irritating headline about me in the *Mail* that said, "Glad to be sad". And obviously, if someone has died, then it's sad. But people do like to pigeonhole you as "tears of a clown" – it suits the *Daily Mail* reader to think that all gay men are unhappy. But although Christopher was dying, and he died, it was quite a happy relationship; he was not a miserable person.'

Then Julian had a very unhappy relationship which ended with his being abandoned. He went 'completely doolally' and bought a large family house in Holloway, somehow planning to fill it with animals and children, but, of course, 'It was just me, in Holloway.' So he was almost relieved when the Norman Lamont débâcle gave him an excuse to sell the house (with his stage costumes still in it) and go to Australia. 'I did have a horrible time of it for a while. I can't bear to talk about it really. I'm not being difficult . . . It just brings on a panic attack, you know. How *can* I talk about the most painful experience I've ever had? And how does it benefit me to have that in print? There is a big gap, I think, between the service I offer, which is a couple of hours of camp light entertainment and lots of buggery jokes, and me having a broken heart from some horrible love affair.'

When he returned from Australia, he still kept a low profile and said he was quite happy not to work. He tried doing straight theatre, playing a gangster in a Jean Genet play, but it was not a success – he had become addicted to audience laughter. But on the other hand, he could no longer bring himself to go on stage with the opening line, 'There's nothing I like more than a warm hand on my entrance' – he just didn't find it funny any more. Nor did he want to dress up and ponce about in glitter costumes.

In fact, he may have wanted to go straight – for a couple of years, he was obsessed with the desire to have children. He thought of adoption, or coming to an arrangement with a lesbian friend. 'That got quite serious. She was very up for it and we talked about buying the flat downstairs – it could have worked out. She went off to sort out her menstrual cycle and work out when I had to deliver the seed. And then I *really* thought about it, and I thought, "No, I can't do it." I didn't want to do it that way. It felt like a selfish thing to do. Because at *some* point you have to explain to this child, although it would undoubtedly be a very wanted child, that it was conceived with a turkey baster or something. And I don't want that responsibility. The thing is, I want to raise a child *myself*; I don't want to share it.'

Of course, he could still have a child, but he says the urge has passed – he got a cat instead. He would like to have another serious relationship, but he is quite happy on his own and believes it is important to be self-sufficient. His days of gay clubbing and pick-ups are over – 'You do *tire* of it.' Sometimes, he says, he even forgets he is gay. He has had bad periods of depression, and was on Prozac for a while. He also had bereavement counselling after Christopher's death, and has tried rebirthing and 'body harmony' and acupuncture. He used to rely on three pints of lager and a joint to get him on stage, but he doesn't now. On the other hand, he says, 'I've been quite interested in sedative-type drugs. I tried opium once – that was marvellous. I like drugs that calm you down. I don't really like speedy drugs, they don't suit me at all. It's often the way, isn't it? I mean, I've got friends who are already very manic and they're the ones who do coke.'

He still asks his mother's advice about his love life because, after all, 'She's a trained counsellor and it seems silly not to tap into it. She's very good at reframing a situation so that, even though none of the factors have changed, you just look at it a different way. And she's very into being responsible for your own actions, and your own feelings, so you can't say, "You've made me unhappy" – you've made yourself unhappy.' Nevertheless, he didn't tell his mother about Christopher being HIV-positive until quite near the end, because Christopher didn't want people to know. Did he consult his mother about seeing me? 'Ooh, no! She'd say, "Why are you speaking to that woman? Fancy letting her in your home."'

At the end, he asks rather sweetly, 'Do you think I'm peculiar?' Well, sort of, I say – being a performer, being gay, he's obviously not Mr Average. 'And I think it's a pity,' I add, 'that you haven't got a happy relationship.'

'I've got the cat!' he shoots back. Actually, what I find peculiar about him is that the things he says about himself just don't tally with the man you meet. He describes himself as 'vicious', 'nasty', 'vengeful', he talks about panic attacks, he says, 'I'm painfully self-obsessed' – all suggesting a turbulent inner life which bears no relation to the poised, serene, confident person you meet. I asked if he was actually on some kind of sedative or Prozac when I met him, but he said no, not any more.

There have been hints, in the past year or two, that he plans to retire. In fact, the programme to his current stage show bills it as a 'farewell tour' and says, 'Let's face it, you can't go on and on and on and on pounding out the same old nonsense.' But actually he can, and apparently intends to. His career, he says, 'seems to evolve by itself, it seems to progress, but it's always been important not to be too calculating about it. I just think I must get through this tour, try and do the best I can do in Tunbridge Wells.' He is probably more ambitious than he lets on: he was deeply disappointed a couple of years ago not to get the *Generation Game*.

What will he do eventually? 'Well, I've got all these pension schemes that mature when I'm fifty, so I could retire then. But I don't know what I'd do, because I don't do anything but work, really. I have this fantasy, you know, of living in a bungalow and growing geraniums and getting up early in the morning and writing a few chapters of a book. I think there's more to life than television, you know. I wouldn't mind doing something with a bit more meat to it. And something that's not funny. But then I quite like being funny . . .' And off he goes, to wow the good people of Tunbridge Wells, with jokes about hamsters up the bottom.

Reproduced by permission of *The Observer*.

Max Clifford told me it's because he suffers from piles – this could be true.

When he edited the *Sun*, he was hardly ever seen outside the office. Apparently, he gave a television interview right at the beginning and Murdoch told him never to do it again. Anyway, he never craved publicity, the way Andrew Neil did, and was quite happy to remain out of sight. The rumour was always that he was epileptic and didn't go out for fear of having fits, but he told me this was a myth.

'No, no. What happened was that I was having lunch with Eve Pollard and I passed out. And I came round and thought, "What was that?" I felt all right but I went to the men's room and looked in the mirror and I looked bloody terrible. And I came back and looked at my plate, and Eve Pollard had wolfed my lamb chop! Nah, that's not true . . .'

'Shall I put it in anyway?'

'Yes, put it in. *Eve Pollard stole my lamb chop while I was lying unconscious.* Anyway, so I had all the tests and they thought I was epileptic. Which actually alarmed the hell out of me, because I had visions of me frothing at the mouth and being carried out on a stretcher while Mr Murdoch was holding a conference. But in the end it wasn't epilepsy, and they never found out what it was – it could have just been a blood sugar thing. Or it *could* have been that I was bored to death by Eve! No, she's all right.'

He talks crisply and clearly, in complete sentences, as if dictating copy. He never rambles or loses his thread. When he has answered a question to his own satisfaction, he says, 'Right? Go on.' I kept trying to provoke one of his famous bollockings but it never came – I suppose they're reserved for employees. People who have been the butt of them, or even just witnessed them, still blench at the memory. His speech used to be famous for its very high incidence of f-words and c-words, but I hardly heard one. Even more surprising is that he seems to have learned the language of political correctness – he talked at one point about 'the gay community' and I almost fell off my chair.

My big fear beforehand was that he would insist that the whole interview should be about L!VE *TV*, and that he would refuse to talk about the *Sun*. In the event, he talked about L!VE *TV* for maybe five minutes, but when I asked if it was as much fun as working at the *Sun*, he leapt at the opportunity to rave about the past: 'The *Sun* was incredible, you have no idea. There were days of such humour and life and fun that first, you shouldn't be paid to do it and secondly, you shouldn't be *allowed* to do it, to be honest. Was it fun? It was the greatest. It was also a fabulous, successful business, making at least a million or a million and a half a week. And it was important and the reason the *Sun* is important is because almost 4 million people a day *buy* it, so that is 12 million readers.'

Oh right, so we don't even have to pretend to be interested in telly. On the contrary, he spells it out: telly is *nothing* compared to newspapers. 'All this cobblers that's written about popular newspapers being finished is absolute tosh. If you put the *Sun* and *Mirror* readers together, that would be, what, 18 million readers? Channel 5 executives would kill their grandmothers to get hold of that kind of audience. Papers are a great, vibrant business and will continue to be.'

He was born into newspapers: his father was news editor of the *South London Observer*, and his mother chief reporter, though she later became press officer to Sir Horace Cutler, the Conservative leader of the GLC. Both Kelvin's brothers are journalists, as are his wife Jacqui and one of his three children. He left school (Alleyn's, Dulwich, a direct-grant grammar) at seventeen, armed with one O-level, to join the *Kentish Mercury*. Patrick Collins, now a famous sportswriter, was assigned to look after the new boy and remembers him as 'brash and lively, popular, not so much witty as breezy. Like most of us, he was desperately hiding his middle-class accent and trying to be streetwise.' One day, Collins took Kelvin to the magistrates' court and pointed out a reporter from a rival paper, a striking blonde with fabulous legs. 'That's Mary,' he said. 'Everyone fancies her.' Kelvin was delighted: 'That's my mum!'

Kelvin joined the *Sun* in 1973 as a sub-editor. Derek Jameson called him 'the king of the kids', and Murdoch was sufficiently impressed to send him to New York as managing editor of the *New York Post*. Kelvin loved New York, but his wife Jacqui thought it was a bad place to bring up their three children. So he returned to the *Sun* as night editor under Larry Lamb. In February 1981, he moved to the *Daily Express*, but Murdoch was furious to lose him and two months later appointed him editor of the *Sun*. The *Express* made him work out his notice, and for a few months journalists watched in awe as he edited the *Sun* by day and the *Express* by night. He was only thirty-four and his energy was terrifying: they called him 'MacFrenzie'.

His motto on the *Sun* was 'shock and amaze on every page' and, tearing round the office, interfering in every detail of his Curranticus Bunticus, he turned agency dross into gold. That was his supreme skill – not getting great scoops (which the *Mirror* could do as well, if not better), but taking run-of-the-mill stories and giving them a spin, a joke, a headline, that made them special. 'Freddie Starr Ate My Hamster' was the most famous, but one of his own favourites was about a man who mistook a tube of superglue for his piles ointment: 'Our John's Gone Potty And Glued Up His Botty'. Writing catchy headlines is a peculiar, unteachable gift, like perfect pitch, and Kelvin valued it highly. One day a casual sub picked up a story about Frank Sinatra receiving sheep serum treatment in Switzerland and headlined it 'I've Got Ewes Under My Skin'. Kelvin was so delighted he gave him a staff job on the spot. And, despite the fearsome bollockings, his staff loved him. Garry Bushell says, 'He's one of the nicest people I've worked with – funny, mercurial, intelligent. You won't find anyone who's worked with him who does not like him.' (Not strictly true. Janet Street-Porter worked with him and doesn't like him. But it's broadly true.)

Murdoch called Kelvin 'my little Hitler', and said approvingly, 'He's out there, screaming and shouting, and he's good. Somehow it works.' Kelvin in turn called Murdoch 'the Boss', and admired him more than anyone, except possibly Mrs Thatcher. Murdoch would give him occasional bollockings or – worse – long silences on the phone, but was generally supportive. When Kelvin told him that he had pulled 'Gotcha!' after the first edition because they had learned of the death toll on the *Belgrano*, Murdoch told him, 'I wouldn't have pulled it if I was you.'

But towards the end of the 1980s, Kelvin began making costly mistakes. First, there was the Elton John rent boy story that led to the biggest libel settlement in newspaper history – £1 million. Then 'the Truth' about the Hillsborough disaster (blaming it on drunken Liverpool fans), which cut the paper's circulation in Merseyside by 200,000. Kelvin started getting phone calls from the Boss saying, 'You're losing your touch' and knew his days were numbered. In the summer of 1993,

Murdoch gave him such a terrible bollocking that he simply put on his jacket, walked out and faxed his resignation. Murdoch sent one of his most trusted deputies to woo him back, but in January 1994, Kelvin finally went – to Sky Television.

In his autobiography, Andrew Neil says that Kelvin's transfer 'could easily be construed as a disguised firing'. Neil should know because he went through something similar himself, being seconded from the *Sunday Times* to Fox where he lasted not much longer than Kelvin at Sky. The prevailing theory is that Murdoch was forced to move both editors because John Major threatened restrictions on cross-media ownership if he didn't. But Murdoch might have felt they were past their peak anyway.

Kelvin insists – and insists and insists and insists – that he left the *Sun* of his own accord. 'Oh yes I did, I really did. Honestly, I promise you, literally, I'd *done* it. I don't believe anybody should run a paper for that length of time [twelve years]. I just about kept my marbles, which is always the great test of editing tabloid papers: at the end of the day, are you barking mad? A number of things will happen to editors normally. They either burn out, or turn to drink, or they become a mixture of ego and alcohol, right? They start thinking they're running the country. And directly you start feeling like that, go to your boss and say, "I am simply going mad and I need to have a spell in the real world." But Mr Murdoch is a great people person. With a personality like mine, really it was a miracle that he employed me so long. To look at it the other way is very selfish and ego-ridden.'

When he joined Sky, Michael Grade said, 'Kelvin is the only person I know who could take Sky downmarket.' He did his best – but only for eight months. He fell out almost immediately with Sam Chisholm, his boss, who referred to him as 'my little boy scout' in front of the staff. When he got an exclusive interview with Bienvenida Buck, the news editor refused to run it, and when he got the Harkess 'coven' (Alan Clark's nemesis), the news editor resigned. He also seems to have mishandled a boxing deal, losing a series of Lennox Lewis fights and paying too much for Chris Eubank, though Kelvin insists, 'It was a perfectly good deal. Nowadays, they do deals like that ten-a-penny. But it was the first of those deals and people were critical. So what?'

He recently sued *Business Age* magazine for saying he was sacked from Sky. 'I *fired* Sky, which is the way I prefer to put it, because I couldn't stand the chief executive. I think the trouble was that I'd enjoyed my life so much at the *Sun* that it was *unusual* for me to not have an enjoyable working day.' He went on holiday – an unusual event in itself – and discussed it with his wife and finally rang Murdoch and said, 'Boss, I'm going.'

Roy Greenslade said at the time: 'Rupert is genuinely fond of Kelvin. It beggars belief that this is the end of the Murdoch–MacKenzie saga.' But it was. Kelvin hasn't seen or spoken to Murdoch since, though he says they still exchange Christmas cards. He once told a colleague, 'I tell you, Rupert is so sharp . . . He could sack me tomorrow and I'd still like him.' So does he still like Murdoch? 'Yes. Well, he was very good to me when I worked with him. The only thing I would take issue with is that thing in Andrew Neil's book, that it was a disguised sacking. I don't believe that.'

But did he lose out financially? 'Well, yes. I mean, when you say *lose out*, I quit, so there's no question of severance or anything like that.' But surely Murdoch should have given him a pay-off for all his years at the *Sun*? 'No, no. No, no, no. No, no, no, no, no. That absolutely is 100 per cent wrong. I quit. You know, I must have said this about 28 million times, but I'll say it again: I don't regret what I did.' Even if he was finessed by Murdoch, he doesn't seem to resent it. In fact, he probably admires him all the more as a result – he always knew Murdoch was a hard man.

Anyway, Kelvin then found himself out of work for the first time in thirty years. 'And I can tell you, that is *rather* a sort of wake-up moment in your life. You get up in the morning and nobody gives a stuff about you – it comes as a great shock. The next thing that comes as a great shock is that if you call somebody up, they don't return the call immediately. Suddenly you're not of any moment. So there were lots of times of walking the dogs down the road, chatting amiably to my dogs about the philosophy of the position that I found myself in.'

And in the end it was David Montgomery, of Mirror Group, who rescued him from unemployment. It was a bizarre appointment because Montgomery had already hired Janet Street-Porter to launch L!VE and might have guessed she wouldn't thrill to Kelvin. And Montgomery and Kelvin are chalk and cheese: Montgomery very quiet, uptight,

Ulster puritanical and Kelvin, of course, not. But Kelvin says they get on fine – 'He's been great to me, absolutely great.'

What happened next was the subject of a very good television documentary. Janet Street-Porter set up the station as she envisaged it – youth-oriented, designery, a bit like the *Big Breakfast* – but ran into problems with the combination of new technology and inexperienced staff. Kelvin was meant to be setting up a sports channel and keeping out of her way. But when she went on holiday a few months after the disastrous launch, Kelvin moved in. He dumped some of her programmes and started bringing in his own – topless darts, News Bunny, the weather forecast in Norwegian. When some of the women producers objected to topless darts, he said they could have their own equivalent, so they started 'Handy Hunks', which he describes as 'a two-minute show where, for reasons that are not entirely clear, rather good-looking blokes wearing denim shorts change tyres for women drivers'. Janet Street-Porter left. Kelvin never set up the sports channel, but he has made what seemed like a hopeless situation into a financially viable one, mainly by lowering L!VE's ambitions. Nowadays, he says, 'We're in the local news business. And we're small! We're little! We should not be confused with the vast mass of great television, BBC or ITV; it would be as ridiculous as comparing the *Daily Telegraph* to the *Wisbech Guardian*. We are little, local news stations. That's what we are – local, local, local, and we are not big, we are little.'

Got it, Kelvin. So given that L!VE is little and not big, why is he paid the exceedingly big salary of £360,000? And, come to that, what does he spend it on?

Oddly enough, this is the one question that really seems to embarrass him – he suddenly goes all prim. 'I don't know how you talk about wealth, it's a strange sort of thing to talk about. How can I put it? I'm not poor. I've got enough to pay the gardener.' Doesn't he have any expensive tastes? 'No, not really. I don't ever do anything, really. I don't have any outside interests. I invest a little. I like work and I like all the things associated with it. I like meeting people and developing good relationships with people that I work with.'

And television has certainly expanded his people horizons. He actually meets *gays* and *lesbians*, apparently for the first time in his life. At the *Sun*, the atmosphere was so homophobic that gay casuals working temporary shifts learned to remove their earrings before they went in, for fear of provoking another clamour about 'shirtlifters' and 'botty burglars'. And now I find Kelvin talking politely about 'the gay community'. What *happened*?

'OK, right. I have changed quite a lot in that area. I tell you why. A paper like the *Sun* – and this is probably entirely my fault, right? – would almost certainly eschew gays. Because it was a bit like the police force or the army in that respect – there's a lack of understanding and the jokes would be cruel and tough. Well, that is that little world. But when you're away from that sort of newspaper office, that banter doesn't really exist. So if you *don't* change, you'd be a fool. And I have changed. And anybody who knows me knows that I have. So you're quite right. It's a very accurate point, and one that I had to deal with.'

But isn't there something a bit immoral in slagging off gays for twenty years and then, when your circumstances change, saying, 'Oh, they're fine'? 'No, no. I don't know why I got trapped into this particular line of questioning – but people are not as sophisticated as you would have them be, right? The ordinary working guy and woman do not take a naturally laissez-faire attitude. Only journalists, media types who hang around the top bar of the Oxo Tower paying bloody £7 for a glass of Spanish chianti, are like that. But the truth is, everyone can change – why not?'

But the odd thing about Kelvin is that he *hasn't* changed, except in his attitude to gays. Despite twenty years of enormous salaries and chauffeur-driven cars, he never seems to have upped his lifestyle or his tastes. He has no interest in wining and dining or hobnobbing with grandees. He plays squash and golf, walks the dogs and spends the weekends watching Sky Sports – 'I can sit and do that till the cows come home.' His friends are people he and his wife have known for twenty-five or thirty years, since their days on local newspapers. His house near Sevenoaks has a thatched wishing-well in the garden.

His only known excursion into sophistication came in January 1993 when he took a Caribbean holiday with a woman not his wife. She was Joanna Duckworth, a blonde secretary twenty years his junior, from the *Sunday Times* books pages. The *Mail on Sunday* got wind of this fling and sent a reporter to doorstep him. Kelvin handled it smoothly, telling the reporter, 'My wife and I are on very good terms and are in the midst of a very amicable separation.' But he was back with his wife by the summer of 1994. He says the separation lasted two years and 'I had a relationship and ended it and went back to the missus.' Would he call himself a good husband? He is, for once, lost for words. 'Eughh! . . . Am I a good husband? . . . Well, I think . . . neurgh . . . probably on the low side of average I would think.' His wife is features editor of a magazine called *Eva* which he describes as 'I'd better be careful what I say here – not quite into the two-headed baby area.'

What drives him? It's a question he, of course, has never pondered. 'Do you mean, like, I always hated my mother or something? Nah. Honestly. I just like *work*, you know.' Introspection comes under the heading of 'tosh', which means anything smacking of egotism or pretentiousness – and he has a great fear of both. His *Who's Who* entry is the shortest in the book, as if to declare 'I'm just an ordinary bloke.' But he is an ordinary bloke who can hold his own against the highest in the land. When John Major rang him the day of the ERM débâcle to say 'I hope you won't be too hard on me', Kelvin's reply was, 'Well John, let me put it this way. I've got a large bucket of shit lying on my desk and tomorrow morning I'm going to pour it all over your head.' Major thought he was joking – 'Oh Kelvin, you are a wag!' – but soon learned he wasn't.

As editor of the *Sun*, he could be both an ordinary bloke and an extraordinarily powerful one because he was the voice of Everyman, though he would never put it in such poncy terms. But what he did say was, 'The only regret about me not being in the newspaper business is the ability which newspapers have – and the best newspapers should do it on a regular basis – to tip the applecart over. Because that is the fun – confronting some bloody pompous thing and telling your readers the truth. Take *The English Patient*. If I were in the newspaper business, I'd go to someone like Garry Bushell and say, "Now I want you to pour an absolute bucket over this film." Because otherwise, *otherwise* the whole country ends up going to see it and they're all sitting there thinking to themselves, "It must be me, I must be thick."' Which perhaps harks back to how he felt as a schoolboy – and is the nearest we'll get to answering the question: what drives Kelvin MacKenzie?

He still reads the *Sun* and the *Mirror* every day. He says he would *like* to believe that the *Sun* went downhill after he left but, 'Despite me praying earnestly every night, the complete opposite has happened. It remains and will remain a great paper.' In his day it was 100 per cent Tory, but he believes it was right to support Labour this time: it was supporting the readers.

After we'd been talking for an hour, people kept coming with increasing urgency to say he was supposed to be in a meeting with David Montgomery. He didn't seem in any hurry, and when he finally went, we shared the lift down. He said that Chris Horrie (who co-wrote an excellent book about the *Sun* called *Stick It Up Your Punter*) had been on to him wanting to write a book about L!VE. But, he snorted dismissively, 'What's to write about?'

A few days later, he rang to say that maybe he'd forgotten to mention that L!VE is opening a new station in Manchester this month and *that* was why he had agreed to see me. Well, you could have fooled me. If he was meant to plug Manchester L!VE, he didn't do it. If he was meant to convey that he is entirely happy working in television, he didn't do it. I am convinced he has no personal vanity and gets no pleasure from seeing his picture in the papers. So why give an interview at all? I felt that it was aimed past me, past the *Observer*, to some specific, outside audience. Could it be Murdoch? Does Kelvin hope that now John Major is out of the way, he can return to the *Sun*? Should I, alone among my colleagues, prepare to cheer?

Reproduced by permission of *The Observer*.

Neil Tennant

1 June 1997

Neil Tennant is an extremely intelligent, well-read, cultured forty-three-year-old with greying hair and a bald patch, so it seems embarrassing to call him a Pet Shop Boy.

The Pet Shop bit doesn't bear thinking about, and he's as much a boy as I'm a bimbo. He is, strictly speaking, half of the Pet Shop Boys; the other is Chris Lowe, the composer and keyboard player, but for interview purposes Tennant *is* the Pet Shop Boys because Lowe doesn't give interviews or, when he does, doesn't speak. From time to time, while Tennant was chatting away over lunch, I wondered, 'Why's he wearing that funny, shiny pleated shirt?' and then I remembered, 'Oh, because he's a pop star.'

But he's a pop star who talks about almost everything except pop. He is a great Noël Coward fan and is putting together an album of Coward songs, sung by Elton John, Bryan Ferry, Madness and others for the Red Hot Aids Trust, which will be released next Easter. He is also keen on Rodgers and Hammerstein (his favourite song is 'This Nearly Was Mine') and Russian music, especially Shostakovich. He collects modern British painters and knows a lot about Victor Pasmore. In fact, he solved a mystery that bothered me for years – what happened to Pasmore's *Chiswick Reach* which used to be one of the most popular paintings in the Tate? He told me John Major borrowed it for No. 10. (Outrageous!) He banged on about how shocking it was that Andrew

Lloyd Webber got a peerage while Paul McCartney got a knighthood, 'because McCartney is a very serious cultural figure, one of the most serious of this century, whereas Andrew Lloyd Webber has not made a musical contribution to our culture'. He talked about the need to abolish the Royal Family ('a meaningless charade') and the relief of having a Labour Government. (He was one of Ken Follett's Luvvies for Labour, and gave them some dosh: he refused to say how much.) Anyway, we had a wonderful natter over lunch – and I had to ring up afterwards and say, Er sorry, you didn't really tell me anything about yourself. So then I asked some nosy questions and we both got thoroughly embarrassed.

I met him first before he was a pop star, when he was assistant editor of *Smash Hits* magazine in the early 1980s. We were both in New York on a PR junket to interview Boy George's friend Marilyn, who was then trying to launch a solo career, handicapped by lack of talent and manners. Marilyn was deadly but Neil Tennant was more than adequate compensation. He told me then that he was about to become a pop star but I thought it was the wine talking. A year later, 'West End Girls' was number one.

Perhaps the reason he seems one of us, and not one of them, is that he became a pop star so late. He was thirty-one and already balding when the Pet Shop Boys had their first hit in 1985. And, having worked for *Smash Hits*, and being quite a good businessman (his brother works for Coopers & Lybrand, his sister is married to a banker), he wasn't the innocent dupe that beginner pop stars are meant to be. He had plotted to be a pop star ever since he was nine, back in Newcastle, and his parents let him stay up late to watch the Beatles' Royal Variety Performance on television – 'I remember they had Harry Secombe on, and you could hear the fans screaming outside, and I felt literally sick with excitement.' But an early attempt to create a folk group in Newcastle foundered: 'It was called Dust, and it was very "of its time".' So he went to London to read history at a polytechnic, and worked in publishing for ten years, graduating from Marvel comics to tropical fish to *Smash Hits*. With his ordered mind, editing skills and good business brain, he might well have been managing director of one of the big publishing conglomerates by now if he hadn't done this strange, undignified, unsensible thing of becoming a pop star. He describes being a Pet Shop Boy as 'a struggle between total embarrassment and total shamelessness'. But he believes that shamelessness is the mark of a true professional.

The turning point was meeting Chris Lowe, an architecture student five years his junior, in 1981. They met in an electronics shop in the King's Road, Chelsea. Neil remembers: 'I had a synthesizer and I wanted to plug it into my record player amplifier, and they were welding together a – what's the word? plug? point? – I've never been good at electronics, ironically. Chris was buying batteries or something. And he said, "Oh, have you got a synthesizer?" Because in those days, in 1981, it was quite something to have a synthesizer in your bedroom. So we started talking and he came over to my flat a few days later to play the synthesizer. And he was very musical, and that was that really. I immediately thought he was quite good, actually.'

Did he fancy him? 'Oh I can't talk about it, it's too embarrassing! It would embarrass *him* more than anything else. It certainly wasn't the basis on which we became friends.' I always assumed that the basis of their friendship was that Neil fancied Chris but Chris didn't fancy Neil. Neil said no, it wasn't like that. 'We have a very close relationship, but it's nothing to do with sex. I know people always can't believe that. Even our manager wouldn't believe it. But it *isn't* the case.'

Tennant is absolutely sure he wouldn't have got anywhere without Lowe – he would still be writing miserabilist bedsit singer-songwriter moans no one would ever listen to. But Lowe was different: he came from Blackpool and had a vaguely showbiz background – his mother was a dancer, and his grandfather had been in the Nitwits and lived in Las Vegas. Musical life for him started with *Saturday Night Fever*, and he was heavily into clubbing. The only sort of music he liked was disco.

The genius of the Pet Shop Boys was to combine these polar opposites: Neil's wistful introspective lyrics and Chris's mindless, cheerful, upbeat rhythms. They would never have been in the Top 10 without Chris: they would never have engaged an intelligent audience without Neil.

They messed around making music in Neil's bedsit for a couple of years, then Neil went to New York to interview the Police for *Smash Hits* – and managed to contact Bobby Orlando, the record producer who had done wonders for Divine. Orlando agreed to produce a demo for them, and they made 'West End Girls'. EMI heard it and wanted to sign them – but first Neil had to get them out of the contract they had signed with Bobby O. He managed it, but it took time, so there was a strange year (when I first met him) when he was poised for stardom but still unknown. Then 'West End Girls' was finally released, and became a number one hit in nine countries, including the UK and the US. They went on to have three more number ones, and a string of successful albums, selling about 25 million copies altogether, accompanied by brilliant videos and stage shows, directed by Derek Jarman and Bruce Weber among others.

At the beginning, nobody quite knew what to make of the Pet Shop Boys. Neil would chatter away in interviews, offering opinions on anything (I often think he should be a newspaper columnist), while Chris would glower or just not turn up. He once explained cheerily, 'I'm thick as shit, me.' In fact, Neil assures me, Chris is actually very articulate, funny, intelligent, but he never wanted to do interviews and his dumb persona worked well for their image. Neil could some-times sound quite pretentious, talking about how his lyrics were inspired by *The Waste Land* or explaining that the title of 'Can You Forgive Her?' came from a Trollope novel, so it was good to have Lowe being 'moronic'. They always tried to have it both ways – intelligent/moronic, romantic/ironic – and largely succeeded. The soul-searching sincerity of Neil's lyrics was offset by his deadpan delivery and Lowe's insouciant keyboard. Actually, Neil explains, he never meant to be deadpan or ironic: he just wasn't very good at singing dramatically. He relied on the words, sung with choirboy clarity, to get the emotion across.

He has always considered himself a better songwriter than singer, but is now fonder of his own voice. 'I sing the songs because I write the words, really. Having said that, I think I make a very distinctive sound on record. Right from the start, I always tried to sing in an English accent because so much pop music is sung, regardless of the singer's nationality, in an American accent, and I always thought, "Well, I don't speak like that so why should I sing like that?" And I have a very distinctive pop voice – it's not a rock voice at all – because I can sing very high, so when I double-track it, it has rather a sweet quality.

In pop music, I think if you have the choice between being a brilliant singer and a distinctive singer, it's better to be distinctive.'

But it is as a lyricist that he really shines, and he is at his best when mining his own experience. He has almost written his autobiography in his lyrics – 'It's a Sin', about his Catholic upbringing; 'Being Boring', commemorating his best friend from Newcastle who died of Aids; 'Can You Forgive Her?' about a failed heterosexual relationship. He reckons he's getting better all the time: 'You learn about songwriting. And I do think that to express what I feel – there's definitely a *release*. And they can help you to define your life, and help you understand things.'

If his songs have an underlying theme, he believes it is escape – about going somewhere and getting away. Escaping what, though? Boredom? Repression? His Catholic background? Or escaping from himself, from not being quite the person he'd like to be? I'd say his songs are more about yearning for the unattainable. Like all romantics, he is always looking for the ideal love but never finding it – 'I'm always waiting for a red-letter day, For something special somehow new, someone saying "I love you."'

His love life seems to have been quite troubled – and complicated by the fact that for many years the Pet Shop Boys were in the closet. Their original appeal was to a teenage audience and Neil recalls that at the height of their success, in 1987–8, he would get girls fans hanging round outside his house in Fulham, and writing 'Neil is a sex god' in the ladies' toilet at Hurlingham Park over the road. So he never said he was gay in interviews.

He only finally came out in 1994, and said last year that he slightly regretted it: 'Now it's all sort of normal and healthy, it's a bit boring really. It makes me feel like telling everybody I'm straight . . . I mean, fifty years ago I'd have been married with three children and having affairs with men on the side, and frankly, I'd probably be happier.' He still thinks that's true, though he says that lately he hasn't minded so much about not being a father because, 'I have the life I have, and I wouldn't have it if I had children. I know so many people with children and it's such hard work, it would drive me mad. It would be very hard to do what I do with the Pet Shop Boys, I'd just be shattered.'

But it took time to reach this acceptance. There's a song on *Bilingual* called 'Metamorphosis', where he talks about his early confusion: 'I knew what I wanted, I knew how to get it, It didn't make me happy, So I started again. What I wanted to be was a family man, But nature had some alternative plans. So I did without the lot, put emotion on hold, And hoped my instincts would do what they were told.'

In the 1970s, he had two quite long relationships with women. In 'Can You Forgive Her?' on the 1993 album *Very*, a man recalls being taunted by a woman: 'She made fun of you and even in bed said she was going to get herself a real man instead.' By the 1980s, he had accepted that he was gay – but was celibate for most of the decade. He was never promiscuous. 'I just don't have the urge to be. Also I don't know that I have the physical confidence to be. I'm not saying I've never had casual sex. But even before we were famous, I was never like that. There's something about that aspect of the gay world that I find off-putting. It makes sex into a recreational activity, or a sport, and I just can't really think of it like that.'

He didn't finally have a live-in relationship with a man until 1991, and that ended in heartbreak three years later. Even now, when he has had another, happier relationship, he goes a bit tearful remembering it. 'I thought that would last for ever, I was very upset when it finished. I was amazed how depressed I was – because I really wanted the relationship to end, to be perfectly honest, but when it did, I didn't realize it was going to leave me that low. I felt completely defenceless.' The subsequent relationship has also broken up but they remain good friends. One of the advantages (consolations?) of homosexual love affairs, he thinks, is that, 'People stay friends, and you develop a sort of extended family to the point where you end up knowing your ex-boyfriend's ex-boyfriend.'

So is he glad to be gay? 'I don't want to be seen as one of the flipping gays tripping down Old Compton Street wearing a Dolce e Gabbana T-shirt, because it marginalizes everyone. I just don't think it's really that important. I think we all place too much emphasis on sexuality and people view it as a kind of cultural choice as well, and I just don't believe that is the case. People assume that if you're gay, there's a whole range of other boxes you fit in, and that irritates me. When I talk to gay magazines, I always argue against the idea of gay culture and I've argued all the way around, and realized that it quite simply boils down to children. As you know, Janet Street-Porter is a good friend of mine, and she and I have relatively similar lives, and I think it's simply because we don't have children. It means you're out and about more, you socialize more. But I don't go to gay clubs that much, to be honest.'

In fact, he lives a rather 'straight' bourgeois life. He collects arts and crafts furniture and modern British painters, he listens to classical music more than pop, he is obsessively tidy, and he hates unpunctuality – he once blasted Janet Street-Porter for being six minutes late in a restaurant. Ideally, he would like people to be punctual *and* laid back, but given the alternative, he'd prefer them punctual. On the whole, he says, he is known for his cheerfulness, but, 'One of my worst things is I get irritable, I get very irritated when everything's going wrong and people are panicking and flapping about nothing very important, and also there's a certain stupidity to do with pop music which I just find irritating. And as I get older, I make a conscious effort to say, "Oh never mind, it will all have blown over by tomorrow."'

So in many ways he is a control freak. But then his lyrics reveal a romantic, disorganized, impulsive soul. He agrees there is a dichotomy. 'People always assume that I'm very organized and rational. But then you say I'm a romantic. The dots don't really join up. I am an ordered person – but then I'm very easily bored. I have to be in different places all the time. That's why I've got two houses – because when I get bored I get on the train and go to the other one. So yes, part of me is a strong romantic. At the same time, I'm a very strong realist. Sometimes I'm too strong a realist, sometimes I won't do things because I think, "Oh, what's the point?" Our manager thinks I'm incredibly inconsistent and she has to deal with us every day. Actually, I think our manager thinks we're both raving mad.'

He has just done a mad impulsive thing, and bought a house in Wearside, County Durham, another home to add to the ones in London and Sussex. This one is near Newcastle, where he grew up and where his parents still live, and his sister and her husband will live in a cottage in the grounds. He is still rather amazed at himself: 'If you'd told me a year ago I'd be doing that, I'd have said it was a ridiculous idea. But I suddenly thought I wanted a complete change of location. I mean, it's the place where I have roots, though I haven't lived there for twenty-five years – I left home when I was eighteen. But I was struck, going to look at the house, by how totally different it is up there, the way people are, the way it looks – the light is colder and the countryside is definitely wilder. And people have a completely different way of life. I know it sounds corny, but it's less materialistic; there's just less bullshit going on. I felt I sort of belonged there. It seemed to represent a part of me I'd forgotten about.'

But he has always, at least in his lyrics, given the impression that he hated Newcastle, that he never fitted in there. In 'It's a Sin', for instance, he says, 'For everything I longed to do, No matter where or when or who, Had one thing in common too – It's a sin.' So how can he now say he wants to return to his roots? He says it was only *school* he hated, 'mainly because of the football culture. I didn't like sport, I had no interest in it, and if you were bad at sport you got a lot of grief, really. I was quite happy with other things, but I had my social life outside school. I joined the youth theatre in Newcastle when I was about eleven and that was a turning point. One was encouraged to write things, and I wrote a little play that was performed at the University Theatre.'

So now he is returning to his roots in another way – going back to the theatre, which was his first love. Next week, at the Savoy Theatre in the Strand, the Pet Shop Boys will perform their songs in collaboration with the video artist Sam Taylor-Wood. They originally meant to do it for a week and have already extended the run. 'The great thing with this is you can stay at home and just turn up at 6.30 – which appeals to both of us, the idea that the audience will come to us rather than us to them. Nobody has ever done it before – a season in the West End!' And then, of course, there is the long-awaited musical, which he and Chris have been talking about for years, but are now writing in collaboration with the playwright Jonathan Harvey. It will be written for a small theatre: 'It doesn't all have to be a spectacle, it can be about life now and it can be funny as well.'

The Pet Shop Boys are probably on the wane as recording artistes – their last album, *Bilingual*, sold 1.2 million, whereas previous albums sold 2–4 million each – but in a way, that makes their future more interesting. They have always been keen on collaborating with other artists and branching out into experimental forms. Neil says he has no idea what they'll be doing ten years from now. 'I've never had a long-term ambition. We take it a year at a time. I would just like us to do something we found interesting – I'd quite like us to be doing something in the theatre – but we might be doing a 1980s Revival Tour. No, not seriously. We tend to take up opportunities that interest us. We like doing collaborations and are lucky because we are open to other people's influences, and we bring them in.'

Does he enjoy being a pop star as much as he did? 'It has changed. When we started, we were much more pop starry, we were always whizzing around doing terrible TV shows in Germany and we used to scream at everything. And it's not like that now. Now, we're not always being the Pet Shop Boys. Which is a dangerous thing, because people have a very strong idea of you which they want you to adhere to. They have a set idea of what a Pet Shop Boys record should be like – sexy, fast beat, over-produced – but we don't want to do that for the rest of our lives. I don't imagine Chris and I would ever split up. We could find that we lost our audience. But then we would probably still make music together, for fun, like we did before.'

Reproduced by permission of *The Observer.*

Major Ronald Ferguson

24 November 1996

Major Ronald Ferguson, as we all know, is a military man, and as a military man he draws up very strict rules of engagement. The rules in this case are that I can interview him at his home in Dummer provided we talk *only* about his Dummer cricket school, at the end of which I can ask *one* question about his daughter. My editor has rashly claimed that I am knowledgeable about cricket so a futile half-day is spent trying to bone up – I might as well have boned up on quantum mechanics. Luckily, I don't need to ask any questions about the cricket school because the major has prepared a speech and got it all off pat. But we must make a tour of inspection first.

We march across the farmyard, past the dog kennel with all the nameplates of deceased occupants, and arrive at the old cow barn he's converted into his cricket school. Having no idea what a cricket school looks like (or indeed what it is), I cannot tell whether this is a particularly fine example but the major assures me that it is. Then sharp about-turn and report to barracks for briefing. The house is incredibly pretty (how can someone brought up here design a place like Southyork?) and densely cluttered with family portraits and photographs, Prince Andrew and the Queen among them. Major Ron takes off his Barbour to reveal a snazzy striped velour blouson and skintight needlecord trousers – a handsome man still at sixty-five, and very aware of it. He tells me that he works out regularly at the Beechdown Club in Basingstoke.

A housekeeper brings coffee, and the major embarks on his cricket school speech. He is not exactly a master of concision so I will paraphrase. He said at one point, 'This is a bit long-winded,' but before I could agree too fervently, he went on: 'But you'll need it for background.' Oh right. Anyway, he gave up playing polo in 1992 and decided to start playing cricket again, so he joined two local clubs, Farleigh Wallop and Oakley. One of them said they needed facilities to train their colts (not horses, apparently), so he thought of his disused barn. That night he measured the barn and had his great idea, and next day he phoned his old friend Peter Sainsbury to say he was starting a cricket school. 'He said, "You're mad." I told the farm foreman and he said "You're mad"; the estate manager, the bank manager, "You're mad." So the more people who told me I was mad, the more determined I was to do it.'

(Ah, there speaks the authentic Fergie voice! One can imagine his daughter telling her staff, 'I'm just popping out to sit under a pyramid in Islington and talk to a nice Greek lady' and them saying 'You're mad' and her being all the more determined to do it. In non-Fergie circles, it's known as not listening to advice.)

Anyway, the major built his cricket school and opened it in April 1995. It was immediately a huge success with all the local cricket clubs, and now has almost more bookings than it can handle. There are coaching courses for boys during the school holidays and indoor matches in the evenings. Now he wants to get state schools sending him boys in the afternoon but, amazingly, the schools plead poverty. He says that, though he tries to keep the fees as low as possible, 'This is not a charitable organization.'

He loves his cricket school because, apart from making money, he can stride around being good with the lads as he did in the army. He obviously relishes the company of young people – he said, rather wistfully, that his youngest daughter Eliza, aged eleven, is 'a great little companion, even just for boring things like going shopping to Basingstoke'.

So he umpires matches most evenings and ensures that they start on time and everyone is properly dressed. 'Got to maintain proper cricket standards. Everyone appreciates that – it's not as if one was being dictatorial.'

And he hobnobs with all the local cricketers – ostracized as he now is in polo circles, these are his new friends. 'Initially, they didn't know quite what to expect from what they'd read and heard about me. And I didn't set out to be extra nice to anybody. But I welcomed them and talked to them, and in a very short space of time, any slight reservations were completely broken down. Now it's great fun because it's a wonderful atmosphere and there's a lot of what you might describe as normal after-sport chitchat, sort of "Why the hell did you run me out?" mickey-taking – a very, very healthy atmosphere. Marvellous!

'Let's face it, it's not quite the same social structure as it was on the polo ground – I mean, naturally, because it's people from every walk of life. But the social side of polo never concerned me at all – unlike other people who shall remain nameless – and now, with cricket, it doesn't even come into it. I'm not a social person in Hampshire. People think because you live in Hampshire you're out at cocktail parties every night. A lot of people are – maybe my wife would quite like to be – but I'm not. It's not my scene, never has been.'

His polo friends dropped him in 1993 when he ceased being the Prince of Wales's polo manager after a series of unhappy incidents. First he was exposed as a regular attender at the Wigmore Club, a dodgy massage establishment. The major thought it was a great joke and wrote to the *Sun* requesting the original of their Wigmore Club cartoon – unfortunately he wrote on Guards Polo Club letterhead – Patron HRH The Duke of Edinburgh – and the committee was not amused. Soon afterwards, he was dropped from his job as deputy chairman of the Guards – though he seems to think it was as a result of the club's 'unsatisfactory financial position'. He moved to the Royal Berkshire Polo Club where he helped a young businesswoman called Lesley Player set up an International Ladies' Tournament. He also had an affair with her. Lesley Player kissed 'n' told with a vengeance – in her book *My Story*, she claimed that she had slept not only with the major but with Steve Wyatt, and at much the same time.

The major's reaction was recorded in his own autobiography, *The Galloping Major*. 'I had to laugh. In her book Lesley accused me of having terrible legs and of being poorly endowed. Pure fiction, I assure you.' This seemed to be his most serious regret about the affair: his book is characterized by a devastating lack of remorse, and served to alienate him from those friends who had stayed loyal out of sympathy for his wife. He was 'let go' from the Royal Berkshire in 1993 and since then has not appeared on an English polo lawn. For a while, he carried on playing polo in the States but now he's stopped. Was he bitter about the way his polo friends all dropped him? 'I think that in life you find out who your true friends are, and I certainly discovered this over the years, and so has Sarah. Bitter is the wrong word because I'm not a bitter person – disappointed is probably better.'

Mrs Ferguson, who has been out having a tennis lesson, suddenly pops in to say hello. She looks wonderful, glowing in her tracksuit, and I want to shake the major and say, 'How *could* you betray her for a crummy little climber like Lesley Player?' Anyway, the effect is to make me impatient, so as soon as Mrs Ferguson leaves, I pounce: 'Can I ask my Duchess question now? Do you think she was wrong to write her autobiography?'

'I thought the question you were meant to ask is, "How is she?"'

'Oh all right, how is she?'

'She's very tired now and wants to settle down. I've said to her, we'll get through November and then, when you've finished all your publicity for the book, you must settle down.' He recites all her interviews – Ruby Wax, Diane Sawyer, Oprah Winfrey, Larry King, David Letterman ('which I think was a mistake, but that's my own personal opinion') and says that, after Canada, she only has to do a few book-signings.

Wasn't Ruby Wax a bit of a mistake from the Duchess's point of view? 'Well, obviously I saw it through different eyes, as a father, and although this is transgressing from our deal, as a father I think enough is enough. There's been too much recently, it really has been endless, as you know. And not just recently. I hadn't said anything about her for six or seven years, but about a month ago I had to go on Sky, ITN, ABC, *Good Morning America*, etcetera, to kill two stories which had been repeated in the *Washington Post* that she was on suicide watch. Well, as Sarah said the other day in one of her interviews, she hardly knows how to spell suicide let alone even consider it. And secondly, there was an absolutely unbelievable front page of the *Sun* about a month ago where it said she'd done a deal with the Queen whereby she would sell her children to pay off the overdraft. So she said, "Right, you must break your silence." So I did. And at the same time I said to the editors – though I knew it would be a waste of time – "For goodness sake stop this vicious harassment and leave her alone." But then, having said that of course, knowing the book was coming out and knowing the publicity she had to do, it's no good me saying stop this harassment, stop this publicity, because she was doing it herself. So there you are. That's enough on her, I think, don't you? I know it's very tempting . . .'

Knowing the major's record (the Wigmore Club, Lesley Player) in resisting temptation, I take this as my cue to carry on. What did he think of the passage in her book in which she seemed to blame him for her low esteem? ('He was a very, very tough father . . . When my demands became a bore, he would call me selfish and spoiled, and – hated word – an "encumbrance". No daughter of his would get above herself, he'd vowed he would keep me in my place.')

'I haven't read her book yet, I haven't had time. I didn't actually know she said that, but I don't think that's true. But anyhow, I never comment on something which I haven't read.'

'You haven't *read* it? Are you a very slow reader?'

'No. There's lots of other things going on. The most important thing at the moment is that my mother [Lady Elmhirst, eighty-eight] is desperately ill. That certainly takes priority over reading any books, including Starkie and Vasso – which I wouldn't open. So what else would you like to ask?'

Was I right in thinking that Ruby Wax suggested that she'd been an alcoholic or some sort of addict? It was a bit unclear in the torrent of psychobabble but that was the impression I got.

'Rubbish. She didn't say that, or if she did, I must have been snoring at the time. Absolute rubbish. That's as absurd as the suicide watch and selling her children. I never even heard that. None of us take alcohol, I'm virtually teetotal, contrary to what people try to make out. Sarah's never been a drinker as far as I know. I'm trying to think – I'm sure Sarah's had a glass of wine – actually I can't think of when I've seen any of them take a drink.' (Starkie says: 'At night she would down a handful of sizeable vodkas, then take to the wine.' Vasso says she was addicted to slimming pills at one stage.)

'But how else do you account for her erratic behaviour? She did seem to become a bit unbalanced.'

'Unbalanced? Slightly mental, do you mean? Pah! Not as far as I'm concerned, no, not as far as her father's concerned. But don't forget that we're here and she's there, I don't see her every day, I don't talk to her every day.'

I couldn't believe that the major hadn't read his daughter's auto-biography but obviously he hadn't because when I referred to their estrangement after he published *The Galloping Major* in 1994, he said: 'Estrangement? Who says so?'

'She does in her book.'

'Oh does she?'

'Shall I read you the passage? I've got it right here.'

'No thanks.'

(The passage reads: 'That book left me feeling totally forlorn, irretriev-ably alone. It wasn't the content of what Dads had written. It was the fact that he had traded upon our relationship for a few thousand pounds, without so much as consulting me. He had taken my most cherished possession, my privacy, and auctioned it off, as though it were his seigniorial right . . . I ultimately forgave Dads, but for a time his book carved a deep rift between us.')

I asked again, incredulously, have you *really* not read it? But the major was on a different tack. 'Under whose influence was she at that moment?'

'Bad John Bryan, you mean?'

'Right. And what was John Bryan trying to do?'

'Make her divorce Prince Andrew and marry him?'

'And? And? And try to get her totally away from those who might be opposed to his plans.'

'Would you have seen through him?'

'I *did*. Yes. So did Jane in Australia.'

'And tried to warn her against him?'

'Oh we did. But he certainly could turn on the charm. He didn't do it with me because he knew it wouldn't work with me but I know from other people.'

Do you think he was cold-bloodedly exploiting the Duchess for commercial gain?

'This is where you're straying outside our charter. I'm sorry, but with everything else going on, it's totally counter-productive for me to start sounding off about John Bryan. It's no good for her, and no good for anybody at all. So please, please remember that we agreed I wasn't even going to mention the word Sarah. O K, well, we have transgressed, fair enough, but please, please this mustn't be an opportunity for anyone to say, "Oh God, now here's Father sounding off." It's awfully tempting, I know . . .'

Maybe at that point I should have produced a socking great cheque. As it was, I made my goodbyes. The awful thing was I liked him.

Reproduced by permission of *The Observer.*

Gilbert and George

13 October 1991

We are in Fournier Street, in Spitalfields, and the scene is already familiar from every Gilbert and George interview ever published. The artists, in their matching thick tweed suits and George VI haircuts, are poised on hard-backed chairs with a tea-tray between them, ready to deliver their views on art, life and everything, speaking in antiphon and finishing each other's sentences. The well-documented rows of Brannam pottery frown down from the Christopher Dresser sideboards, the floorboards gleam in the grey East End light, and George, the English one, leans forward to ask politely, 'Milk?' while Gilbert, the Italian one, leans forward to ask politely, 'Sugar?'

They have been doing this in every interview for at least twenty years. They met as sculpture students at St Martin's School of Art in 1967 and within two years had decided to make art together. More importantly, they would *be* art together, they would be 'living sculptures'; they would wear the same clothes, adopt the same mannerisms and express the same opinions. At the time it seemed a good gimmick, a profitable ploy for the playful sixties. What is astonishing is that they have gone on as a double act for more than two decades and, moreover, gone on to be taken more seriously than perhaps any other British artists of their generation. Their work is international: it has been exhibited in Moscow and is currently on a tour which takes it from Krakow to Rome, Zurich, Vienna, Barcelona and The Hague. In 1986 they won the Turner Prize. It is a rare critic, nowadays, who is prepared to call them charlatans.

Of course, I have tried hard to persuade them to let me interview them separately. I talked to their dealer, Anthony D'Offay; I talked to their friend, Daniel Farson; I talked to them. The answer was straightforward: No. Never in a million years. The interview would be with them together, or not at all. And so together we are.

They express delight with the present I have brought them – a little Devonware sugar bowl bearing the legend 'There's no fun like work' – and reciprocate by giving me an enormous tonnage of books about themselves. There are probably more books about Gilbert and George than about any other living artist, for the simple reason that they pay publishers to publish them. But when I say something snide about vanity publishing, George explains patiently, 'We believe in it very much because it's democratic – by subsidizing the publishers we can bring our pictures to a wider audience who otherwise wouldn't see them. We want to be available. Because we remember as art students, being interested in contemporary art, the access to it was nearly impossible.' The latest book is an account by Daniel Farson of their Moscow exhibition called *With Gilbert and George in Moscow* (Bloomsbury, £9.99), which has the great advantage over all the previous G & G books of being readable. But although Farson travelled with them and, more importantly, got drunk with them, he seems to have fared little better than most interviewers in separating the Gilbert from the George.

Physically, of course, they are quite easily separable: George looks like Eric Morecambe and Gilbert like Ernie Wise; Gilbert speaks with an Italian accent; George in a wonderfully genteel BBC English. But what they *say* is identical: they talk as one; they even seem to think as one. They quote themselves endlessly; you can find the same bits of G & G dialogue going back in the cuttings file over more than a decade. They are brilliant propagandists for art, and their interviews are as formal, and as manipulated by them, as any of their artworks. But even off-duty (for instance, at Farson's launch party) they never drop their act – if it *is* an act, which of course is the big question.

They have taken considerable trouble to organize their lives in a way which minimizes friction. They share a house, but have separate bathrooms, 'so we don't have to row about toothbrushes'. They have assistants and cleaners to do the chores. They go to the same tailor and order the same suits. They have eaten at the same restaurant – the Market Cafe down the road – for the last twenty years. At weekends, they take the train from Fenchurch Street to Shoeburyness or Leigh-on-Sea and walk along the Thames Estuary. In the evenings, they watch *Coronation Street* ('It's really *very* good,' says George) but have given up the 'wireless' because they can't abide phone-ins. They never socialize; they don't have a car; they try to be alone. 'All that,' Gilbert explains, 'makes a free life, which is very, very good, and we try to keep even our studio very clean. We like very much order, it is important for us, then we can be disorganized in our vision. Then we can create. When everything is in order, then we are free to say something. We only have one vision and that is our art.' George: 'Everything else has to base itself around our sense of purpose. We are driven, mental people. We want to achieve lots of things and everything we do has to serve that.'

They are never apart. Gilbert used to return to Italy for a week every year, but not any more. They believe in being together, in unison, for mutual support. Other people criticize them, so they must never criticize each other. George: 'You see couples rowing in every restaurant, very boring. We're based on common agreement. We don't think it's interesting what Gilbert thinks about this, or George thinks about that, we're interested in what *we* think.' Gilbert: 'We became self-less.' George: 'We leave aside all the personal, unimportant details. We're not finickety about that.'

But it is of course 'the personal, unimportant details' that intrigue. And just occasionally, accidentally (or perhaps by way of bait?), they let slip individual differences. For instance: 'When I'm worried,' says Gilbert, 'I get ill in the stomach.' George: 'And I get drunk.' Gilbert: 'But George getting drunk doesn't help me *at all*; it makes me much worse.' George: 'But Gilbert getting stomach-ache worries *me*, so I get drunk.'

And, as the hours of conversation roll on, certain deeper differences emerge. It becomes noticeable that it is always George who fields the really difficult personal questions; Gilbert waits, amused, to take his lead. Gilbert seems to enjoy my nosiness; occasionally he even acts as my accomplice, urging George to show me photographs of himself as a child ('You see, he looks so serious!') or volunteering bits of information ('You know his brother is a vicar'). George, however, is deeply agitated by personal questions: I believe he is the real enforcer of their secrecy and the one most threatened by intrusions into it. According to their cleaner, Stainton Forrest, who told Daniel Farson, George has a terrifying temper: 'Do I ever see it! I do! And you wouldn't like to see it. When George really loses it, he really loses it.' Hence, perhaps, the fear evinced by all their art world associates when asked for background on Gilbert and George: it is like asking courtiers to chat about the Royal Family, and about as productive.

Anyway, let me tell you what I have managed to find out by way of separate biographies. Gilbert, whose surname is Proesch, is Italian and was born in 1943 in the Dolomites, in an area around Cortina d'Ampezzo, which has its own language, Ladin, which Gilbert says is 'the real Italian, in fact. In Switzerland there is a canton where they speak the same language. The Alps used to be full of these people and then the Germans came down the big valleys and so you have German-speaking valleys and, up in the mountains, Rhaeto-Romansch.'

His parents are both dead now, but his brother and three sisters still live in the area and occasionally come to his exhibitions: 'I am their nice brother.' His parents were working-class and Gilbert has supported himself from the age of fourteen, he says, when he went to the local art school. This was not an academic art school so much as a craft apprenticeship in the regional speciality, which was wood-carving. 'We had to carve Madonnas, and Bambis for the tourists.' More usefully, they also had to copy the works of Donatello and Ghiberti and the great Gothic altarpieces. Gilbert says he was 'the *best* carver – but not of the dead ones, of course.' At seventeen, he took himself off to Munich Academy, supporting himself by doing 'one hundred and one different jobs' and then to St Martin's School of Art, which was then the best art school in the world. There he met George.

George was born in Plymouth on 8 January 1942 and his surname is Passmore. George's father left home before George was born. George told Daniel Farson that he went to find his father when he was twenty-one – 'I always imagined a loving Daddy . . .' – and tracked him down to a pub in Dulverton, but the meeting was not a success and was never repeated. His mother remarried when he was still a child

(Gilbert makes George show me a photograph of himself – tall, bespectacled, swotty-looking, aged about ten – at his mother's wedding). She is still alive and he visits her once a year. Gilbert describes her as 'young and tarty' and George does not demur. He has an older brother who is now a vicar in the North of England; George went to see him recently, for the first time in years. There are hints that George is becoming religious himself.

Although the family was poor, Mrs Passmore sent the infant George and his brother to elocution lessons – 'She was very determined that we should be well-spoken.' And indeed, he has perfect enunciation now. He left secondary modern school at fifteen (he had 'reading difficulties' – he may have been dyslexic) and worked in a stationer's shop in Totnes. But from 1957 to 1961 he also went to evening art classes run by Ivor Weeks at the Dartington adult education centre, and Mr Weeks eventually got him a scholarship to attend the full-time foundation course at Dartington College of Arts from 1961 to 1963. From there he moved to Oxford College of Technology and on to St Martin's.

Ivor Weeks is still at Dartington, and remembers his former student. 'He was a teenager, ill-formed and awkward. But even at that time, he was obviously an extraordinary person – his special qualities had been ignored at school. He was full of intriguing stories; everything he did was interesting. His art was so different and so peculiar – it didn't seem to come from anywhere. It seemed naive or primitive, but incredibly detailed and well observed; I remember one still life of jewellery in particular – an unusual subject for the late fifties – and it had a feeling of loving care, a bit like Morandi.'

Mr Weeks encouraged him to develop his talent in his own way – 'To have demanded normal art student behaviour from him would have been disastrous' – and protected him from the other students who seemed to dislike him. 'There was a hint of some strangeness,' says Mr Weeks, 'I didn't go into it.' George would often go to meals at the Weekses' and babysit for their four children, regaling them with stories of how he planned to be a super-tramp. Once, by way of a return match, he invited Mr and Mrs Weeks to a meal at his tiny semi-detached home in Totnes: his mother served the meal but didn't sit down. 'I think he had rather a difficult home background,' Mr Weeks recalls. 'He found his brother very difficult and used to say he couldn't sleep because of him turning the pages of the Bible.'

Mrs Weeks remembers the teenage George as 'very quaint, with rather a Devon accent and a bow-tie, a pork-pie hat and a stick. He was given to practical jokes, like exploding cigars. He seemed eccentric then and always stood on his dignity.' It did not occur to either of the Weekses that George might be gay, and indeed he had girlfriends. One was a student at Dartington Hall school and was reprimanded for going out with a 'town boy': George, on his dignity, went to see her teacher to remonstrate. But he also told Mrs Weeks how, when he was twelve, he befriended another boy at school and the headmaster called him in to say, 'I hope this is nothing unsavoury.' Recounting the incident, George added, 'Don't you think that was a *horrible* thing to say to an innocent child?'

This, then, is the George whom Gilbert met at St Martin's on 25 September 1967 – Gilbert remembers the date. George had been at the art school for a year; Gilbert was the new boy and spoke no English at all; George befriended him. Gilbert explains, laughing, 'George likes foreigners. He is able to be much freer with foreigners, like every English person – they misbehave much better in say Barcelona than in London! He was the only one who was so friendly to me. I couldn't speak English, not one word.'

They were both on a special sculpture course run by Frank Martin on the top floor. It wasn't official; it had no status at County Hall, but it drew some of the best sculptors of the time – Frank Martin himself, Phillip King, Anthony Caro. The term sculpture was loosely applied, and would become more so in Gilbert and George's hands. 'Anything can be a sculpture,' says George. 'Sculpture was making thought, feelings,' adds Gilbert. 'We think art is a vision, nothing to do with materials.'

They are annoyed by the accusation that they lack basic skills, like drawing. George responds angrily, 'I think we're the most trained artists we know. I did seven years studying painting, sculpture, graphics, pottery, and Gilbert did eleven years.' Gilbert: 'But this whole idea that you have to draw is completely nonsense because in the nineteenth century everyone could draw, even Queen Victoria. It doesn't mean anything. Turner was accused of not being able to draw, but what was important was his vision. If you are able to understand the world, that's art.' George: 'You mustn't confuse art with skill.' Actually, Ivor Weeks believes that he can identify their separate drawing styles in some of their early works: George, he says, was a naive and rather awkward draughtsman; Gilbert far more fluent. Nowadays, of course, by using photographs, they have eliminated drawing altogether.

They cannot pinpoint the precise moment when they became 'Gilbert and George'. At St Martin's they exhibited together, but that was quite normal – many of the students formed groups of two or three to show their work. They sent out invitations saying 'Gilbert and George at home' – one of their early best-remembered 'at home' exhibitions was in a tea-shop. But although they didn't *plan* to become a partnership, George explains, 'We were working together and people commented on it, and then we realized . . .'

George remained in touch with the Weekses for some years after he left Dartington, and took Gilbert to meet them. Mr Weeks believes that 'the George of now happened when he met Gilbert – the George I knew *could* be articulate, but he lacked the confidence to speak out. That came from Gilbert.' On the other hand, 'The artistic drive was always there, and also a sort of precision which I see still in the work of Gilbert and George.' Mr Weeks recalls that the first time he saw them together in the late sixties, dressed in their matching suits, 'They talked about how they would become internationally famous artists and manipulate the art world.'

This was when they started calling themselves 'living sculpture' and wearing identical suits and haircuts (they showed the barber a head of George VI on a coin and said 'We want it like that') and talking in unison. They first gained attention with their 1969 'singing sculpture', *Underneath the Arches*, when, wearing suits and bowler hats and bronze make-up, they sang the song for seven hours non-stop, without even going to the loo. They repeated it recently for the twenty-first anniversary of the Sonnabend Gallery in New York, but only for three hours – Gilbert had stomach trouble.

By 1970 at the latest they were established as Gilbert-and-George. But what exactly *is* their relationship? Is it a working partnership, like, say, Rodgers and Hammerstein, or a marriage? When they met at St Martin's, did they fall in love? Gilbert waits for George's answer, which comes after a pause: 'I'm sure it was love.' And did they then decide to start working together? George again: 'No, just to be innocent, moving along – life carrying you along. Because even as students we were very innocent, and not at all self-conscious. We never read newspapers, we never watched television, we were just two lonely people, country boys.'

Most artists would feel it was a sacrifice to merge their individual identities in a pair, but George explains: 'We feel it was a strength – more than a doubling, in fact. Don't you think it's the most normal arrangement in life, two people, it's the most common grouping? All artists are two, mostly.' Really? Rembrandt, for instance? Gilbert: 'He had a wife, he fought for the wife, he went in prison. The attacks that we've had in the last fifteen years, one person alone could not withstand: we have to protect ourselves from people who would like to destroy us.'

They were asked by the *Sunday Correspondent* magazine: 'What or who is the greatest love of your life?' and answered, as one might expect, 'Each other.' They have given enormous sums of money to Aids causes; they move in gay circles; their paintings often seem (though more on this later) homoerotic. And yet . . . I still have a hunch that they are not really a gay couple. When I asked them explicitly if they are homosexual, George (always George for the tricky ones) answered smoothly: 'We never use that word. We just say sexual. We believe that every person is *sexual.*' Gilbert: 'The whole of life is sexual, not homosexual, not heterosexual, dividing up. We believe in different freedoms. Complicated life, no? Because people *are* complicated. And we have to accept that, not having strict rules.'

George's life is particularly complicated because, some time between leaving Dartington and arriving at St Martin's, and probably in 1966, he married. The existence of George's wife has long been rumoured in art circles, but nobody seems to have met her – Mr Weeks recalled that the one time George visited him with his wife, he left her outside in the car. However a friend of the Weekses who *did* meet her told them: 'I assure you she's not the sort of lady to be ashamed of.'

But when I tried to raise the subject, Gilbert laughed mischievously, 'Don't look at me!' while George became agitated and said sternly, 'We never go into details of actual sex. I mean I'm sure we have very elaborate and complicated love lives and sex lives behind us, but we never like to go into details about that. We're probably more frank in our pictures than any other artist alive, but our art is not personal in that way, not autobiographic.' And Gilbert agrees: 'We eliminate all that stuff, in fact; we eliminate personal lives.' When I persist in asking about their private lives, George exclaims like a child throwing a tantrum, 'Not telling! Not telling!' while Gilbert snaps, 'It wouldn't be useful.'

The marriage lasted long enough to produce two children, an older girl and younger boy. The boy is now nineteen, which indicates that George was still involved with his wife for at least three years after he met Gilbert. There are those who maintain that George is still married and signs off at Spitalfields every night to go home to a normal family life: a more credible view, however, is that the marriage ended in the early seventies. They told the *Sunday Correspondent* their greatest regret was 'Not having discovered bad behaviour earlier in life', and they told me that they discovered it together in the early seventies. George explains that at art school, 'We weren't the wild students, we were the well-behaved lower-class people brought up to behave, and we tried to be good. We didn't realize you could go to nightclubs. Every other student was going off to have drugs and sex, but we weren't: we were late developers, you could say. It was in the early seventies that we first discovered nightclubs, and parties, and being able to speak to strangers in the middle of the night.'

They tried to make up for lost time by going out every night and getting wildly drunk and even arrested. The drinking is reflected in their work from about 1972 (*Any Port in a Storm*) to 1975 (*Bad Thoughts*). But nowadays, says Gilbert, 'We're not involved in parties or clubs in that way. George just gets paralytically drunk at every opening.' What's he like when drunk? 'He's very nice, very kind,' says Gilbert. 'He's a happy drunk.'

Soon after they left art school they published a photograph of their two heads together smiling. It is the last photograph in which they ever looked happy: henceforward their image would be unremittingly serious. Gilbert explains: 'We were much more innocent then. We didn't realize that art was going to be so hard.' *Were* they happy then? George: 'Only in the same way people are when they grow up, nothing to do with being arty.' Gilbert: 'And we were happy at the beginning to have some shows, to get some recognition. The first time we sold an artwork we were so happy – £800 – we thought it was *incredible*. Maybe that is why we started to celebrate so much! It was a big drawing called *Walking, Viewing, Relaxing* and we exhibited it in Germany. Unlike art students today, at that time you didn't even think about selling; there were only about three collectors of modern art in the *world* at that time. So when the dealer said, "How much is this?" we hadn't even thought.'

Such naivety didn't last long: they were actually more successful, much earlier in their careers, than any other artists of their generation. Yet they feel they have had to struggle against an overwhelming weight of prejudice and hostility. They both talk of being 'beaten up' by the critics, and when I ask if they mean bad reviews, Gilbert exclaims, 'That is beaten up! They call us drunks, fascists, paedophiles – all kind of stupid names!' while George counters passionately, 'People always say "Why do you mind criticism?" and they don't seem to realize . . . Have you ever been walking at night and you hear a most horrible row going on in a house between a husband and wife? And you get that *dreadful* feeling in your stomach? It's an *awful* feeling. If we were sitting in a restaurant and I was to say "You are the biggest stupid cow we ever met," you would be very affected, I'm sure, wouldn't you?'

Yes, but . . . It seems an over-sensitivity. The only critic who has *really* beaten them up is the *Evening Standard*'s Brian Sewell, in an article entitled 'Beware of Strange Men who do Funny Things' – but he beats up quite a lot of people. Anyway, if they wanted to be popular they'd be painting every-blade-of-grass landscapes. But saying that they are reviled and 'beaten up' is good self-advertisement: it goes with their stated aim to 'attack the viewer, to affect them'.

The criticism most often heard is that their art is fascistic – this began with works like *Britisher* and *Patriots* in 1980 and has lingered ever since. George says it's meaningless – 'Fascists are what teenagers call their parents in sitcoms when Daddy refuses to let them borrow the car.' Still, there is something menacing about the armies of bare-chested young men who march across their canvases, and the occasional presence of swastikas – though, as George points out, the swastika existed long before the Nazis.

When I asked Gilbert if his family had supported Mussolini, he said angrily that no, on the contrary, his family hated Mussolini because he tried to abolish the Ladin language, and half the male members of his family were killed by the Nazis. 'We *hate* the blackshirts, because they want to dictate what we can do, what we can't do. You see them in Brick Lane on Sundays with their *Socialist Worker*, some crummy disgusting title – they are dictating all the time. But our art is just to do with flowers and humanity, complex life. That's what we like: complex life.' However, Ivor Weeks recalls a meal with Gilbert and George in the seventies, when 'They said some things that if it had been anyone else, would have made me get up and walk away. But I never understood whether that fascist stuff was just part of the game.' Or just a phase, like their drunkenness, which they tried out and then discarded? I suspect that much of their 'philosophy', if one can call it that, is no more than a reaction to prevailing pieties, in the same way as they adopted suits and short haircuts in the sixties when everyone else was into beads and kaftans.

They reject the label 'fascists' but they are not actually *upset* by it. What really gets them going is my casual remark that their work is 'obviously homoerotic'. Gilbert yelps, 'Not at all, it's not so clear,' and George agonizes, 'How can you say that? What do you *mean*?' I mean all the muscular, bare-chested young men who feature in their canvases; the total absence of women and children; the prevalence of phallic symbols. The young men are not blatantly eroticized, as in Mapplethorpe, but they are sex objects none the less. 'But they are just boys we find in the street,' wail Gilbert and George, 'they are not gays. You can't sex a person on the street, anyway.' Gilbert: 'In the eighteenth century, every man was bisexual.' George: 'It wasn't even called that; it was just being a gentleman. He would have a wife and a friend. It's only fashion that makes people think that they personally like this kind of sex or that kind of sex. It's conditioning: people are just dragged along by conditioning.'

This is the first time I have seen them, especially Gilbert, so agitated. They are far more bothered by the suggestion that their *art* is homosexual than that they themselves are. Why does it worry them so much? George: 'We don't like these clichés being applied to us when they're so unfair to life, when they're unfair to people.' Gilbert: 'We never did gay art, we *never* did, *ever*.'

But their denial would be more convincing if they had not taken me to see the 'model shots' in their studio. The studio is in the back garden, purpose-built and heavily protected with locks and alarms, as high-tech and state-of-the-art as the house is old-fashioned. Here they periodically hold casting sessions when they advertise for male models – what they call 'normal humanoids'. They showed me the results – boxes and boxes of contact sheets, all colour-coded into head shots, torso shots, bottom shots, genital shots – more than 2,000 of them, and as boring as reading the phone book. When I objected, 'But these are pornographic,' George told me off: 'Where's pornographic? Is nakedness pornographic? Are you pornographic when you get into the bath?' No: there is a difference. But what is really creepy is not so much the photographs themselves as their desire to show them to me, with George going, 'What do you think of this one then, hm? hm?' over my shoulder. It is like his use of rude words – I am particularly struck by 'jobbie', his word for faeces – suddenly dropped into the middle of conversation, or the way when I am leaving he hands me a two-ended lingam and tells me, 'This is the Gilbert and George model.' Schoolboy stuff – but disturbing, too, and vaguely hostile in intent.

George denies he hates women, but he has a weird view of them. He said the only reason women weren't turned on by pictures of naked men was because they 'accept the conditioning that they have to stay at home, read magazines, eat chocolates and not look at naked men, because they'd be dirty tarts if they did. If their husbands ever knew, they'd chuck them out of the house.' Where does he get this bizarre vision of women from? Was life in Totnes really so peculiar? Maybe it was.

We reverted to the normal G & G interview script at the end, when I asked if they were content, and George gave the familiar answer: 'Content? Certainly not. We'd be most unlikely to use that word. We've always said that we're the most miserable people we've ever met. But we accept that. We're not miserable about it any more. People always ask, "How do you feel *now*?" as though when you're forty you've succeeded, or when you're fifty, but there is no such thing – art is a life's work.'

But what is all this life's work in aid of? What do they hope to achieve by their art? George again: 'We would like to give the individual greater opportunity for individualism. Everybody should be able to rise out of their bed in the morning and feel what they are as a person, not that they have to belong to some group and be terrorized by this or that. It's fantastic to think of all those individuals alive in the world today; we close our eyes and think of them all poking out all over, in the jungles, in the cities. Every one has death; every one has life; every one has hopes; every one has fears. That is our inspiration.' It is a wonderful message – but how strange that this hymn to individualism comes from a man who has voluntarily amputated his own past and submerged his personality in a double act.

Reproduced by permission of the *Independent on Sunday*.

Sir Anthony Hopkins

27 July 1996

The odd thing about Sir Anthony Hopkins is that although he often sounds, as we shall see, like an absolute monster of selfishness, he is actually far nicer to meet than many actors who present themselves as sweetie-pies. He tells you his faults readily enough – he is restless, impulsive, unreliable; he won't be tied, he won't 'commit'; he's a good starter but a bad finisher, he often walks out of things (most spectacularly his Macbeth at the National in 1973); he has godchildren he doesn't see, a daughter he neglected for many years, friends he never rings – all that. He doesn't hide the fact that his career comes first and everything else a long way afterwards – he says he would act the telephone directory if anyone asked him to. Nevertheless, you believe him when he says, 'I'm not a bad man.' But trying to capture him is like catching smoke.

We met at the Miramar in Santa Monica, which is his Los Angeles home from home, and staff kept rushing up to ask, 'How's Muriel?' Ooh, Muriel! I thought, sniffing scandal (his wife's name is Jenni), but Muriel turns out to be his mother, the Port Talbot baker's widow, who stays at the Miramar whenever she visits him. The Miramar staff like Tony but they *worship* Muriel.

Then there's his manager, Bob Palmer, amazingly laid back for a star's manager, who says he's sorry Tony is running a bit late but there are these two ladies . . . He nods towards them, two very grand ladies in hats, sitting ramrod-straight in the corner. They wrote to ask Sir

Anthony to autograph their Shakespeare, and this is their moment. Bob, meanwhile, is such good company I completely forget who I am talking to and confide that I hate interviewing actors because I never go to the theatre. 'Oh well,' he says easily, 'that's something you've got in common with Tony.' Huh? 'He hates going to the theatre.'

When Hopkins has finished chatting to the old ladies, we amble over to a private bungalow to have lunch. He is meant to be telling me about his new film, *August*, which is rightly called 'a film by Anthony Hopkins' because he directed it, stars in it and even wrote the music. It's a sort of Welsh *Uncle Vanya*, with a mainly Welsh cast – in fact exactly the sort of 'heritage' film that Virginia Bottomley wants to see more of, dripping with charm, nostalgia, picturesque scenery and maids in mob-caps. Chekhov transposes to Wales surprisingly well. What makes the film important for Hopkins is that it is his début as a director. He found directing a doddle, seldom needed more than two takes ('my Welsh meanness') and brought it in for £3.5 million, which is petty cash by Hollywood standards. He filmed it over two months in the summer of 1994 but has taken this long to find an American distributor.

The trouble is that Hopkins doesn't seem to remember it very well. So much has happened since then – he has made four more films, including *Nixon*, for which he almost won a second Oscar; he has moved from England to Los Angeles; he has been through tabloid hell over an alleged affair and possible divorce; he has been in hospital with a bad back and has just spent six months deliberately resting for the first time in years. So filming *August* two years ago seems like two lifetimes ago. At the time, he gave interviews saying he was enjoying directing so much he thought he would do it full time and give up acting. Now, reminded of this, he looks amazed and says, well, he enjoyed the shooting but the editing and post-production was a night-mare and of course he couldn't possibly ever give up acting.

Doing *August* was part of a 'giving back' phase when, in gratitude for his knighthood, he sat on committees and launched Snowdonia appeals and even said he would like to retire to Wales. But he has always been an uncomfortable Welshman. His childhood in Margam, near Port Talbot, was 'awful' – not because of any lack of parental love, he hastens to say, but because he was so hopeless at school – he thinks now he might have been dyslexic. And he never spoke Welsh or played rugby or sang in a male voice choir or did any of the things that boys from the Valleys are supposed to do. He was a moody, lonely, only child whose main pleasure was playing the piano and whose father, a baker, worried about him not being like other boys. Salvation came only when the local hero, Richard Burton, returned to Port Talbot to visit his sister, and Hopkins saw him whipping past in his Jaguar with his first wife, Sybil, and went to get his autograph and thought, '*That*'s who I'd like to be.'

What made Burton important for Hopkins was not his stage acting (which he never saw) but the fact that he was a Port Talbot boy who made it in Hollywood. He has no sympathy with people who say that Richard Burton sold out – 'He didn't sell out. He did what he wanted to do and why *should* he stand around in the Old Vic for the rest of his life?' This has always been Hopkins's own attitude. He made his name in the English classical theatre but he never had any love for it ('I hate wearing tights and all that verse') and headed for Hollywood at the first opportunity. The irony is that, though he lived in Los Angeles from 1974 to 1984 and chased after every part, he never really established himself. He made a few good films – *The Elephant Man*, *The Bounty* – but he made many more bad ones and finally gave up in 1984 and returned to London, to the classical theatre he loathed. At least – he might have thought – he would earn himself a knighthood. But in fact his Shakespearian offerings drew mixed reviews, though his *Pravda* and *M Butterfly* were highly acclaimed. And then, absolutely out of the blue, Hollywood summoned him back again because Brian Cox, who had played Dr Hannibal Lecter in *Manhunter*, didn't fancy playing him again in *The Silence of the Lambs*. Brian Cox must have been kicking himself ever since.

Hannibal Lecter made Hopkins a star and won him his first Oscar in 1991. Since then he has made fourteen films, including the much admired *Howards End* and *Shadowlands*, *The Remains of the Day* and *Nixon* – he received Oscar nominations for the last two. Having rather belatedly caught on to the idea that he is a great actor, Hollywood now can't get enough of him. After *August*, we shall see him in *Surviving Picasso*, which he filmed in Paris at the end of last year, and soon he will start shooting his next film, which he describes as 'like *Deliverance*, with a script by David Mamet' in which he plays a bookworm who perforce becomes an action hero.

Even he, with his gnawing insecurity, has to admit that now he is a success. His Oscar gave him the film recognition he knew he deserved; his knighthood in 1993 healed his rather chippy attitude to the English theatre, where he had always felt at the mercy of clever-clogs directors. He believes that success has made him a nicer person. 'I feel more responsive to other people because I'm not so insecure. Of course I get bad-tempered or irritable sometimes – but I just feel reassured that I wasn't the moron I thought I was. I don't set out to be an *example*, but to be . . . kind, you know. I'm not a very trusting person. I used to be very guarded and hostile, especially with journalists. But now I think, "Oh well, to hell with it." It's only recently I've begun to feel a little more – no, *much* more – sociable. I used to be withdrawn, a bit reclusive.'

But he is still wary of people he thinks are cleverer than him – and he thinks most people are cleverer than him, or at any rate better educated. He claims he was a dunce at school (though he was musical enough to get into the Welsh College of Music and Drama) and that all his teachers considered him useless. He says that his one regret is that he is not better read – he buys books, in enormous quantities, but seldom reads them. He likes to say that he is simple-minded, or even stupid. Obviously he is not stupid, but he is instinctive rather than intellectual, and in truth not a good talker. He conveys the impression of eloquence but often lacks the words to convey what he really means. I suspect all this makes him a better actor: he acts from the heart, not the head.

Although his acting fee is now reckoned to be about $2 million per movie, he lives terribly modestly by Hollywood standards. He has a two-bedroom wood cabin in Pacific Palisades, above Malibu, and says his biggest extravagance is buying new plants for the garden. He has a Spanish maid who comes three mornings a week, but he always cleans up before she arrives because, 'I have this working-class ethic, you know, that I don't want to put people to trouble. If I use a dish I wash it immediately.' Similarly, when filming, he travels alone, with none of the normal film star retinue. He once tried taking a hairdresser but it was a disaster, so since then, 'I've decided it's not worth it, because once you get involved in all that, having a minder, or having assistants – it's so expensive apart from anything else and so they laugh at all your damn jokes and everything but it's not necessary.'

He has never liked consorting with other actors and avoids them as much as possible. His social life revolves around Alcoholics Anonymous. He gave up drinking in 1975 when he first moved to Hollywood, but he has attended AA meetings ever since, not only in LA but wherever he happens to be – he went to AA in Wales when he was filming *August*. He says it keeps him 'comfortable'.

Why, I asked him, are so many actors alcoholics? 'Oh, because we're just babies, that's why. A bunch of wimps, self-centred. We're attracted to what is exciting and challenging because we're *greedy*. Greed is at the centre of all alcoholics, insatiable greed for life, for sensation. The sad thing is that we want so much of life that it's constantly disappointing us, because we're not realists. Whereas people who are quite happy with their lives and are normal, sensible people – and I mean that without any facetiousness because I'm married to one, my wife Jenni – they face life and say, "Well, that's the way it is."

'Jenni is very normal, not greedy, not gluttonous, not at all avaricious, just sensible, decent, and much smarter than me. She says, "Why do you have to kill yourself over a bad review? So what? What about all the good ones?" But me, of course, I always remember the bad ones. I think it's just basic immaturity – a terrible, aching immaturity so that nothing is ever satisfactory. But that has changed considerably in the twenty years I haven't had to kill myself any more. You know, I *am* happy, I am content with a lot of what I've got, but there is still that sense I want more. I want to write more music, I want to star in a bigger movie. But now I don't want to beat myself to death if I can't get it.'

The only thing that seriously interferes with his contentment is his thinning hair. He mentioned it at least a dozen times in the course of our conversation until finally, exasperated, I said, 'Oh come on! Your hair might be receding but it's not *that* bad.' Then a thought struck me – 'Or have you got one of those nasty bald spots at the back?' He leant forward and I gravely inspected his scalp. 'Oh yes, you have.' It is not nearly as bad as, say, Prince Charles's but I suppose in Hollywood it counts as a major life disaster. He is trying to face it with equanimity.

'I don't want to cover it, or wear a hairpiece, I don't want to pretend that I'm younger than I am, because then it becomes ludicrous, then you lose *any* appeal. So if people like me for the way I look now, if women go all funny over me, that's fine, I don't want to change. I'm fifty-eight, I've got good teeth but I'm losing my hair, I'm going white, I'm slowing down a bit, I can't run as fast as I used to, I have to fight to keep my waistline down, but the funniest thing, the oddest thing, is that I'm getting these attractive parts to play where women seem to like what I do.'

He is still bemused by the fact that Hannibal Lecter made him a sex symbol – he had never been one before. He finds it embarrassing to talk about – I get the impression he is very prudish and rather innocent about sex. There was one moment when he uttered the word 'orgasm' – he was talking about the Californian obsession with better health, better sex – and then looked appalled.

Anyway, he says, Hannibal Lecter made all the difference. 'It's the oddest turn in my life, the strangest thing and I don't know what to say about it. When I was in the theatre, I always felt so unattractive, so . . . unwatchable. I just couldn't walk around in tights. But then, I think because Hannibal Lecter was such a dark, shadowy, *erotic* figure, I guess, I started getting fan mail and women would come up to me in the street and say "Can you do this?" [slavering his lips like Lecter] – and then they'd scream, and I'd think, "I know what that's all about!"' But however much women might throw themselves at him, he was, until very recently, known as one of the most impregnably married of all Hollywood actors.

I was told on no account to ask about his marriage, but in fact he talked about Lady Hopkins – Jenni – readily enough. He has been married to her for twenty-three years. She met him in 1971 when he was filming *When Eight Bells Toll* and she was working as a production secretary. She was sent to pick him up at Heathrow – he was drunk, as he usually was in those days – and deliver him back to his wife, Peta Barker, and their baby daughter, Abigail, in Putney. But a few days later Hopkins walked out on his marriage, never to return, and in 1973 he and Jenni were wed. They have never had children. He says it was not a conscious decision but, 'Probably selfishness. I'm not easy with children and Jenni's not.'

Friends tend to describe Lady Hopkins in similar terms to Norma Major – everyone is so quick to tell you that she is not really mousey, not 'suburban', not a doormat, that you inevitably conclude, OK, so she's a mousey suburban doormat. In 1974, right at the start of their marriage, she gave an interview to the *Sunday Mirror* in which she said, apparently without any resentment, 'Tony has nothing in his life but his work. He is obsessive about it. There are times when Tony is working so much that his sexual energy is sublimated into the work. But I don't get paranoiac about it. Sex is a part of our marriage, but it's not the thing that keeps us together.'

In the early years, Jenni would accompany him everywhere, acting as his PA on location. But the long months of boredom filming *The Bounty* in Tahiti finished her off, and since then she has mainly stayed at home, in South Kensington, busying herself with Anglo-Catholic church groups.

Until last year, Tony Hopkins lived with her in London, but he was increasingly keen to return to Los Angeles. He had owned a house there till 1984 but then sold it when it seemed his film career wasn't going anywhere. Still, he always longed to return and eventually, a couple of years ago, bought his little cabin in Pacific Palisades. When Jenni came to visit him on the set of *Nixon* he took her to see it. He recalls, 'She said it was nice, but she was dubious about it. She said, "What are we going to do?" And I said, "Well, the thing is, you like it there, and I like it here. I can't change my likes just to suit you and I don't expect you to like this." So we got a bit of a stalemate. Then I said, "Well, I'm doing it. I'm going." I know it's a drastic thing to do, but I had to because I would have stagnated. I don't know what's wrong with me, that I can't sit still too long in London. That's the way I'm made. I don't feel I'm a criminal, that I've done anything terrible. I am what I am. And as I said to Jenni, "You knew when you met me you were taking on a pile of trouble." And she's wonderful, she's come to terms with it.

'I'm not a monster, I'm not a *bad* man. I am a little wild and a little more spontaneous than she is – she loves everything to be organized – she is very consistent in her life. I'm inconsistent about *everything*. And I've tried deeply to change that part of myself, to be consistent, to be a stable member of society, to be worthy of my knighthood and all that – I've sat on boards and committees with Richard Attenborough but I can't do it, I can't wear a grey suit. And so I got honest with myself and maybe hurt a few people, but I thought, "Well, this is the life I want, I'm fifty-eight years of age now. I'm going to do it before it's too late. I want to do it because I don't want to live with regrets."'

He moved his stuff out of their house in South Kensington and into Pacific Palisades at the end of last year, as soon as he finished filming *Surviving Picasso* in Paris. But immediately he was struck down by terrible back pain, a trapped nerve between his shoulders. The pain was so severe and so depressing he actually thought at one point, 'I'm glad I don't keep a gun in the house,' because he felt he couldn't carry on. And when he landed up in hospital, 'I heard it loud and clear from the Messenger Above, from the ceiling of the hospital – "That's it. Next time you're going to have the big one, a heart attack, if you don't stop." I was treating myself like a tank. I never took any rest. In days between work I'd be racing all over the place. So that's what I did; I decided just to slow down and take a long holiday.'

I wonder: was it a trapped nerve or a trapped conscience? He had just bought a house in Los Angeles, against his wife's wishes, and was geographically, if not legally, effecting a separation. Moreover, he was having an affair. This all came out at the New Year when someone snitched to the tabloids that Hopkins had told a Los Angeles AA meeting, held to celebrate his twenty years on the wagon, that he was in love. The woman was Joyce Ingalls, forty-five, a reformed alcoholic whom he met through AA and who stayed with him in Paris when he was filming *Surviving Picasso*. He is supposed to have told the AA meeting, 'Joyce has brought sunshine into my life. Her smile alone brightens up my day. This is the first time in my life I feel alive and feel passion. Thanks to Joyce I can live again. I was dying, but she has brought a kind of passion I have never known before, feelings I was afraid to have all of my life, even as a child.'

He denies that he spoke those words; however, he does not deny that the affair took place. But it was no sooner reported than over. By March, his 'friends' were telling the tabloids that Hopkins was devastated when he found out that Ingalls had previously had affairs with Sylvester Stallone and Tom Jones, and concluded, 'That woman was just using me. She was only after me for my fame and money.' Apparently the crunch came when she left her husband and tried to move in with him, and he felt cornered. Soon afterwards Lady Hopkins flew out to accompany him to the Oscars and told the *Daily Express*, 'It is absolute rubbish to say our marriage is over – we have never been happier. I know about Anthony's relationship with this woman, but that is all over now and we are looking to the future.' Hopkins agrees that it is all over, that 'Jenni is fine', and there will be no divorce. Jenni will come and stay with him in the summer, and he will stay with her next year when he makes a William Golding film in England and, 'We can talk about our differences and hopefully things will resolve themselves. I don't know what's going to happen.'

He is obviously perfectly happy living alone – when I asked if he might have a girlfriend moving into Pacific Palisades he actually shuddered: 'No, no! Oh God, I've been through that. Oh, please, no, that's too much!' He is not really cut out for living with anyone, he told me. 'Maybe I should never have married. Maybe I'm a misfit, I always have been, I'm a bad boy, a rebel. I have friends who know what I'm like and they stick by me – that's up to them. I'm a loyal friend up to a point, but I'm not a very committed friend. I'm godfather to a couple of children I never see. If people can accept that, then fine. I'm not a cruel man, I don't relish hurting people, but if anyone wants to hold me back, then I will move them out of my way, I will just say, "Leave me alone, don't hold me." But you know I've played by the rules for a long time and now I've made up my own rules. I'm just going to live here – I'm having a good life, I feel more at peace now.'

This search for peace is something he often mentions. But even when he is sitting still, talking, there's a sort of turbulence about him – a constant, restless, undirected energy, like a piece of paper blown along the street. It is his strength as an actor but his weakness as a person. He has more energy than he knows what to do with – he often jumps into his car and drives for miles, then walks up mountains. He can't see the point of sleeping more than five hours a night. But now, he says, he is training himself to slow down. His worst time used to be between five and seven thirty in the evening, when he would always have to drive somewhere, anywhere, but now he is training himself to stay put. 'I tell myself, "Now stop", and I sit out on the deck and I have a cup of tea, don't even read or turn on the music, and I see if I can sit there for at least half an hour without doing anything, just watching the birds. And the other night I did it and thought, "This is indescribably beautiful, this is so peaceful." And that's what I want. And to be alone in that is wonderful.'

The key to Anthony Hopkins, I believe, is his extraordinary imitative ability. He is a brilliant mimic – he treated me to a wonderful bit of Jeremy Irons telling him, 'I say! Your Nixon! A bit *good*!' But this mimicry applies to life as to art. He lives in borrowed lives. He watches someone and thinks, 'Oh, I could be him.' But he only *sees* the person, he doesn't understand their inner life. Thus, he told me that while he was directing *August*, he kept thinking: 'Here I am sitting in a chair, answering questions, making decisions. I've seen directors doing that, I look just like a film director.' It made him feel mellow, 'grown-up', and for a while he wanted to stay in that role. But then it came to all the parts of a director's job he hadn't pictured – the editing and post-production – and his enthusiasm died.

He has total visual recall and he remembers his life in vignettes that have extraordinary poignancy for him. He told me, for instance, that once he was in a studio canteen and Clint Eastwood walked in, by himself, and ordered a beer and a salmon sandwich: 'That was so impressive.'

But why? Why was it so impressive? He can't put it into words, but it is obviously linked to his own decision not to be starry. He saw Clint Eastwood, admired him, and thought, 'That's how I'll play it.' When he was fifteen, there was the ur-vignette, when he saw Richard Burton returning to Port Talbot and decided to be him. And there was another important vignette in 1973 when he was visiting Los Angeles and saw a man come out of a coffee bar on Wilshire Boulevard and go into the bookshop next door and he thought, 'God, I just want so much to do that!'

And two years later, having been signed up by the William Morris agency and moved to Los Angeles, 'I was going down Wilshire Boulevard one Saturday morning, pretty high, you know, with my nerve ends tingling, and went into this bookshop and I was standing there reading this book and as I came out, into the beautiful, blazing sunshine, I looked across the street and thought, "That's where I stood two years ago and there's the coffee shop and I'm *here*." Now this is magic, this is really amazing. And this is what my life has been from that point onwards. It's been wonderful, it's like a fairy story, like some kind of dream I used to have when I was a kid.'

His favourite novel is *The Great Gatsby* and one can see why – like

Jay Gatsby, he is someone who has concocted the externals of a life, but not the inner workings. He has succeeded in everything he set out to do, except somehow being himself. The most difficult role is the one he is just embarking on now – being Anthony Hopkins, alone on his sundeck in the evening, at peace with himself.

Reproduced by permission of the *Telegraph Magazine*.

Calvin Klein

9 September 1995

There is some heavy PR flak before you get to see Calvin Klein. I was strongly 'advised' not to mention the book, *Obsession* – a riveting biography by Steven Gaines and Sharon Churcher – whose publication it is said Mr Klein tried very hard to prevent and succeeded to the extent of having it dropped by its original publishers. Mr Klein also took the trouble to write to his friends and associates telling them not to talk to the authors. But, luckily, not all of them obeyed, and when *Obsession* was finally published last year it portrayed a gripping saga of gay sex, drugs, orgies, tears and tantrums which made boring old Calvin Clean seem not so clean and boring after all.

Klein claims that he hasn't even read *Obsession*, but if so he's a fool – it's infinitely more interesting than the hype. The hype is all about clean-living, glossy-haired WASPs getting excited about having his name on their knicker elastic. The book is all about the struggle of a poor Jewish boy from the Bronx to survive and finally conquer the snakepit of the fashion industry and then, at the pinnacle of success, to almost blow it away in the cocaine-fuelled frenzy of Studio 54. At the most hectic period of his life, when he was launching Calvin Klein jeans, his eleven-year-old daughter, Marci, was kidnapped and there was a sensational courtroom scene when one of Marci's kidnappers declared she was Klein's lover and that it was all a put-up job to get publicity. It wasn't so – but it added to the whiff of danger around Klein's name.

Throughout the eighties there were rumours that he was dying of Aids, and at one point his death was actually announced on American radio. In 1986, having been thought of as gay for years, he amazed everyone by marrying Kelly Rector, a 29-year-old assistant on his staff, and in 1988, just as he launched a new scent, Eternity, he announced that he was going into rehab to cure his drink and drug addictions. In 1991 it seriously looked as though his business might go bust and the *Wall Street Journal* talked of 'turmoil within the House of Klein'. But now he is flying high with a new range of goods for the home, and the launch of his own store in New York. And lo and behold, he is in the news yet again – this time for withdrawing his new jeans campaign in response to complaints that it 'eroticizes children'.

The gaudy helter-skelter of his biography forms a striking contrast to his clothes, which are uniformly calm, reticent and monochrome. Not for him the ladies who lunch in their Valentino fuchsias and golds: he remains committed to low-key, low-colour, no-frills minimalism. Such austerity seemed somewhat passé a couple of years ago when the style-troopers of the Royalton came out of their long dark night of the soul to swoon over Versace, but Klein's little slip dresses were a hit this spring and everyone predicts a successful autumn. Klein's loyalty to his look makes one think that perhaps he is a more serious designer than one had imagined. When he started, in the seventies, he was perceived as the 'American Yves St Laurent', but his signature has emerged more clearly over the years. In 1993 he won both the men's and women's awards from the Council of Fashion Designers of America – the first designer ever to take the double.

Calvin Klein Inc occupies several floors of an office block on 'Fashion Avenue', the heart of the New York rag trade, and his PR, Noona, a six-foot sun-kissed Amazon who speaks fluent PR speak in seven languages, insisted on showing me every floor. They were all so eerily the same – white walls, white vases of daisies, white slip-covered sofas, white receptionists of daunting youth and beauty – that it was quite a relief eventually to reach Klein's sanctum and find a fairly normal middle-aged man. He still looks young for his age (fifty-two), but more because of his thick hair and jug ears than his fiery-red complexion. He was racked by terrible coughing fits periodically, which made me think he should never have given up smoking.

After all the PR jitters beforehand he seemed perfectly relaxed about being interviewed, rather *too* relaxed in his readiness to lapse into a form of self-advertising patter – 'The woman I dress cares about quality, luxury, value' blah blah – that is only marginally more interesting than watching fish in an aquarium. This, you feel, is the voice of Calvin Klein Inc rather than Calvin Klein. But occasionally you get a sharp, different voice, disconcertingly wisecracking and knowing – the voice I imagine is familiar to his friends in the so-called 'Velvet Mafia', a group of predominantly gay American businessmen. It was this voice that told me, with a sinister chuckle, 'I understand instant gratification. *Totally* I understand it,' but then refused to expand. All questions about his bad behaviour in the seventies produced similar teasing responses – he seemed delighted to be asked, but then delighted to thwart my curiosity. But awkward questions produced yet another response – a sudden disconcerting blankness, almost like a *petit mal* attack – when I felt he was beating down the desire to strangle me with his bare hands.

Anyway, we bowled off easily enough with me asking him to describe what he was wearing. He told me: black Calvin Klein jeans, white Calvin Klein shirt over white Calvin Klein T-shirt, gold wire-rimmed Calvin Klein glasses, black Calvin Klein lace-ups, Rolex watch. I asked how one would know they were Calvin Klein jeans and, leaping to his feet, he did a funny, campy pirouette, ending with his bottom stuck towards me, and said, '*There* – they have a big CK on the label.' It was a big day for him, he added, because he'd changed into black jeans after wearing khaki chinos for weeks – 'That's like a major shift.' But the only startling feature of his attire was something he didn't mention. He was wearing lace-up shoes with *no socks*. Was this, I wondered delicately, a fashion statement? 'My first editor at *Vogue*, who was the Baron Nicolas de Gunzburg, was someone who never wore socks. He had his shoes lined in silk so that his feet would be comfortable. Well, I don't go that far, but I got into the no-socks thing with the black shoes. It's the look – so yes, it's a fashion thing.'

Fancy. He showed me a photograph of 'the Baron', presumably sockless, though it showed only his head. He was one of Klein's many early mentors – Diana Vreeland, Giorgio Sant'Angelo, Eve Orton, Chester Weinberg were others, all of whom are now dead. Perhaps the deaths of so many friends, plus so many acquaintances lost to Aids, makes Klein particularly vulnerable on the subject of age, but I was shocked at how shocked *he* was when I asked if he was the oldest person in his organization. After a stunned pause, he came back with a shaky laugh, 'What a frightening thought *that* is! I used to be the youngest person. I used to say I was older because everyone who worked here was older than me. What a horrible thought.' Didn't he ever get fed up with being surrounded by young people? 'Never – it's inspiring, especially when they're very beautiful.' Anyway, he consoled himself, he was not the oldest person in the office, because his partner, Barry Schwartz, is six months older.

Barry Schwartz is the Horatio to his Hamlet, or as he puts it, 'My oldest and best friend, the person who believed in my talent, and who put up the money and the support to enable us to start this business.' They became friends at school in the Bronx in the fifties, though they always made an unlikely pair – Klein the sensitive, artistic boy whose favourite plaything was a sewing-machine, and Schwartz the tough supermarket owner's son whose passion was gambling. Schwartz, in fact, was originally friends with Klein's older brother, Barry, who shared his love of betting, and later became a New York cab driver. Calvin was very much his mother's favourite, the apple of her eye. It was she who chose his bizarre first name, much to the horror of their Jewish relations. She was obsessed with clothes and would take him shopping at Loehmann's, the Harrods of the Bronx, where she would spend 'outrageous amounts' on shoes and hats. Klein recalls, 'My mother had excellent taste. Still does. She loves the same colours that I do, she was never loud and never extremely feminine – she loved tailored and soft, rather than pretty and frilly and silly. She had a real passion for clothes and it certainly rubbed off on me. My grandmother was a dressmaker and she had very good taste, too.'

It was natural for Klein to go to design school and then to work in the rag trade, where his first job was designing what he called Clothes for Hookers – pink and red suits and coats with long-haired fox cuffs, collars and borders around the hem – 'kind of frightening'. He was a good sketcher with a very quick eye, who could glimpse an outfit and remember every detail, so his employer sent him to the Paris collections to sketch as many clothes as possible, with a view to copying them. Klein was unimpressed. He loved Paris but hated the collections. 'The couture just seemed to have no relevance to the way we lived in America.'

He already had his own clear vision of how clothes should be – not fur-trimmed or fake Parisian, but clean, simple, tailored and American. In 1968 he could bear Clothes for Hookers no longer and decided to make his own collection. He turned to his old friend Barry Schwartz, who lent him $2,000. Schwartz was busy running the Harlem supermarket he had inherited from his father, but a few weeks after Klein started, the supermarket was wrecked in race riots and Schwartz and Klein went together to survey the damage. Suddenly Schwartz started running up and down the aisles smashing everything that remained – he would never reopen it, he had always hated the place. The next day he joined Klein as his partner.

Their success was rapid and enormous. One day a Bonwit Teller buyer got out of the lift at the wrong floor, saw Klein's clothes through a doorway and bought the lot. By 1971 their turnover was $5 million. In 1973 Klein won his first Coty award, the youngest designer to win it, and then won it again the next year, and the next. He was able to buy his parents a new apartment and – typically – insisted that they should bring *not one thing* from their old apartment, but should live in all-new beige surroundings, designed by him.

In 1978 he noted the advent of Gloria Vanderbilt jeans and launched his own – a huge success, with Brooke Shields in the ads purring, 'Do you know what comes between me and my Calvins? Nothing.' They sold 200,000 pairs in the first week. In the eighties, he had a similar hit with underwear, selling $70 million in his first season, and then an even bigger money-spinner with scent – Obsession, Eternity and Escape, all helped on their way by brilliant advertising campaigns. (According to the biography, there was an initial problem when Klein entered the fragrance industry – he didn't like any smell except musk. Klein says this is untrue, but he concedes that the success of his fragrances is largely thanks to Schwartz, who has 'a good nose'.) By 1984 he and Schwartz were paying themselves salaries of $12 million a year.

However, while his business was rocketing, his private life was cracking up. He had married a nice girl from the Bronx, Jayne Centre, in 1964 and had a daughter, Marci, in 1967. But Jayne could not match his sophistication (according to the book, she had to have the plot of

Clutter, right. I don't need things. You know, I can live like a monk.'
This must cause problems at home – supposing Kelly suddenly said
she wanted glazed chintz everywhere? 'It's unimaginable. It's just
unthinkable, *fortunately*.'

What, I asked him, was the point of being 'American royalty' if you
have to work in New York in August when the temperature is in the
high nineties and the air is like mulligatawny soup? Klein laughs. 'We
all work in August in New York. It's not sixteen hours a day all the
time. But there's a lot that we're doing. And I love it, so I do it. Work
is fun, that's the thing.' He is excited about having his own store on
Madison Avenue and getting into 'luxury homeware' – the homeware,
needless to say, is in his usual austere palette of grey, beige and neutral.

The recession, he says, has been 'scary'. There was a very sticky
patch in the late eighties after he borrowed heavily to buy the jeans
manufacturer, Puritan Fashions, for $66 million, then watched the
bottom fall out of the designer jeans market. He had to refinance the
loan with $80 million of junk bonds. In 1990, further hit by the success
of The Gap, his jeans division lost $14.2 million. In 1991 the whole
company was in trouble with profits of $2.6 million against long-term
debts of $54.6 million and the *Wall Street Journal* reported, 'Mr Klein
appears to have lost his Midas Touch.' It listed all the firings and
defections within the company and quoted an employee as saying, 'You
live with paranoia.'

But in 1992, when his junk bonds were due for repayment, he was
dramatically saved by his good friend David Geffen, the record company
billionaire, who bailed him out to the tune of $50 million and took
over all his debt. Klein has since repaid him. Last year he sold his men's
underwear company to Warnaco for $64 million – he will still produce
for them under licence. Since Calvin Klein Inc is privately owned, and
coy about sales figures, it is impossible to know just how well he is
doing, but the industry estimates that his annual fragrance sales (owned
by Unilever) are about $600 million retail, his jeans about $300 million,
and his men's underwear $100 million. The opening of the new store,
designed by British architect John Pawson, indicates confidence, and
his new unisex scent, cK one, looks like a winner.

The usual picture of the Calvin Klein–Barry Schwartz relationship
is that Klein is art, Schwartz is commerce. But several people who have

dealt with them testify in *Obsession* that Klein is the harder businessman. Klein admitted to me, 'You know, designers today have to be businessmen. You cannot be a successful designer and not have a sense of reality. I mean it's not the thing that I really love to do the most, but it's a must.' Thus, while Klein the designer, the image-maker, rabbits about how the beauty of his home with Kelly made him want to share this vision with the world (by selling a lot of grey blankets), Klein the businessman explains that, 'We've done research and we see that luxury home products keep increasing every year in sales, while ready-to-wear luxury clothes stay the same. So we know that people *are* spending in the nineties, but they're spending on different things. Will they ever spend it on clothes again? I think so. I think it's all cyclical.'

The one person who will certainly not be shopping in the nineties is Calvin Klein. He says flatly, 'I don't shop. Ever. I used to have suits made at Anderson & Sheppard in London, but even that was a chore because you'd have to go for a fitting and I just couldn't bear it.' (In fact, he once flew over on Concorde for a fitting, found it was a Bank Holiday and flew home again. Nowadays his visits to London are spent hiring design assistants fresh out of art school – the Brits, he says, are the best.) Apparently, he doesn't even look at shops, though he admits, 'I probably should. But I'm really not interested in going shopping. I mean – I'm a worker.'

Well, yes, but you'd think that *looking* at shops was quite important for a designer. And this implied contrast between people who work and people who shop is a bit of a slap in the eye for his customers. So too, I thought, was his declaration that the way to tell a pair of Calvin Klein jeans was to look at the label. He sometimes seems rather shockingly uninterested in fashion: when I mentioned Moschino he said he didn't know his work – 'I don't have much time to read fashion magazines.' He also said, 'It's not all that serious, the way people dress. I'm impressed by men and women of real style. I'm a visual person and when I see something of great style, it really gets to me. But my *passions* are in other areas and they tend to be more about work rather than trying to change the way someone looks . . . I really don't care.'

The secret of Klein's success has always been his unparalleled ability to surf the zeitgeist, to catch the new idea just as it is about to break big. But now, like everyone else in retailing, he seems to be adrift on a flat sea. One minute he is talking about 'Generation X', the next about how the new focus is all on staying at home. Maybe he just says whatever he thinks you want to hear. He is very difficult to read. His recent decision to withdraw his new jeans campaign after complaints that it was 'child pornography' (the ads, by Steven Meisel, presented a singularly sleazy view of teenage life) looked like a failure of nerve – after all, he survived as many or more complaints for his Brooke Shields ad. But then again, maybe cancelling the campaign was yet another brilliant publicity ploy – it certainly earned him a whole new crop of headlines. With Calvin Klein, you just never know.

He is not happy to be reminded of the Brooke Shields ad. He hates any references to his past, not just the scandalous bits but *everything*. It is as though they are indecent allusions to his age, or mementos of a previous existence he now wishes to forget. When I asked him how he would encapsulate what he stood for in just three images, and suggested that one would probably be the Brooke Shields ad, he became extraordinarily agitated: 'Oh that didn't come to mind. I mean Brooke Shields is really sweet, she's lovely and she looks more beautiful than ever, but my involvement with Brooke was twenty years ago and she is the *furthest* thing from my mind. You know, I'm not *good* about the past, I'm so in the present, in the moment, so focused on what I'm doing right now. I don't think about the past. I'm thinking about today and what I'm planning for the future.'

I suppose you need this immediacy to be a fashion designer, but it makes for an odd persona – a 52-year-old man without any patina, without a past.

Reproduced by permission of the *Telegraph Magazine*.

Rachel Whiteread

1 September 1996

Rachel Whiteread is not an easy interviewee: she tries to be co-operative, but she hates giving pieces of herself away. She grumbled at one point: 'This is like being on the couch.' In an ideal world, she probably wouldn't even reveal her name. She still feels battered by all the media controversy over *House*, for which she won the Turner Prize in 1993, and has resisted press attention since then. Much of her biography is still unknown. Nor does she like talking about her work because she doesn't want to influence viewers' reactions to it. It was striking with *House* that whereas some people, including me, found it touching, even sentimental, others found it brutal, aggressive, alienating. But she likes that ambiguity – her art is not meant to preach. Nowadays, she no longer titles her work because 'it gives too much away'.

So, in the temporary stalemate of wanting to be friendly but not wanting to give too much away, she shows me round her studio. It is an old Yardley's scent factory in Hackney, north London – a huge, light, airy room, not too odd or sinister at first, though it gets odder as you go round. The biggest object is a black plaster-cast bath that looks like a sarcophagus. On the wall are two old-fashioned light switches, but they are casts, too. Then there are two shop-bought dolls' houses, which she is planning to 'do something with' – one of them already contains strange sci-fi blobs.

There are three ceramic mortuary slabs leaning against the wall and, pinned to a noticeboard, a yellowing page from the *Guardian* careers section with a photograph of a mortuary assistant with his instruments and slab. On a table lies a black plaster hand with, beside it, the rubber glove from which it was cast, also a stack of hot-water bottles cast in transparent resin. When I remark that the hot-water bottle casts look rather like bodies, Rachel agrees enthusiastically: 'Yes – like headless, limbless babies.'

Then she shows me her downstairs workroom, which is dark and evil-smelling, with a huge humidifier wheezing away like a bronchitic dinosaur over her latest work, *Untitled (Three Tables)*. All around are stacks of yellow plastic containers saying 'Warning! Children can fall into bucket and drown.' She has, perforce, become an expert on industrial chemicals and has laboratory contacts who tell her of new developments. Nowadays, she leaves most of the mould-making to assistants because 'I don't have the patience', but she always makes the plaster positives herself. Having trained as a painter, she is fussy about the colour and texture of plaster used.

Next week, the Liverpool Tate Gallery opens a major retrospective of her work, from her earliest piece, *Closet* (1988), to recent studio pieces; it includes photographs and videos of the now demolished *House*, and maquettes and plans of the memorial to Holocaust victims that she is currently building in Vienna. Her design is for a concrete cast of an inside-out library – like *House*. It looks familiar at first, but then increasingly puzzling. It is an enormous honour for someone as young as she is – thirty-three – who is neither Austrian nor Jewish, to be asked to build such an important public monument, but she was one of ten international artists and architects asked to submit designs. She recalls having to go to Vienna to meet the jury in the Town Hall. 'It was like something out of Kafka – there were about twenty-five people in this wood-panelled room staring at me. Basically, they just harangued me for about an hour. I left thinking it was like I'd taken my driving test and killed five people.'

That night, she drowned her sorrows with some of the other artists, and went to the airport with a hangover the next morning. Just as she was about to board her flight, a message came over the tannoy: 'Rachel Whiteread. Do not get on the plane.' It was the organizers in Vienna telling her to come back for another meeting. She had been shortlisted.

Her response was typically abrasive: 'You need to give me better odds than that, otherwise I'm going home.' They told her it was down to two, so she returned to Vienna and was told she had won the commission. Next morning, she was made to give a press conference and decided then not to do it again. 'My job is making the work, I don't see myself as having to stand there and justify it or pander to people.'

Given that she claims to have hated all the media brouhaha about *House*, it is surprising that she accepted the Vienna commission – it is bound to be highly controversial. In fact, it has already had wide press coverage in Austria and the States with, as she grumbles, 'everybody putting in their two pennyworth. It just drives me mad. I'm probably one of the very few people involved who has had any experience of that kind of press and I say to everyone, "I don't want to know; don't even tell me." I don't read the stuff – all it does is kind of paralyse you with worry and it just makes your job a lot harder.' She is very clear that you can't design a work of art by committee or through public consensus.

Stubborn is the word she uses of herself; she is well used to digging her heels in and refusing to budge. In a rare flash of self-revelation, she provided a clue as to why. I asked if there was anything odd about her childhood, and she responded with typical prickliness: 'Why? Should there be?' But then she volunteered: 'I've got twin sisters – that's quite strange.' The twins, two and a half years older than her, were inseparable when small and spoke their own language, so Rachel had early experience of holding her ground against superior force.

She was born in Ilford, east London, in 1963. Her father was a polytechnic administrator, originally a geography teacher, and active in the local Labour Party. Her mother, Pat Whiteread, was and is an artist, socialist and feminist who, in the seventies, helped to organize the first feminist art exhibition, 'Women's Images of Men'. Rachel believes she gets her drive from her. 'She has an incredible tenacity, she keeps going. There's not that much interest in her work, but she's just continued to do it and I think that's amazing.'

When Rachel was four, the family moved to Essex and lived in the country, then moved back to London, to Muswell Hill, when she was seven. The move provoked what she calls 'a kind of breakdown', which lasted for almost a year. She refused to go to school and would run home if anyone tried to take her. She ascribes it to being unsettled by the move – though her sisters tease her that it started with the death of her pet hamster. 'It was just a kind of general unease. My sisters were finding it difficult, too, and my mother. Not that it was an incredibly unhappy time, but quite disturbing. I used to hear voices. A lot of the time I didn't really understand what they were saying, but they were like a communication. And it was a male voice, I remember, quite a deep voice. This is going to sound incredibly strange if you write this . . . But often you hear of children hearing voices and a lot of people think it's a spiritual thing . . . I don't know. I was a sensitive child. I just thought it was normal. But when I told my mum she was worried. It's a difficult thing to talk about now because it was such a long time ago, but I think it affected me quite a lot, and I do remember it and often think about it.'

Has she ever felt a glimmer of it coming back? 'Very occasionally, yes. You know, sometimes you just feel incredibly lonely and it's almost like you're rattling round inside yourself and there's nobody that can be a part of you? There have been moments like that when maybe I start hearing a little voice, but it's not something I worry about.'

Does she believe these voices might have anything to do with her becoming an artist? The shutters come down again: 'I've no idea. It's a good soundbite.'

At Creighton (now Fortismere) comprehensive, she embarked on science A-levels – possibly, she thinks, as an act of rebellion against her mother – but at the last minute switched to art and found herself 'incredibly thirsty for it'. She went to Brighton Art School, where she had a typical Whiteread tussle with the authorities. She was meant to be studying painting, but by the third year she was spending more time in the sculpture department and making 'these strange things that came off the wall and went on to the floor – almost like three-dimensional drawings made from rubbish I picked up off the beach'.

Her tutor suggested she switch to sculpture, but she refused. 'I wanted to stay in painting to prove a point. I remember my tutor saying, "If you don't pull yourself together, you're going to fail," which for *me* – I mean, I'd worked so hard and *loved* what I was doing . . . But anyway I ended up getting a first, so it kind of came good.'

She had a similar problem over whether to do painting or sculpture for her postgraduate course. She applied to Chelsea for painting and the Slade for sculpture and got both – 'which was even more confusing. But I was stubborn. These people were trying to stick a label on something and I didn't want that.' Nowadays, she calls herself firmly an artist, not a sculptor. While she was at Brighton, Richard Wilson gave a workshop on how to make casts and she loved the technique immediately. 'It was just incredibly liberating – that you could make an impression in sand and pour molten metal into it and then you had an object. I liked the simplicity and the directness of it.'

But why does she find casting so satisfying? Surely it's just copying something that exists? 'But you're also *changing* something that exists. If you're casting a spoon, and you push it into sand and then pour in metal, it's not like a spoon any more. That's what I like, that you can subtly change people's perception of the everyday.'

She sees a clear line of development in her work from about 1985 onwards, though gradually moving from the personal to the formal. At the Slade, she made body casts and personal mementos including childhood blankets and a little table from home, but when she left college, 'I decided I didn't want to be so specific about my own childhood.' Nevertheless, her first exhibition in 1988 included several personal pieces – *Mantel* (a cheap dressing table), *Hot Water Bottle*, *Shallow Breath* (a cast of the space underneath a single bed) and her best-known early work, *Closet*, the cast of an ordinary utility wardrobe covered in black felt.

'They were all very particular pieces of furniture – cheap, postwar furniture – which I somehow wanted to immortalize, to give a kind of grandness. I was trying to make a space that I was very familiar with and that a lot of people would be very familiar with. And I have a very clear image of, as a child, sitting at the bottom of my parents' wardrobe, hiding among the shoes and clothes, and the smell and the blackness and the little chinks of light, and I was really trying to illustrate that, which is why I used black felt, to absorb all the light. I was trying to make that space solid.'

Were they all her hiding places as a child? 'Yes, in a way. Kind of happy places, I suppose, where you went and dreamt. Places of reverie. And where you'd mutilate your dolls, cut their hair and everything.' To me, these early works seem terribly sinister, more redolent of fear than of reverie. She agrees: 'There's always been a kind of sinister aspect to most of the work, but I don't really know what that is. I mean, when you tell people that something is cast from a mortuary slab they immediately think it's sinister, but the actual object is incredibly simple, beautiful.' But did they feel sinister to make? Was she investigating her own fears? 'Very much so, yes.'

The most frightening to make was *Ghost*, the cast of the space inside a room, for which she was nominated for the Turner Prize in 1991. It was a room in a condemned house in the Archway Road and at the end, in order to cast the door, she had literally to wall herself in. 'I felt like a nun who'd done something terrible and had to be bricked into her cell.'

The originals of the mortuary slabs that she mentioned are still leaning against her studio wall and I asked how she came to acquire them. 'I don't really want to talk about my interest in death, but there was a period when I made a lot of work that was obviously very connected with it. And at that point, I used to go to an architectural salvage place in Dalston – I kind of used it as a sketchbook. And one day, I bought a ceramic drainage board from a butler's sink. And I said, "You don't happen to have anything like this, but bigger?" I didn't know it was a mortuary slab I was indicating, but he said, "Oh it just so happens I've got a couple down Mile End, come with me."

'So I went with him and there were these two mortuary slabs just lying out in the yard and they were covered in moss and algae and I bought them. I had them in the studio for about six months, not really knowing what to do with them, and I cleaned them. And I remember the process of cleaning them very clearly because it was almost like cleaning a body, you know? Being kind of disgusted, but intrigued at the same time. And one of them had a plug in it and I had to remove this plug and it was full of hair – it was just completely revolting, but quite intriguing, too.'

The theme of death in her work seems to have centred on her father's death from heart failure in 1989, soon after she left the Slade. He had had rheumatic fever as a child which left him with a heart condition. But in fact, Rachel says, she had experience of death long before that. 'I remember after my father died and I was incredibly upset and finding it very hard to come to terms with, I went to this extraordinary woman who's a death counsellor at St Joseph's Hospice. And she said, "Well, for someone of your age, you've actually known a lot of death, it's kind of bizarre."'

At that age – her mid-twenties – Rachel reckons she'd known about ten deaths. She was particularly upset at thirteen when her best friend's sister died suddenly of a heart attack while on a school trip. She found it 'absolutely devastating'. But none of the deaths – apart from her father's – involved close family: it sounds more as though she had an unusually strong fear of death, perhaps from knowledge of her father's heart condition, and sought it out. As a teenager, she worked on the restoration of Highgate cemetery and enjoyed the Hammer Horror ghoulishness of its broken graves. 'I was fascinated by the cracks in these solid surfaces and knowing there was a body underneath – it was full of macabre, sinister fascination.'

She worries about her death perhaps more than is normal in someone of thirty-three – 'I try not to think about it too much' – and was upset recently when she was told that she ought to write a will. She will do it for the sake of her partner, Marcus Taylor, with whom she has lived for nearly ten years. He is also an artist, best known for his see-through perspex refrigerators and his distorted forms in stainless steel. Rachel would like to have children, but is not sure when. She fears that motherhood might interfere with her creativity, but recognizes that 'all artists have wilderness years – I'm sure I will'.

The huge international interest in her work means that she is now, in her own eyes, a wealthy woman (though still in the five-figure rather than six-figure bracket). 'It's something I find quite complicated because I never thought I would make any money from art and I'm still trying to figure out what you're meant to do with it.' She has bought a house in Haggerston, and is now buying her own studio, which she will share with Marcus. She solved the problem of the £40,000 she was given by the K Foundation (an anarchist art group) on the day of the Turner Prize, by giving it all away – £10,000 to Shelter and the rest to young artists.

She has a packed diary, preparing for the Tate retrospective, giving lectures and discussing projects in America and flying regularly to Vienna, where she is supervising every aspect of the Holocaust Memorial, though not casting it herself.

'From the outside, it must seem that I have this extraordinary life –
I have a house, a car, I travel a lot – but actually it is incredibly hard
work and very stressful and the onus is always on me. If I make
something bad, that's my fuck-up. And there are all these other people,
gannets everywhere, feeding on you, all wanting a little bit. Because of
Damien [Hirst], everyone wants access. Damien does it incredibly well
– for him, column inches mean everything and he loves it and that's
his personality. But my personality is much quieter and I like my privacy
and don't like it being invaded. When you open the paper and there's
an article about "the New Left Bank in Hackney" and they pinpoint
where you live – I think that's just outrageously intrusive.'

There is more, much more in this vein, grumbling about the price
of fame and how appalling that people should come up to her in the
street and ask for her autograph. It seems at odds with her socialism.

Exasperated, I finally snapped why couldn't she give people autographs if they wanted them? And she said, sourly: 'Oh, of course, I'll
sign a bit of paper.' But then she went into another jeremiad about
how she could never really enjoy *House* when it was built because of
the crowds of people whispering 'That's her', so she had to sit in a
parked car, wearing dark glasses, peeping out from behind a newspaper.
When she gets on this hobbyhorse, she sometimes sounds like an Anita
Brookner heroine complaining that a man has touched her arm; one
need not doubt the sincerity of her outrage, but one can also find it
arrogant and faintly absurd.

She *is* arrogant – but she has every right to be. I asked whether she
considered herself the greatest living British woman sculptor and she
said, well, she wasn't sure if Dame Elisabeth Frink was still alive . . .
(She died in 1993.) Clearly, she is aiming for that status and beyond:
she would prefer it without the 'British' and without the 'woman', too.
She says she is beginning to think about posterity. She has to for the
Holocaust Memorial, which, unlike *House*, is built to last. She has
designed it so that it cannot be climbed on, and any parts that are
defaced or covered in graffiti can be replaced. 'It's terrifying that this
piece could actually be around for centuries.'

While the Vienna memorial clearly derives from *House*, her studio
work is moving in a new direction. 'It's becoming more formal – the
pieces are becoming more unforgiving, they don't have that residue of

everyday life on them so much.' What did she mean, unforgiving? 'They have a sense of shape, form and colour – they don't have a sense of shape, form, colour, and oh-is-that-granny's-fingerprint-underneath-that-table.'

A pity, I said. For me, it was precisely granny's fingerprint that made her works accessible. But, she said, perhaps people like me could develop along with her work? So that having learned to love *Ghost* and *House*, we could move on to the next stage?

I hope so – I want to interview her again.

Reproduced by permission of *The Observer*.

Joseph Heller

1 March 1998

Everyone told me beforehand that I would *love* Joseph Heller, and, of course, I already loved his writing. I belong to the generation that wore 'Yossarian Lives!' badges on anti-Vietnam marches: *Catch-22* was our Bible. Although it was written in the 1950s about the Second World War, it seemed to have been written precisely *for* Vietnam. Meeting Heller then would have been like meeting God, and even now – when he is seventy-four and long past his best as a writer – I sit up straighter when his terrible rasping Brooklyn accent comes on the phone. 'Do you like food? Do you like clams? We'll talk, then go to this restaurant that has the best clams.'

He instructs me to take the jitney from Manhattan to Armagensett, Long Island, and he will meet me at the bus stop. When I get there, it is pouring and there is no one to meet me and no shelter. There is a church but it is locked. Eventually, I notice a Christmas tableau in the church garden and snuggle in between Mary and Joseph and the ox and the ass while the New York rain buckets down, and I curse Joseph Heller from the bottom of my heart. He is full of apologies when he arrives fifteen minutes later, but I'm not sure; I'm sure I saw him drive past earlier. I think he thought it was a good joke to let me wait a while. He is one of those loud-laughing, wisecracking, back-slapping, supposedly 'jovial' characters who always, in my experience, have a heart the size of a pea.

Later, he decided he liked me and switched into flirtatious mode and even kept urging me to miss my jitney home, but I felt as you do with a dog that has once nipped you on the ankle – 'Yeah? You wag your tail now, but I'm not fooled.' Anyway, he drove me back to his house on Long Island, with a short sightseeing detour to the rain-lashed beach. 'My wife likes the beach, she likes seeing all the children. I don't do children.' Then on to his house – a pretty and presumably very valuable bit of real estate, with a guest cottage in the garden where he writes. His wife was on the phone upstairs so I didn't meet her until later – we talked in the kitchen. He told me I was to correct his English when I quoted him (I won't, though) and he said, 'Can I take it that you've read all my novels?' I lied and said yes. Actually I skipped *Picture This*, which even his publishers prefer to forget: it is no longer listed in the front of his paperbacks.

He is the hardest of all the Great American Novelists to place, partly because his oeuvre is so small (only six novels) and also because *Catch-22* is that freakish and impossible thing – a 'cult' novel that has sold more than 10 million copies. Some cult! His second novel, *Something Happened*, though agreed by all critics to be his masterpiece, was far too dark to be popular. Personally, I have a soft spot for his third novel, *Good as Gold* (which his first wife's divorce lawyer described as 'The *Mein Kampf* of marriage'), but it is more conventional than the others. After that, it is downhill all the way – his last novel, *Closing Time* (1994), got a million dollar advance on the strength of calling itself a sequel to *Catch-22*, but it was a mess. He is also hard to judge on stylistic grounds. I was brought up on the 'practical criticism' theory that you could assess a writer's quality from a mere paragraph of his work, but that just doesn't wash with Heller. There are no dazzling passages of fine writing. He achieves his effects by repetition and accretion, circling round and digging deeper, like the process of psychoanalysis, so that by the end you know his protagonists so well you feel you have lived inside their brains.

That is why his new autobiography, *Now and Then*, is redundant. He has written it all already, and much more successfully, in his novels. And he has said often in interviews that he is no good at facts. I get the impression that his heart was never in it – the chapters have titles like 'On and On' and 'And On and On' and 'And On and On and

On', which is exactly how you feel. We know about his growing up in
Coney Island from *Closing Time*; we know about his Jewishness from
Good as Gold; we know about his war experiences from *Catch-22*; and
his early career in advertising from *Something Happened*. We know from
almost every novel that he was an unfaithful husband and an unfond
father. And he wrote a non-fiction account, *No Laughing Matter*, of his
1982 brush with Guillain-Barré syndrome (a paralysing disease) during
which he fell in love with his nurse, Valerie Humphries, and divorced
his wife, Shirley, to marry her. So *Now and Then* is an orange from
which we have already sucked the juice. If you have not read Joseph
Heller, don't start here – start with *Catch-22* or *Good as Gold*. Then take
a deep breath and read *Something Happened*.

Still, we must talk about *Now and Then* because that is what he is
plugging and he is a great believer in publicity. He said he decided to
write it because he couldn't think of an idea for another novel after
Closing Time, but he had some leftover writing about Coney Island
which he thought he could develop. 'I had all these words, and I was
set to mind thinking about my past and, lacking an exciting idea for a
novel, I began blocking this out. It was not a task; it became almost a
form of psychoanalysis. I mean, recalling so many things about family
life and friends which had gone from my mind completely, it was an
enjoyable experience. Often painful, recalling certain details.'

But his recall is never total. He can never really remember his father's
death, when he was five, which was obviously the key event, the
'something happened' in his life. ('Something did happen to me somewhere to rob me of confidence and courage.') His family never spoke
about it and nor did he – they were not much given to emotion. He writes
in *Now and Then* that, 'I am walking proof of at least part of Freud's theories
of repression.' He had psychoanalysis when he was going through his
divorce, but he regards it as a failure because he could not recall anything
before he was six years old. All he remembers of his father's funeral
is that an aunt gave him a dollar, and since then he has associated
money with life, and the absence of money with death. He used to say
that he would commit suicide if he ever went broke.

Nor does he write about what made him a writer, or how he
developed as a writer. He remembers being hugely impressed by Don
Passos's *USA* when he was at school (though he doesn't think it stands

up now), but it wasn't till he went to college after the war that he could read Dickens and Tolstoy and Dostoevsky. Up till then, he'd only read contemporary novels and, 'They tend to have a great deal of plot and they move very quickly. And it turns out, my novels have very little plot and they don't move quickly – that's not a matter of aesthetic judgement so much as my author's personality and my imagination.' But he didn't put all that in his autobiography: 'My feeling is that there is nothing unusual about my career. Had I written what I think of as a full autobiography, I would have said more about that and more about my children, my marriage, more about the individual experiences, but it's not that kind of book. Above all, I wanted this to be a book in which I come through as modest.'

Can he be serious? He says it with a straight face, but it could be another of his tricky, deadpan jokes. Modesty and Joseph Heller do not belong in the same sentence. He is outrageously egocentric – however much you might ask about his wife or his children or his views on other novelists, he always brings the conversation back to himself. There was a delicious moment when I asked whom he considered the greatest American novelist of the twentieth century: I mentioned Hemingway, he mentioned Faulkner. But he was growing tetchier and tetchier as the discussion continued – obviously I had forgotten the main candidate – and finally he came out with it: 'I would say that *Catch-22* has remained highly regarded since 1960 so it may be *the* novel that still has life and worldwide respect and readership.' It is a source of annoyance to him that Saul Bellow won the Nobel Prize and he didn't. 'I would like to get it – God knows I deserve it – but I don't expect to get it. But on the other hand if I get it, I won't be that surprised!'

When people tell him he has never written another novel as good as *Catch-22*, he replies, jovially, 'Who has?' But actually he is certain that his second novel, *Something Happened*, is his best. 'I think it's the deepest book in terms of effect upon readers, and I also think it's the most difficult book of mine to have been able to have brought off successfully – I want you to correct my English when you quote me – because it's a book about boredom, ennui, monotony, hopelessness, and to write a book about that and create the feeling, not merely state it, and yet to have the book be interesting was not an easy thing to do.'

It took him thirteen years to write – he was fifty when it was published and only then could he afford to give up his day job, teaching English. He used to worry terribly about money, because he is a painfully slow writer and also, 'I was always at the mercy of my imagination – if I did not come up with something to write, I would not be able to write. Other novelists choose a subject – they choose Lee Harvey Oswald or Picasso – but I just can't write like that.' But then, two years ago, he had to have a spinal operation and went over his finances beforehand and realized that he was very well-off and could stop worrying.

He is not a 'natural' writer, not a wordsmith. He reckons to write only about 250 words a day and plans each tiny segment while he pounds on his treadmill in the morning. 'It's not easy, emotionally, but I want to get three handwritten pages done and if I do those three pages then I've got the equivalent of a typewritten page. And once I've done that I usually can't go much beyond it. I don't have the language. I know how I want to proceed but I don't know what the transitional phase should be. "Days afterwards, looking back, he felt . . ." I don't have that. It does not *flow*.'

He realized early on that he could never 'do' realism because he didn't observe – 'I don't notice the colour of your eyes and if you asked me what the colour of your scarf is, I couldn't tell you.' But he also seems to lack the easy command of vocabulary that most writers take for granted – he talks of 'running out of words' or not being able to find the word he wants. He got very excited when I asked if he was an oppressive parent, and said, 'Oppressive! That's another word I wanted to use – I couldn't find it.' He once told Martin Amis that, 'There's some kind of psychological quirk in me which still has me feeling I'm not a writer, not at home with literary language.'

Similarly, ideas for novels come very slowly and infrequently – he never even thinks about the next novel until he has published the present one and even then an idea might not come to him. He says he 'hopes' to start another novel this summer and he has had a few ideas but they are unsatisfactory – 'I have the sense that I've written them before. They're amusing ideas – amusing openings to books – but I don't think I can write them.' He has long wanted to write a sex novel from a woman's point of view, and has already thought of the title, *A*

Sexual Biography of my Wife, but he has no idea of the content. 'I don't know what really intimate thoughts pass through a woman's mind. It's not simply a matter of how a woman feels the first time she's masturbating . . . Most women don't want to talk about it, they deny that they ever did it . . .'

There is a rather uncomfortably long pause. Am I supposed to do my bit for literature and give him a description? Instead, I agree fervently 'Right.'

He once rebuked an interviewer for calling him a 'womanizer', explaining that 'a womanizer is someone who is passionately attracted to women. I wasn't.' But if he wasn't attracted to women, why did he sleep with so many? 'I'll tell you why. First of all, there were not that many. And second, it was part of the male culture. It was not a *sexual* drive, it was just . . . I was in New York City working in an atmosphere where men did that, we'd have parties and a couple would go into a room together. I think twice I fell in love – it lasted a year – I never had a wish to end my marriage, and when summer came and I went away with my family for the summer that was usually the end of it, a very peaceful ending. Those were what I would call affairs, the others were just individual sexual encounters. It was a delightful phase, it mostly started after *Catch-22*, and I felt very good about myself. Looking back, I don't feel so good about it because the effect on my wife was devastating. I regret much of the outcome. On the other hand, I enjoyed very much the experiences and if I had to do it all over again, I don't know which I would do.'

He says his wife Shirley never *accurately* detected his affairs, but she knew he was unfaithful. Still, the marriage tottered on for thirty-five years until 1982, when he contracted Guillain-Barré syndrome and fell in love with his present wife, Valerie, who was his nurse. In the end, *he* filed for divorce. He never spoke to his first wife again, though he sent her flowers when she was dying. 'Conversation was impossible between us, that's one of the reasons we separated.'

Significantly, perhaps, his son and daughter are still unmarried in their forties – he says it's because, 'they don't relate as openly to people as I do'. Perhaps it's because he set them such a bad example? 'Not *me*! They had a mother, too, and they had a grandmother who was a tyrant.' But he agrees that he was probably an 'oppressive' parent and that fatherhood was not his thing. There are some truly harrowing scenes between father and daughter in *Something Happened*, the father clearly loathing the daughter and making no allowance for the fact that she is a child. He says dismissively, 'I don't relate to children particularly, or even young people any more – there's no basis for conversation.'

I ask what attracted him to his present wife, Valerie, and he says, 'Well, you'll see when she comes down. She's attractive. She was my day nurse, she was single and it developed. One thing I say which is amusing but true is that we were intimate before we were friendly.' Soon afterwards, Valerie joins us – slim, elegant, probably in her late forties. Unfortunately, she seems to be boiling with rage. She ignores me and says to him, 'You know what – we have some things to discuss!' It seems she has just read his publicity tour itinerary and doesn't like it – not enough free time between America and Europe. Then she announces, 'I'm hungry, I'm starving,' so we pile into two cars and go to the restaurant in Easthampton. Previously, I had asked if his wife still treated him like a nurse and he says, 'Does that answer your question – is she bossy? She's as bossy as can be!'

Over lunch, I asked Valerie what he was like when she was nursing him, and she said, 'Different. He was a very happy person, very agreeable, even though he was almost paralysed, he was very happy and he really did not realize that he might not recover. The doctors said, "You'll be fine," and he believed it. A lot of times, when people are sick, there is a different personality to when they are well.' Heller butts in: 'When I met her in the hospital, I was flirting.' Valerie: 'And now he flirts with everybody else!' Heller: 'We've been married over ten years. I'm sure my character has changed, and she has changed to an extraordinary degree – barely tolerable!'

Had she heard of Joseph Heller before? 'Yeah, but I didn't know what he looked like. I thought he looked like Norman Mailer!' She had never read any of his books, not even *Catch-22*. 'I was so busy, I had no time. After we were home from the hospital, *then* I read the books. I remember running down the stairs when I was reading *Catch-22* and I said, "You wrote this? You're crazy! I can't believe you wrote this!"'

Heller remarks, menacingly, 'You may have noticed she talks more rapidly than I do . . .' Valerie immediately responds, 'Have you ever heard his daughter speak? She speaks in entirely slow motion. I've never heard anyone speak like that in my life. Never. It's very strange to me. Real . . . slow.' Heller comes back: 'What she's saying is that she talks rapidly, and I get irritated by people who talk rapidly.' Valerie: 'I think the British speak *very* rapidly and the Southerners speak even more rapidly.'

The whole lunch is like this: I'm never sure if they're joking or rowing, but there are strange turbulent undercurrents whirling through the meal. He eats an enormous number of oysters, she eats some huge Mexican thing, they both keep asking if I like the clams. 'Mmm, yes, yum-yum,' I go, dreaming of cigarettes. I ask for a glass of wine. 'Look at the size of that glass!' she says. It is a standard wineglass. 'You'll never drink all that!' I could easily drink a tanker, the effect of the Hellers together is so unhingeing. When I talk to him, she gets annoyed, when I talk to her, he does.

The only way to appease them both is to talk about England – they both like it. He went to Oxford on a Fulbright scholarship in 1949 and is very proud of the fact that he is now a Visiting Professor of his old college, St Catherine's, though he admits that disliking young people is a bit of a disadvantage. He also turns up regularly for literary festivals (Cheltenham, Hay-on-Wye) and says he enjoys such junkets, 'for vanity, excitement. I enjoy very much having expenses paid, and being *a* centre of attention if not *the* centre of attention'. He has several friends in England – Craig Raine, Galen Strawson, Ian McEwan – and was a friend of the late Peter Cook. He loves the *Spectator* 'because it's so uptight and right-wing'. Valerie loves English sitcoms, especially *Ab Fab*, but he doesn't: 'Comedy doesn't make me laugh. Tragedy does!'

Later, driving me back to the bus stop, he seemed in mellower mood and burbled fondly about Valerie as if they hadn't just been verbally beating each other to a pulp – maybe it's their normal form of conversation. He says she gets lonely out on Long Island; he does, too, but he's got his work. Their neighbours are mostly rich businessmen whom he finds, he says, very egotistical. 'Really?' I choked. 'Some people might say *you* were a bit egotistical.'

'Do you mean egotistical, or self-satisfied?'

Actually, I meant egotistical, but he went on, 'Well, I am satisfied and I'll tell you why. I'm well into my seventies. I'm in good health, I have a nice personality, I can live comfortably. It doesn't mean I don't go into periods of depression and anxiety – like now, waiting for reviews to come out, wondering even what *you're* going to write about me – but I'm no longer anxious about things like money, and I'm no longer really anxious about sexual activity – that's in the past. I wish I was younger, I wish I was as virile as I was, and I wish I was ambitious, I wish I had as much energy – but all those things waned with age. Consequently, I feel I'm in retirement and I have been in retirement for about ten years. There's none of the pressure of ambition and ego telling me to write. So, yes – I'm very content and complacent now.'

Reproduced by permission of *The Observer*.

Rupert Everett

14 September 1997

Just my luck to meet Rupert Everett at the very moment when he decides to put his bad boy past behind him and start reinventing himself as a fine upstanding member of the Hollywood film community. Until this August, he was always reliably outrageous, but now he's become as wet and timorous as any other actor. It's so sad. It's so *corny*. It happened almost overnight. One minute he was babbling away to *US* magazine about how he used to be a rent boy, and the next he was a *huge* success in *My Best Friend's Wedding* and had clamped the gag over his mouth.

So now he was never a rent boy, never a junkie, never called Kevin Costner a frump, never sent a snipping of his pubic hair to a theatregoer who complained, never screamed or queened or misbehaved. He *is* still gay, thank God, but that's about as far as it goes. Just a few months ago, he was furious with Hugh Grant for going on American television to apologize for the Divine Brown incident – 'I thought how fantastic for him to have been given head by Divine Brown and how brilliant a career move it was, but the moment he said it was an abomination, he really lost me.' But now he's doing much the same himself, bowing under the yoke of middle-American morality as part of the price of Hollywood success. I suppose it's inevitable, but, oh, it's depressing.

Of course, I didn't know all this when I went to meet him in Paris, in the swish rooftop penthouse suite of the Hôtel Meurice. He couldn't come to London, he explained, because his dogsitter was on holiday – his Labrador Moise is his one true love. He lived in Paris for ten years, but sold his flat this spring, because he thinks Paris has stopped being fun. From now on, he plans to live mainly in New York, though he has a life and circle of friends in many different cities. He won't live in Los Angeles because it's too far from anywhere else and he doesn't like flying; he can't live in London because of the quarantine laws.

He was having breakfast, dressed in jogging clothes, looking like one of his own aftershave ads – tousled and vaguely damp. His manner is vaguely damp too – whether you call it languid or laid back, it reads to me like rude. He indicated that I should sit at his side while he ate breakfast at a huge dining table facing the French windows on to the terrace. The disconcerting thing was that there was an elderly Chinese lady sitting on the sofa who showed no signs of moving. Had she come about the feng shui? I found the feng shui pretty odd. Everett eventually got round to introducing her, saying that she had brought him two silk dressing-gowns bequeathed by a friend – he leapt up and modelled them for me – but having gone ooh! and aah! and smiled a bit, we all resumed our awkward places. Eventually I got him to move out to the terrace where at least I thought I'd be able to see his eyes when he talked. But he immediately cried, 'Ooh, we can tan!' and adopted a head-back tanning pose.

Is he vain? I don't even need to ask – I saw his bathroom. He was only in Paris for two days but he must have lugged an entire suitcase of unguents with him – night creams and day creams, exfoliants and moisturizers, vitamins and royal jelly and tinted pomade for his hair. Yes, he agrees, he does spend a lot of time looking in the mirror, but it's not a source of pleasure. 'I think vain people don't really like what they see, that's why they're vain. They're thinking they're looking terrible all the time and they've got to improve. It's quite exhausting, being vain. It's a full-time job.'

As a boy, he was painfully thin with huge buck teeth. But he cured the latter with braces and the former by going to the gym. By the time he went to drama school (Central), he was modelling for photo stories in *My Guy* and being hired for menswear shows in Milan. He still does modelling jobs – he is the face of Opium aftershave – and says that, 'Modelling has always got me out of a lot of financial scrapes. Because the secret of a cinema career, at least at my kind of level, is that you have to shop around if you want to do a reasonable piece of work, or you have to *wait* around. So modelling has always kept the wolf from the door.'

But there won't be many wolves at the door after *My Best Friend's Wedding*, which grossed $34 million in its first weekend. He is extremely good and likeable in it, playing Julia Roberts's homosexual confidant. Before the film was released, the studio showed it to focus groups who all said they wanted to see more of Rupert Everett. So they reshot the ending to give him more screen time. It is an extraordinary late revival for a Hollywood career that seemed to have petered out ten years ago. But he explains, 'I don't think revival is the word. I don't think I've had one.'

He went out to Hollywood in 1983, after he had finished filming on *Another Country* and *Dance with a Stranger*, because he was supposed to be making a film with Orson Welles, but it fell through. Then he stayed on, looking for work but not finding any – it was the junior bratpack era with no parts for young upper-class Englishmen. So, although in theory he was 'hot', he was also unemployed, and he remembers it as the worst period of his life.

He returned to England to try to establish himself as a pop star, and co-starred with Bob Dylan in a rock epic called *Hearts of Fire*. Both efforts were a total disaster – people still howl at the memory of 'Generation of Loneliness', his pop single, and *Time Out* said that in *Hearts of Fire* he was 'hilariously typecast as a talentless wanker'. He also did a stage production of *The Vortex*, which might have been good if anyone could hear it – he had decided to adopt a Brando-esque mumble. When a theatregoer wrote to complain, he replied with a brattish letter: 'Please accept my heartfelt apologies – and this bunch of my pubic hair in the hope that it will make up for any inconvenience.' One way and another, he made himself a *lot* of enemies, so in 1987 he decamped to Paris, planning to make himself a star of European cinema.

He says that actually he did some admirable work in Europe, though nobody in England noticed it. He was in a couple of good Italian films, and spent a year and a half in Russia filming *And Quiet Flows the Don* for Sergei Bondarchuk. He did *The Importance of Being Earnest* at the French National Theatre – the first foreigner to play there since 1922.

So his European career was not undistinguished. But his American career dwindled to playing tall, dark, handsome strangers in terrible television mini-series. It was only his performance as the Prince Regent in *The Madness of King George* that, he says, gave him back 'some kind of credibility'. But he had enough time out of work to write two novels, *Hello Darling, Are You Working?* and *The Hairdressers of St Tropez*, both greeted with jeers and derision in England, but lauded elsewhere, especially in the US.

He seems to have aroused a peculiar degree of hostility in England, perhaps because he comes from what he calls a 'hooray' background and doesn't bother to hide it. Nowadays, he won't talk about his family, beyond saying 'I had a very comfortable, secure upbringing', but he has talked about it often enough in the past. He was born in 1959, the second son of an army major who later became a successful stockbroker. He and his older brother, Simon (who is now a pilot in Nairobi), lived with their maternal grandparents while their parents were stationed abroad, but that was fine – they had a nice nanny and a beautiful home in Norfolk.

But at seven, he was sent away to boarding school and hated it: 'It's completely wrong. It makes you grow up too soon. It makes you come across real unhappiness and rejection too early in life.' He became 'difficult' and had to be sent to another prep school before going to Ampleforth, the Catholic public school, at thirteen. Incidentally, he now describes himself as 'definitely a Christian, but not necessarily a Catholic. I think Jesus is very misrepresented in the Catholic faith.'

It all sounds like a fairly conventional upper middle-class childhood, including the conventional trauma of going to boarding school at seven. But turning to Everett's first novel, *Hello Darling, Are You Working?* (1992), we see a more exciting picture – and one given extra significance by the fact that the book started life as an autobiography. The opening paragraph reads: 'By the time he was eight he knew he would never be a Great Actress. There it was, sticking out in front of him like a sore thumb: his penis – and his first showbiz disappointment – shattering all his dreams.' In the first scene, the boy causes a sensation when his aunt asks what he wants for his eighth birthday and he screams, 'I want a wedding dress!' But whereas his aunt is shocked, his parents explain

kindly that boys don't really wear wedding dresses. They are extraordinarily tolerant: 'No word of anger greeted his appearance on his father's
grouse moor in another of his mother's nighties.'

The picture that emerges is of a strange, difficult, sexually confused
boy but with very loving and supportive parents. So it was odd to find
Everett recently telling *US* magazine that as a boy he used to walk to
a secluded spot near his parents' house and pray for the Virgin Mary
to appear, so that the Catholic Church would build a huge hideous
basilica for pilgrims and it would ruin his parents' favourite view.

Everett defined himself as 'artistic' from an early age and started
dreaming of being a star from when he saw his first film – *Mary Poppins*
– at the age of six or seven. 'I completely identified with Julie Andrews.
My fantasy – the first way I worked it out – was that I wanted to be
Julie Andrews's child. And the weird thing was that about twenty-five
years later, I did a film with her, *Duet for One*, in which she gave a
fantastic performance as a violinist with MS, and I was her protégé,
so it really was the trippiest moment.' Later, at Ampleforth, he switched
his affections to Bette Davis and Montgomery Clift, and it was the
latter who inspired him to become an actor.

He started acting in school plays with his good friend Julian Wadham
(who appeared in *Another Country* and *The Madness of King George*). 'We
did all the school plays, him and me, we were the stars. We used to
have this amazing fantasy life. We were obsessed by Franco Zeffirelli
and we were always sending each other letters saying "Mr Z's assistant
would like very much to meet with you next week". We were very
highbrow. We put on a production of Schiller's *Mary Stuart* and Julian
played Queen Elizabeth and I played Queen Mary. I remember when
they were casting *Boys from Brazil*, Julian wrote to the casting director
and said: "I am very interested in your film *Boys from Brazil*. I am a boy,
and here's a photograph of me as Queen Elizabeth."'

Everett left Ampleforth immediately after O-levels and went to
Central School of Speech and Drama in London. This was the period
when, he told *Hello!* in 1989, 'I discovered sex on a massive scale.' He
also told *Hello!* something very interesting, though inexplicable at the
time: 'Once, my father found me on the street. I hadn't seen him for
months. I said, "Hi, Dad", and he just hit me really hard on the head
and walked on. I understand him now.' I asked him to expand on this

interesting vignette but he said, 'I don't want to talk about it. Really, I just don't want to get into my family. I'm sorry.'

Perhaps his father suspected what he was doing at the time – working as a rent boy. Everett first talked about it to the *Sunday Times* in 1992. Asked if he ever hustled, he said, 'Yes. I didn't do it very often, and I don't particularly want to enlarge on it. I was on a sort of crash course when I came out of school, desperate to throw off everything that I'd been brought up to believe.' Three years later, he confessed it again to the *Independent*, saying that he got his first offer outside Gloucester Road station when he was sixteen. 'And I was very pleased with the money!' But the press ignored it. His career was at a low ebb then, and he probably could have said he was a mass murderer without anyone noticing.

But then, in August this year, he confessed it yet again to *US* magazine, and this time it made headlines round the world. He said, 'I didn't set out to hustle, but this guy offered me such a massive amount of money, well, it was like a year and a half's pocket money and it just came in really handy.' Prostitution, he said, provided his main source of income for a year or two, though not without its risks: 'The first time out is fine, and then you get knocked about a bit on your third night of work and you go back four days later with a bruise and you get knocked about again, but you've got a knife, so you're OK. It becomes second nature.' Probably he was relying on the fact that *US* magazine is not widely read here, but he reckoned without the British tabloids and the *Daily Telegraph* which repeated it all. That must have caused some consternation at the parental breakfast table.

Anyway, when I started to ask him about it, he cut in immediately. 'Don't want to talk about it.'

'But you *have* talked about it.'

'Yes, but not any more. Enough's been said on that subject. I'm not trying to deny anything, but that particular story is one that I don't want to give any more time to. As a matter of fact, it was in the newspaper *years* ago and nobody cared, and I just don't want to go on about it. It really pisses me off. I'm sorry – but it's not just me that's involved, there's my family.'

What is more amazing is his newfound unwillingness to admit he was a junkie. He always *used* to say he was a junkie, there's hardly an interview in the cuttings file in which he doesn't say it. But to me he said coolly, 'I was never a junkie.' Huh? Why did he used to keep saying he was, then? 'I don't think I said I was a junkie. A junkie is an addict. I don't think I was an addict.' But did he use heroin? 'Yep. But luckily I was saved from drugs by a bigger desire, which was partly vanity but mostly ambition, to be a star. And it was the thing that protected me from getting too muddled up, too completely pulled down by that type of thing. I had some stronger desire, that I wanted more than a line of smack – I was *obsessed* when I was a kid with becoming a star. Luckily for me really, because I think otherwise I would have fallen head over heels into that.'

He thinks this obsession with becoming a star is also what has prevented him forming relationships. He claims he has never been in love, though he has sometimes been infatuated. He told *Attitude* magazine that he had his first gay encounter aged eight, and full gay sex at thirteen. But he also had girlfriends and it wasn't until he was twenty-six that he decided he was totally gay. 'I mean, I definitely knew I was partly gay, but it wasn't till I was about twenty-six that the last earth ray of my heterosexuality fizzled out.'

I wondered if it was his parents' absence in his childhood that made him so wary of relationships but he said, 'No. I think it stems from a career in show business much more. Because you're always – well, less now, but in the formative, early adult years – you're forced to think about yourself, what everyone thinks of you, how you're going to make it better, how you're going to make up for that mistake. You are your product. What people find very difficult about actors is that their focus is completely inward-looking. There could be a murder going on on the next terrace, and I'd be giving this interview and wouldn't bother to intervene. It's not really our fault. It's just – that's how it happens. I don't think I'm any less giving than most people, but I do think a lot of the actor's state is inward-thinking and obsession about oneself and getting parts and all that stuff.'

He reckons he is a bit more relaxed about it now, but he is still very ambitious. He has a film coming out next year called *B Monkey*, in which he plays an Old Etonian drug dealer, which is rumoured to be good. Meanwhile, he is doing a short season of Tennessee Williams's *The Milk Train Doesn't Stop Here Anymore* at the Lyric Theatre, Hammersmith. He plays Flora Goforth, the part originally played by Elizabeth

Taylor, although he is playing her as an old queen with dementia. But isn't he famously the man who said, 'British theatre sucks'? 'Yes. I don't like the theatre in general – I never go. It's so *long* normally and so visually unstimulating and the audience is so depressing. But for an actor, it's rather like manure – it's nourishing. If you can't get a part in cinema, it's always a good idea to do a play because someone might see you and maybe give you a part in the cinema. And Philip Prowse, who I work with always, is a theatrical genius, so there is not a dull moment in the plays I'm in – but that is unusual.'

Obviously, he wants to capitalize on his success in *My Best Friend's Wedding*, but he's in no great hurry. He feels he's achieved a lot, in Hollywood terms, by being a gay playing a gay and being liked for it. He is not sure whether he could play straight, or even whether he'd want to. But what he is really excited about is two commissions to write screenplays – one a spy film starring himself, the other a film for him and Julia Roberts. 'For me, that's really the best thing that's happened for ages. And I'm not a bad writer, and I could become a really good writer if I went on writing, I know that. And that's really an exciting thought.'

Given that he seemed languid – the polite way of putting it – throughout our interview, I asked whether he found interviews boring. Oddly enough, this was the one question that seemed to fire him. 'I don't think it's *boring*, I think it's more unpleasant really, because there's always so much to lose. Especially when you're trying to deal with the English press; it's like a thin-ice-skating competition. I don't mind particularly for myself being slammed by the press, because it's happened so often and after a bit you don't really care. But then you have people like your family who you have a responsibility to . . . It's so difficult, it's scary. When you're dealing with things like I'm dealing with, they're really difficult subjects. If you're talking about, say, your homosexuality, even after five years, it still feels like someone's shining a really bright light on you. And to be a big star in America, you can't digress from the straight route. It's very difficult because you *want* to be honest. I don't want to contribute to the huge lie that everyone's always telling – because everyone's lying endlessly – but it's very difficult trying to conduct your life in public. So it's kind of unpleasant, I think. The English press is revolting, I think. Revolting.'

I feel very torn about Rupert Everett. He can be charming when he wants to be. He is intelligent and original and capable of honesty when not constrained by Hollywood. But I felt all the time, could try harder – could concentrate harder, could make the effort to frame proper sentences and not keep repeating himself (he has a terribly lazy, limited vocabulary for someone who fancies himself as a writer). And there is something careless about his transactions with other people – I didn't like him leaving that Chinese lady on the sofa. Maybe he's spent too much time hanging out with models and hairdressers, where merely being beautiful is enough. When I asked why we couldn't photograph him in Paris but had to have him photographed in New York instead, he said, 'I don't like doing paparazzi snapshots for newspapers because they always make you look terrible, and I like to take more time.' *Paparazzi shots?* I almost choked. 'You're talking about *Jane Bown*!' But he only shrugged – she is probably not a name among the hairdressers of St Tropez or whatever ghastly milieu he inhabits.

For me, the nub is whether we believe that his sudden discretion is motivated by care for his family, or care for his career. He claims the former, of course, but it would be more persuasive if he hadn't talked about being a rent boy three times. If his family were going to be upset, they would have been upset the first time, when the story appeared in the *Sunday Times* (hardly an obscure newspaper) and he should have shut up then. The sheer timing suggests that Hollywood had more to do with it. I haven't written him off, though. He is certainly *interesting*.

Reproduced by permission of *The Observer*.

Gerry Adams

22 September 1996

The abnormality of Gerry Adams's life is apparent as soon as you see Sinn Fein HQ in the Andersonstown Road. It might once have been a sweet suburban villa with a big garden. Now the house is a fort, the garden is concreted over and encased in a steel cage. A big silent man ushered me into the cage, across the yard and into the house and left me in an airless brown room with boarded-up windows. After five minutes, I started imagining firebombs coming through the door, so I decided I'd be safer with the big man in the yard, even though he wouldn't talk to me.

So by the time Gerry Adams appeared, as if by magic, strolling around the side of the house (had he been there all the time?), looking friendly, handsome, *normal*, I was almost gibbering with gratitude to see him. Perhaps this is not a good stance for an interviewer: I can only say I liked him immediately. He said we should sit in the back yard, because it was too gloomy in the house. I tried not to throw myself to the ground every time a car backfired in the street, but it didn't help when he told me that the building had been hit by a rocket, bombed, shot at and that a man had been killed just outside. Three people were killed in his constituency office down the road by an RUC man posing as a journalist, 'so naturally we have to take precautions'. Yes indeed – I rather wished we could conduct the interview lying down or preferably somewhere else entirely, like the Groucho Club. I never wanted to be Kate Adie.

Thus we got off to a rather nervous start, with him talking somewhat robotically about his autobiography, *Before the Dawn*, and not looking at me. But later he relaxed and even laughed at some of my questions – No, he never dyed his hair, 'Never say dye', and no, he did not own an Armani suit, even though his supporters have taken to shouting 'Tiocfaidh Armani' instead of 'Tiocfaidh Ar La' (Our day will come) whenever they see him. When I suggested that maybe he'd been corrupted by all his American hobnobbing with the stars (he met Donald Trump and *liked* him!), and would soon start developing a taste for fine claret, he completely disarmed me by saying: 'Well I do have an aspiration for expensive claret! I think everyone should have it!' When I harped on about his working-class background, he said, reasonably, that John Major had a similar background (I got the feeling he really likes John Major) and that you don't have to travel to meet interesting people. 'You know, all life can be here. I have met people who are unlettered, some who might even be illiterate, but very, very gracious and decent people. It isn't about Armani suits.'

He was firm about what he wouldn't talk about – his family. He wouldn't even tell me if his son Gearoid, now twenty-three, is still a student or working. He never speaks about his wife of twenty-five years, Colette, and has not been photographed with her in public since 1984. He doesn't say much about her in the book either, beyond that he proposed to her when he was on the run from internment in 1971 and didn't kiss her till their wedding day. He says that keeping her and his son out of the public eye was a mutual decision. 'They have their own lives and even if I was a different type of political figure or even if we were out of this conflict, I would still advise them to keep out of the public eye. Because there's nothing as nice as being able to walk down that road to go to the shops or go for a pint and be anonymous. Of course the local people know them, but not outsiders.'

He protects his family by moving around continuously and seldom spending a night at home, though it didn't protect them in 1993 when the house was hit by grenades with them in it – he says the attackers must have known he wasn't there and deliberately targeted his family. He was shot in the neck and shoulders in 1981, sprayed with bullets as he emerged from a courtroom – he says that he still feels the pain

when he's tired or when it's about to snow or rain. He took himself
out of hospital very quickly, because 'people were getting a bit hyper',
and consequently walked round with an undetected bullet in his arm
for weeks. He gave me a gripping description of what it smelt like
when the surgeon slit his arm open, and then apologized for being so
'personal'.

He travels in armour-plated cars, or the famous taxi that once
belonged to Liz Taylor. He says: 'That's not exceptional. I mean if
leaders of other parties come, they have police escorts, or whatever.
Ours is more of a ramshackle do-it-yourself thing, but it's just a normal
precaution in these abnormal circumstances.'

Maybe, I suggested cynically, some of these aspects of his life which
are seen as sacrifices – having to keep moving around, not spending
time with his family – could be things that suited him anyway? Rather
to my surprise – because he is not versed in the byways of psychological
analysis – he understood exactly what I meant. 'Well, I think that could
be true of some people, but not me. Obviously, I've been very politically
involved and I think most things are political, but when I go on holidays,
I don't feel bored, you know? I know it must look very strange to
someone coming from outside – this guy sleeps in different houses –
but so do a lot of other people in the movement. If it was just me, it
would be both intolerable and absolutely mad. But you're talking about
an entire communal thing, hundreds of Sinn Fein activists, maybe not
to the same degree, but being affected. So over twenty-five years, a
struggle throws up its own sort of support mechanisms. And I know
that republicans aren't the only ones who have suffered, and in fact
republicans have inflicted hurt. Think of someone visiting a prison for
the past nineteen years or of someone visiting a grave for the past
nineteen years. Without being too overburdeningly morbid about it all,
it's a very abnormal way to spend your life. And especially on the
families. Because at least I'm occupied and engaged all the time, but
what is your family doing, you know?'

Time and again, he emphasizes that he is nothing special, that he is
merely one of a movement. It's a problem with his book, and with this
interview, that his socialist ideology does not allow him to be personal.
He wants to be seen as a typical product of the Belfast Catholic working
class or perhaps of oppressed minorities everywhere – he actually told

me: 'I think my childhood is almost universal, not just in terms of Britain or Ireland but different parts of Europe.' But seeing yourself as a universal social atom does not make for good autobiography. The description of his childhood in *Before the Dawn* – 'All of us were scrawny, browned by the sun, freckle-faced, muddy-kneed' – is as mawkishly sentimental as a Hovis advert.

When I told him I wasn't interested in his similarity to all the freckle-faced muddy-kneed boys he grew up with, but in his difference – after all, *he* became the leader, not anyone else – he grew wary, thinking I was trying to lure him into – what? – a cult-of-personality trap. I suppose I was. Thus he was not very helpful in my attempt to understand the dynamics of the Adams family. He conceded that he probably took after his mother (whom he describes as 'gentle') more than his father, and that being the eldest of ten probably gave him an early sense of responsibility. From the book, one gathers that he was a shy, serious-minded, possibly rather priggish boy, who took his Catholicism seriously and thought at one stage of joining the Christian Brothers. The important influence was his Adams grandmother, with whom he lived for much of his childhood. She counselled moderation in all things – he remembers her telling him you could never trust a man who was completely teetotal.

I wondered about the effect of growing up as effectively the crown prince in a great republican dynasty – both his parents came from long lines of republican martyrs going back to the Irish Republican Brotherhood and nineteenth-century Fenians. Adams's father, 'old Gerry', was sentenced to eight years, aged sixteen, for the attempted murder of an RUC man, and served five. He ran a club called the Irish Republican Felons' Association for former prisoners. There was also a whole raft of uncles who'd served their time for the cause. Surely there must have been pressure, or at least an unspoken assumption, that Gerry, as the eldest son, would head dutifully the same way?

No, he said, this was not a factor for him, though it probably was for his younger brothers, because the 'armed struggle' was dead as a dodo throughout his childhood, the Belfast IRA virtually non-existent (it had just twenty-four members in 1961). Until he became 'active' himself, he was only vaguely conscious of his father's past. So no one was telling him to join the IRA and his Granny Adams, 'who had seen her sons go in and out of prison', was keen to discourage him.

So why did he leave school and join Sinn Fein at seventeen? He says it was just one of several 'hobbies' at the time, and he was planning to go to Kenya to build dams on International Voluntary Service. He believes that if he had been born in, say, Finchley, he never would have been a political activist though he would probably have been a community worker. 'But what happened here in 1969 was that there was a huge convulsion. If you can imagine all these areas under barricades, like a Sarajevo, and then people coped with it – people who were mothers or housewives, who were unemployed, or at school, had to start organizing their own lives. And I was just swept up into all of that.'

The call came on 14 August 1969, when someone ran into the Duke of York where he was a barman and told him: 'You're wanted. You should pack in work. The wee man's looking for you.' The wee man was Billy McMillen, an old IRA leader who was gathering volunteers to try to organize direct action. Adams writes in his book: 'I disagreed, feeling that any attempt to militarize the situation, to bring the IRA into it and to engage the RUC on their own terms would take it out of the hands of the people and bring the entire situation down to a gunfight, which the RUC would surely win. Anyway the discussion was to some degree academic, since the Belfast IRA had scarcely any weapons.' This is perhaps the explanation for how he can say (as he always does) that he never joined the IRA. There was hardly an IRA to *join* in Belfast when he started; it was more a case of the IRA joining him. At all events, by 1972, he was sufficiently recognized as a leader for the British Government to whisk him to a secret meeting in Cheyne Walk, Chelsea, with Willie Whitelaw and Paul Channon.

Kevin Myers of the *Irish Times* claims that he was in a pub in Andersonstown in 1973 when there was a fight in the men's room and he overheard someone telling Adams of the incident and Adams saying: 'Shoot him.' When I quoted this back to Adams he said: 'Well, first of all, it's totally untrue. So I don't even need to get into defending it. I didn't frequent pubs, you know? I mean Kevin Myers could have written about things in which I was involved, and he could have drawn conclusions from that. But to totally fabricate this silly story was just off the wall. Actually, I pass all of these things, as a matter of course, to a solicitor, but . . .'

Was that a hint of threat? I find it hard to picture Adams as the 'cold-blooded killer' standing in a pub and casually dispatching people to their deaths. But there was one sentence in his book that really shook me. It was towards the end, in his chapter about the hunger strikes of 1981, when he had described the deaths of Bobby Sands and the other strikers – in propaganda terms, it was an enormous boost – then continued: 'But when some ended their fasts and it was clear that this was the beginning of the end, I had no regrets whatsoever about their decisions.' No *regrets*? Wouldn't the normal reaction be to be overjoyed? 'Sure. But that's probably part of me responding, almost subconsciously, to the accusation that's been made that the hunger strikers were "ordered to die" and that we were sorry the hunger strikes ended.'

He goes into such painstaking detail about his last visit to the hunger strikers before they died, that it sounds as if he is trying to clear his conscience. Does he feel that he could have stopped them killing themselves? 'I don't think they killed themselves.' Well, then, could he have ordered them to stop the hunger strike? 'Of course I could have. But I don't think they would have. And I think if I had done, I would in a sense have betrayed them. Our big pitch, my big pitch, was trying to prevent the hunger strike before it started.

'Once it started, rightly or wrongly, it became almost . . . it wasn't a pact, there was no formal pact. They were my friends, I was their friend. I didn't want to see them in that situation. Having said that, of course, we're all profoundly troubled by different events in our lives, and I do find – I mean the hunger strikes were very emotive and very troubling for anyone who was involved in them. Have you read David Beresford's *Ten Men Dead*? To me, it's the best book out of Ireland in the past twenty years. I looked at it again the other day. I was travelling in the car at half-eight in the morning, and even just glancing through it, I could feel myself getting emotional. And rather than put myself in bad form, I closed the book.'

He is wary of getting emotional – when I asked which of the many funerals he has attended he remembered most vividly, he snapped: 'I don't have a favourite!' Obviously, he remembered his mother's in 1993 and his Granny Adams's. He remembered one where the congregation stood out in the graveyard and wouldn't go in the church because they were annoyed with the church leaders' political stance. He remembers the 'Battle of the Funerals' and of course he remembers the hunger strikers' funerals. 'I just have a sense of going to too many funerals, and being absolutely riven, gutted by the thought that somebody else had been killed. It's all a huge argument for getting it resolved. And I say that while very conscious of the public image there would be of me and *my* role in all this. I don't know who said politics is the art of the possible, but whoever said it was reducing it to mediocrity – politics has to be the art of the *impossible*. Why can't we get away from soundbite politics and move the whole thing along?'

He says that although Sinn Fein is currently excluded from the peace process, their peace strategy is still in place and he is in close contact with John Hume and with the White House. 'It's actually a period now of immense frustration for me, both personal and political, because we're locked out of the talks, and I think we should be involved in them, because I feel a responsibility, because I feel *entitled*. I'm not caught up with notions of leadership – I do it through a sense of duty – but I would like to continue to make a contribution for as long as God spares me. It is my conviction that we *will* get peace but I genuinely don't know when. I think we're into the endgame.'

If he is a hypocrite, he's a very good one: he certainly convinced me he wants peace in Northern Ireland, though of course he ultimately wants a socialist united Ireland. He might once have been a fanatic, but doesn't seem like one now. He has more 'hinterland' than most politicians – he talked about writers he admires (Alice Walker, Sean O'Faolain, John Steinbeck) – and about the need to keep in touch with a life outside politics, 'because I do not think that the struggle can be so all-consuming. There has to be a connection into the big picture, into music, into love. Obviously, the political struggle has become my life, but I like to keep little bits of my life for myself and my family, and we escape into that every so often.'

After the interview, he said he'd take me to a church hall down the road where the Long Kesh POW Drama Group was rehearsing a play based on the writings of Bobby Sands. It was weird, stepping out of the Sinn Fein fort into a normal shopping street. Adams became the suave politician going walkabout, smiling and nodding at his grateful electors. And indeed they did greet him warmly on every side and cars tooted their horns, and a father pointed him out to his son, and both of them were beaming – he is very much the local hero. I was meanwhile twitching and dodging, scanning the rooftops for snipers and wondering how far away from Adams I could decently walk while still technically accompanying him. Fortunately, it was not far to the church hall and he introduced me to the cast or whoever they were – they were all talking Gaelic – and I read the programme about 'theatre of the oppressed' while he prepared his speech for the opening. Then he walked me back along the street, shook my hand, said: 'I'm disappearing now, see you soon.' And poof! he was gone.

Reproduced by permission of *The Observer*.

Lord Rothermere

29 June 1997

Five weeks ago, the third Viscount Rothermere convulsed the Establishment by announcing that henceforward he would be supporting Labour. This was only three weeks after his leading news-paper, the *Daily Mail*, had run a pre-election front page featuring a Union Jack and the apocalyptic message: 'There is a terrible danger that the British people, drugged by the seductive mantra "It's time for a change", are stumbling, eyes glazed, into an election that could undo 1,000 years of our nation's history.'

He 'came out', not in the *Daily Mail*, but in its sister paper, the London *Evening Standard*, with an article in which he quoted Nurse Cavell's dying words, 'Patriotism is not enough.' It was the clearest possible rebuke to that Union Jack front page. Everyone confidently waited for Paul Dacre, the editor of the *Mail*, to resign. It hasn't happened. Nor has Rothermere shown any signs of wanting to sack Dacre. On the contrary, he praised Dacre warmly to me as the best editor in Britain. He probably enjoys demonstrating that he is not the sort of tyrannical proprietor who countermands his editors. And also, perhaps, he likes to make mischief.

The *Daily Mail* is the middlest of middle England newspapers. Lord Rothermere, on the other hand, lives in Paris and has done so for the past twenty years, making only occasional sorties to England. He recently married his long-standing mistress, a Korean-Japanese former hand model called Maiko Lee. Although the *Sunday Times* lists him as the ninth richest person in Britain (worth £1.2 billion), he owns no property at all or at any rate no houses. '*This* is my property,' he says, banging his hand down on a copy of the *Daily Mail*. 'It is the only property I want.' He describes himself as a Buddhist and believes in reincarnation. He reads history and writes poetry. He says British education is useless and the only good schooling he ever got was in America. He believes the Royal Family cannot survive and does not deserve to. He wants to expel hereditary peers (such as himself) from the Lords. When I ask if it is true that he was once a playboy, he booms confidently, in his fine patrician 71-year-old voice, 'I *am* a playboy.' It is not the typical profile of a *Daily Mail* reader.

He is known to be eccentric, mischievous, disconcerting and some-times plain baffling. No one can ever agree whether he is incredibly stupid or incredibly clever – a common verdict is that he is twice as clever as he looks, but only half as clever as he thinks he is. When he was a young man, he was taken for a complete buffoon, but now – when he is the last surviving British press lord and has seen off all the Aitkens and Astors and Berrys who used to be his rivals, and when his newspapers have virtually demolished the *Express* opposition – *now* one thinks that people who once called him stupid look pretty stupid themselves.

Rothermere is the third generation of the Harmsworth dynasty. The two Harmsworth brothers – his great-uncle Lord Northcliffe and his grandfather the first Viscount Rothermere – built a mighty press empire, starting with magazines and going on to launch the *Daily Mail* (which last year celebrated its centenary) and the *Evening News*.

Rothermere is keen on history, and particularly his family history. When Associated Newspapers moved from Fleet Street to Kensington in 1989, he had Northcliffe's office moved panel by panel. I met him in his Paris office, which still has a carved stone lintel over the door proclaiming *The Continental Daily Mail*, but, of course, there are no printing presses now, no messengers dashing in with telegrams. The offices seem to be home to a rather glamorous Dutchwoman called Thérèse Lenoir, who tells me she is Lord Rothermere's arranger. 'I arrange his flat and buy his cars, because he was being crooked by everyone, you know? And I am one tough lady. I have great admiration for him because he is the kind of man who is really seeing things as though he is from another planet . . .'

Even as she speaks, there is a great woosh of brown fur and a dog the size of a sideboard comes trundling in, towing Lord Rothermere on a lead. He is absolutely the French idea of an English 'milord' – 6ft 3in of perfect tailoring and a fine head of snow-white hair. He looks as if he would bark, but he doesn't: he has a very gentle, courteous, diffident manner, but just slightly spacey, as if seeing things from another planet. He can turn deafness off and on. He tells me that the dog is upset because he can hear a storm coming. This is nothing to how upset I am at having the dog give me an elaborate gynaecological examination under the desk, forcing me to chat politely to Lord Rothermere while trying to squeeze it to death with my knees. When I ask how you spell its name, he says, 'Well, you can either spell it Ruma or Ruma.' He pronounces both versions identically and I wait for elucidation. None comes. Only the pages of *Hello!* reveal it is actually Ryu-ma.

In 1974, Rothermere said that the *Mail* had always supported the Conservative Party and always would, but now he says, 'Well, it was a different world, and a different sociology in those days – different everything. The world has changed again; that's why I'm supporting Tony.' (He says Tony with an amused, sardonic air as if it were a silly name. His own name is Vere.) 'Tony to me is like a breath of fresh air, a new spirit – he's a modern man who understands the need for social caring and who understands also the need for prosperous business.'

Lord Rothermere is not, on the face of it, a modern man. He has an Edwardian panache – one thinks of open landaus and fur travelling rugs and Monte Carlo gaming tables and yachts moored on the Croisette. The Harmsworths were great playboys – the first Viscount Rothermere told Arnold Bennett that he spent £10,000 to £20,000 a year on women, and 'It's worth it.' Vere's father, the second Viscount Rothermere, took the view that once a family had made its fortune, it should distance itself from 'trade' and leave that to managers. Vere remembers that his father took him riding as a boy and outlined his glorious future – he would go into one of the cavalry brigades, the Blues or the Life Guards, it would be a marvellous life. 'And I listened to all this and I thought, "Oh, how *awful*, how absolutely ghastly!" I saw the prospect of endless boredom stretching before me. I never ever wanted to do anything but work in newspapers.'

He was then Rothermere's only son so he *had* to inherit the business, but he was a lamentably unpromising boy, remembered by his Eton contemporaries, if at all, as dim. He doesn't think he was dim exactly: 'I had a very fertile mind, I was always daydreaming, with a terrific imagination, and British education did not agree with me – the whole atmosphere was so negative. I won the school boxing championship, so I couldn't have been altogether lazy. I don't know – I don't want to go into my own personal psychology.'

'Why not?'

'Well, why would one? I don't want to know about those things, how you got on with your parents and whose fault was it – mine or theirs – it doesn't get anybody anywhere. I think most human beings spend a great deal of their adult life getting over their upbringing – you spend the second twenty years of your life getting over the first twenty, and I think that was really my problem.' His first wife told Nicholas Coleridge, 'I just couldn't understand him, suffering so many hang-ups with his parents.'

His parents separated when he was three and divorced, after a long, scandalous, public court case, when he was eight or nine. He was shunted between their multifarious homes, acquiring two stepfathers and two stepmothers along the way. He says he and his sisters became 'very disoriented – we were early divorce casualties, I think'.

In 1940, he was evacuated to America and spent a year in Kent School, Connecticut, which he loved. But then he was shipped back to Eton 'and the general British negativism slowly re-entered my soul'. Almost uniquely for an Etonian, he failed his army officer selection board and had to do his four years' national service as a private. His fellow conscripts were mainly from the Gorbals. But he got on very well with them – it helped that he had been a boxing champion – and developed an affection for 'people' (he means working-class people) which he has never lost. 'You see, when you're standing above a tree, you can only see the branches and the leaves but when you're underneath the tree, and you look up, you can see all the things inside the tree, and that's a very valuable experience.'

(Lord Rothermere loves these big, poetic metaphors. In his *Evening*

Standard article he wrote that the Conservative Party had exhausted itself 'like a magnificent salmon, that, overcoming all obstacles, spawns the next generation and drifts spent and ruined back to sea'. Many took this as a sign that Max Hastings, editor of the *Standard* and a keen salmon fisherman, had written it, but the piece was classic Rothermere. He confirmed to me: 'I wrote the whole thing. I also am a salmon fisherman.')

After national service, he worked for a year in a Canadian paper mill, learning about newsprint, and then moved to Fleet Street for his long apprenticeship under his father. He was Vere Harmsworth in those days, known as 'Mere Vere' – his biggest apparent contribution was to invent a promotion called Win a Pub. But he had an incredible piece of luck – or maybe good judgement – in that in 1956 he met and befriended the features editor of the *Daily Sketch*, a slightly younger man called David English. They plotted Win a Pub together, which entailed spending much time in pubs, and formed a friendship which has stood them in good stead for more than forty years.

But his father clung to power, and clung and clung, even when he was obviously suffering from Alzheimer's. When he finally surrendered control in 1971, having failed to bring off a merger with the *Express*, his papers lagged miles behind the opposition. Mere Vere's first act was to appoint David English as editor of the *Mail*. They then relaunched the paper as a tabloid (Rothermere prefers the term 'compact'), and began the long, slow climb to overtake the *Express*. In 1979, Rothermere closed the *Evening News* in return for 50 per cent of the *Evening Standard*, and in 1985 he bought the other 50 per cent, so that he now wholly owns London's monopoly evening newspaper. In 1982, he launched the *Mail on Sunday*, which has now overtaken the *Sunday Express*. As Lord Rothermere says, he inherited two ailing newspapers and now owns three successful ones. He has done better than his father.

Yet despite his enormous success, he still has this lightweight, playboy image. He says he doesn't mind. 'I like to play. But I also work hard. I was never socially very popular as a young man – too shy. I can't see any *point* in parties to tell you the truth. I like meeting beautiful women, but I like taking them out to dinner! But parties – I'm not very good at them, that's why. I'm rather jealous of people who *are* good at parties, like Jocelyn Stevens, who can make a party go. I can't do that, that's not my thing.'

Nevertheless, he married a great party girl, the Rank starlet Patricia Beverley Brooks, widely known as Bubbles, though he hates that name. They married in 1957 and she bore him two daughters and then, with great difficulty, a son. Her doctor had told her she would die if she had another child, but when Vere's father suddenly produced another son – a rival heir – at the age of seventy, Bubbles got busy and studied how to influence the sex of a baby. In December 1967, her efforts were rewarded with the birth of Jonathan. Nigel Dempster claims that, 'for that alone, I know that Vere believes he owed Pat an eternal debt'.

But she was a troubled woman. In later life, she became very plump and often seemed over-loud and hysterical. She died of a heart attack brought on by an accidental overdose of sleeping pills in 1992. Lord Rothermere was deeply shocked, and read a very moving poem at her funeral – 'Oh, lady with the Mahler soul/Why have you me in thrall?' Disconcertingly, he still talks about her in the present tense, telling me: 'We still love each other very much, we've always loved each other. You can, of course, love more than one person – I have ten grandchildren and I love them all. I loved her very much up to when she died and still do – we have an enormous bond together.'

He concedes that she was 'difficult', but he believes it was not of her making. 'I think she suffered from postnatal depression. I didn't know about these things, but one of my daughters had postnatal depression and I suddenly realized when I was talking to the psychiatrist that that was very likely the problem with Pat. She'd had a very bad time with the birth of Geraldine [in 1957] and this was probably the reason for her behaviour. But it was never treated and it became endemic, and that was the basis, I think, of her difficult, her eccentric behaviour.' Growing agitated, he goes on, 'That's one of the reasons I'm a modernist, why I like Blair, because he is a modernist and I *hate* this old rubbish. She would probably be normal and healthy and alive today if it wasn't for all this old rubbish, these old prejudices, these old people who don't want to see anything new, want to cling to the past! The past is like a dead sheep! If you cling to it, you start to stink!'

But although he obviously loved Bubbles, he left her in 1978 and moved to Paris with his new love Maiko Lee. He met her at the Dogs'

Hospital Charity Ball in New York in 1976 (when she was twenty-eight) and fell in love with her immediately. Why? 'Oh, she was beautiful! And I like beautiful women! And then I suddenly discovered that I was in love with her, and that was it really. Within twenty-four hours.'

Maiko was a hand model based in New York – he still sometimes recognizes her hands in advertisements for scent or jewellery – but she moved to Paris with him immediately, sharing his little bachelor flat on the Ile de la Cité. Bubbles was angry at first and called Maiko 'that geisha', but she came to accept her, though they never met. Maiko was Rothermere's consort in Paris and Japan, where they often visited her home in Kyoto, but for formal events in London, Maiko would discreetly disappear. They married in Paris in 1993, a year after Bubbles's death.

'I fell in love with Maiko, but I did not cease to love Pat. Maiko's love is so calm and peaceful. Pat was tempestuous and exhausting, like a tropical storm that takes its energy from its surroundings.' Lord Rothermere has a great theory about the difference between innocence and ignorance, and he describes Maiko Lee as, 'innocent in the religious way. That is to say, she knows about this world very well so she's not ignorant, but she has a pure heart – which is what real innocence is.'

His marriage to Maiko Lee is one of many factors that set him apart from the British Establishment. Although he talks about crossing the floor of the House of Lords and joining the Labour benches, he rarely goes there. He is not one of the Great and the Good, he is not a club man. He agrees, cheerfully, 'I think the British Establishment has a great problem fitting in newspaper proprietors. I think they always have had; it was true of Northcliffe and my grandfather, and I've seen it with others – it's no accident that newspaper proprietors tend to live abroad, or tend to be Canadian or Australian – that's not new.'

What would he have done if he had not been a Harmsworth? 'Journalism. I would have been a journalist. I would have liked to have been a feature writer, not exactly Lynda Lee-Potter . . . well, I *could* do that actually. Lynda Lee-Potter is *fantastic*!' Sir David English chuckles when I retail this, and says he can't quite see Vere as Lynda Lee-Potter. 'He's always said he would love to have been a working journalist, but sometimes he'd like to be Ian Wooldridge, sometimes he'd like to be the chief sub-editor. I think he would be a better layout man, because he's got very good instincts about layout and typography.'

The conventional view of Lord Rothermere, especially among journalists, is that he is a very stupid man who just got lucky in finding David English, who, they believe, is the brains behind the whole operation. The one loudly dissenting voice comes from Sir David himself. He says of Rothermere: 'I think that, being very clever, he tries to give the impression that he's not very bright, which is a wonderful negotiating technique for succeeding in business. And that is how people are often enmeshed and entrapped and outmanoeuvred, as Mr Maxwell was. I think it's now recognized that he *is* very bright, he's got a gut instinct about newspapers. And that is what bonds us.'

English points out that it was Rothermere who decided to make the *Mail* tabloid and go for a women's readership; it was Rothermere who decided to launch the *Mail on Sunday* and who brought off the merger between the *Evening News* and *Standard*. It was his idea recently to buy a newspaper and printing works in Hungary, even when advised not to – he said the business would be profitable by the next century and, in fact, it is profitable now. And finally, it was Rothermere who had the inspired idea of resurrecting the *Evening News* when Maxwell launched the *London Daily News*, just to confuse everyone. The board said it couldn't be done: Rothermere rang from Japan and told them how to do it. English concludes: 'That was a key tactical decision in destroying Maxwell. So, if he's not very bright, gee, I wish I was as not-bright as him!'

Five years ago, Lord Rothermere stood down as chairman and promoted Sir David English to replace him. It was a sudden move, brought on by Paul Dacre being offered the editorship of *The Times* and saying he would only stay if he could edit the *Mail*. In practice, it seems to have made little difference: Rothermere and English still run the company in tandem, while Dacre edits the paper. But one day – and surely not too far into the future – Rothermere will have to hand over to his son, the Hon. Jonathan Harmsworth, who is waiting eagerly in the wings. In 1987, Rothermere said he would retire in 1996; he said, 'I want to spend the rest of my life living on a mountain top, skiing down it every morning and being carried up it every evening.' But now the mountain top seems to have receded and he says that only fools fix dates. *He* waited a terribly long time, till he was forty-six, to take over from his father. But, in fact, his father stayed too long, watching the paper slide into decay while he slid into Alzheimer's. Will the same thing happen again?

Jonathan Harmsworth will turn thirty this December. His father will then be seventy-two and Sir David English sixty-six. English shows no signs of retiring; in fact, he says only three things would make him retire: death, extreme ill health or Rothermere going. 'We more or less agree that we will work on together for as long as we can. We've always worked as a team and we've decided to go on doing that.' Rothermere seems slightly more willing to go and says, 'I've got to face the fact that my health won't always last in its present state. I've got to find some sort of gentle decline.' But he probably feels he owes it to Sir David to carry on as long as English wants to, which could mean well into the twenty-first century. And then the dynasty rolls triumphantly into the fourth generation, having long survived the point at which family businesses traditionally decline. Who now can sneer at Mere Vere?

Reproduced by permission of *The Observer*.

Alexander McQueen

15 December 1996

Hubert Givenchy, I seem to remember, used to be photographed standing deferentially behind his client wearing a white coat like a purveyor of high-quality meat to the gentry. If he had a personality, we never knew about it. But couturiers, like chefs, have come a long way socially – it's a mark of how the art/commerce axis has shifted that the modern couturier is not only not servile, but preferably rude, in-yer-face. Only then can he sufficiently terrify the pusillanimous fashion crowd whose idea of 'loud-mouthed' is anyone who would say boo to a goose. They are all impressed to death by Lee Alexander McQueen who is so wonderfully 'real' and yobby – a genuine East End taxi driver's son from genuine working-class Stratford East. He left school at sixteen! With one O-level! And worked as a tailor's apprentice! How thrillingly, shudderingly real can you get?

McQueen has recently prettified himself with a tattoo on his shoulder, a Japanese fish symbol because he is a Pisces and very fond of water. As a schoolboy, he swam for Essex. More – he did synchronized swimming, the only boy with forty girls, wearing a hula skirt and performing a Hawaiian dance. He wanted to learn how to swim underwater and come up legs first but he never graduated beyond the Hawaiian dance because his mum was so embarrassed.

He was 'pretty gorgeous' as a boy, he says, with near-white hair and blue eyes, but not so much now, at twenty-seven. 'I'm not the typical sort of Adonis-looking bloke. I'm more the typical East London bloke with a bit of a stomach.' His one concession to beautification was to have his protruding teeth capped as soon as he got some money because he had a complex about them. 'But I'm not that shallow as to think of myself, or want to be, an Adonis, because I think at the end of the day, everyone gets old and everything goes south – and with me it's started a little bit earlier!'

I was prepared for what Alexander McQueen looked like, because I'd seen him at the end of his last fashion show, paddling round with rolled-up trousers like Mr Prufrock. But I wasn't prepared for how he speaks. Put it like this: if a Spud-U-Like could speak, it would speak like Alexander McQueen. It takes a while to sort out the words from all the adenoidal snuffles and snorts, and half the time they're only space fillers like, 'know what I mean'. But once you've got the hang of it, you start being impressed. He may be inarticulate but he's not stupid.

His appointment as head of Givenchy was announced in mid-October. Before that, there'd been endless rumours about whether John Galliano would move to Dior and who would replace him. McQueen claims he 'didn't pay much interest'. He didn't know Galliano – they only met a couple of weeks ago in Paris – and he sees him as someone from a different era. 'He's a really nice guy. But he comes from a time when fashion was about élitism – in the 1980s designers were seen as kings. The 1990s is no longer about élitism, it's about the general public and not putting yourself on to a plane higher than anyone else.'

The first McQueen knew that he was being considered for the Givenchy job was when Bernard Arnault, the head of LVMH, which owns Givenchy, summoned him to Paris. 'He'd seen my shows and he said I was his horse. Like in a betting race? But I've got rather a stagnant view of fashion and I'm not that much swayed about people's opinions about myself. I was grateful for the offer but it was something I could take or leave. But I'm glad I took it because it's turning out to be a lot of fun.'

He opted for a two-year contract – though they offered him longer – and was happy with the salary of 'a bit more' than £100,000. He has already designed his first couture collection and is working on the ready-to-wear. It is a staggering workload for someone who just three years ago was on the dole. At Givenchy, he has a staff of sixty and is expected to design ten collections a year. He seems to have no plans to learn French – which, given his mastery of English, is perhaps just as well – but says it's quite easy to communicate 'international fashion language', like the shape of a sleeve. And he is dead impressed by all the brilliant atelier staff at Givenchy who produce special buttons or flowers overnight when in London it's a case of 'Oo, special order' and takes weeks. But he will still be based in London – he has just bought his dream house in Islington – and will continue to design under his own name.

Who are Givenchy's couture customers? McQueen won't say – 'It's private' – but they tend to be ladies from the Far East or Middle East. I must say I find the idea of Alexander McQueen trying to schmooze some Saudi princess quite hilarious, but McQueen doesn't see the joke. 'The thing is, because of my background, I'm quite humble and respectful about money and these people are as well. They know there's problems in the world and that spending more than £10,000 on a dress is in some people's eyes obscene. So they like to keep that private.'

One suddenly sees why Arnault chose McQueen as his horse: 'respectful about money' must be music to the ears of a backer. He puts all his fantasy and extravagance into his clothes, but he views the world with a coldly realistic eye. When I asked if his Givenchy clothes would be like his own collections, he looked at me as if I were mad: 'You don't design a spaceship to go into space if it hasn't got no wings, if it doesn't make sense. In my own collection I like the spaceship not to have any wings because I want to see how it falls back to earth, but people at Givenchy want to come back to earth slowly, not with a bump!'

He has a 'stern head' on his shoulders, as he puts it. It wasn't easy growing up in Stratford East as the youngest of six children of an East End cab driver with all that that implies. You weren't supposed to be gay, you weren't supposed to keep drawing ladies' fashions, as he did obsessively from the time he could hold a pencil. Only his father's sister, aunt Renee, 'a fantastic dresser', encouraged him and supported his ambitions to go to art school. His mother didn't dare because 'she had the restraint of my father or brother so she never got that leeway to let me do what I wanted. So she was always putting the thumb down on me because my father was putting the thumb down on her.'

Actually, I spoke to Mrs McQueen later and she said all her children were good at drawing, but Lee was the one who brought art books home from the library and advised his older sisters what to wear to the disco – and they took his advice. Though she describes herself as 'not fashion conscious' – she dresses at Marks & Spencer – she loves going to his shows 'once the first shock has worn off. I'm a bit Victorian.'

He says he was 'the pink sheep of the family' – not the black sheep, because they never rejected him, but an oddity, a misfit. He realized he was gay when he was about six and went in for a 'Prince of Pontins' competition at Pontins holiday camp. He came first. 'But I wanted the boy who come second to win because I fancied him! I just knew I had feelings for boys rather than girls, from six years old, maybe earlier.' But he kept quiet about it because it would not have gone down well at home. 'My father comes from a rather large East End family with mental attitudes from the past. It's just the era they were brought up in really.'

He is quite bitter about the social circumstances he grew up in – the hopeless sink school where 'you're just another East End oik going nowhere fast', the general poverty of expectation. He believes that most of his family had talents that could have been developed if they weren't stifled by circumstances. His mother actually went to art school, briefly, but gave it up to get a 'proper' job as a polytechnic social science teacher. Now she's a genealogist – writing a book on the history of their family. 'She was on the verge of actually becoming a separate identity to my father then all of a sudden it stopped, which was kind of sad. But that's just the way it is.' Likewise, his sister Jackie went to art school, hoping to become a graphic designer, but gave it up to become a secretary, and his brother Michael was an 'even better artist' and painted 'muriels' but ended up a taxi driver like their dad. 'It's sad. But that's the situation we grew up in – it's not heard of to be a fine artist in an East London family. But I always had the mentality that I only had one life and I was going to do what I wanted to.'

What he really wanted was to go to art school, but he left school at
sixteen with just one O-level, in art ('I had to draw a stupid bowl of
fruit') and worked for a while clearing glasses in his uncle's pub. Then
he saw an advertisement for tailor's apprentices at Anderson & Sheppard
in Savile Row. He remembers it as a 'romantic' time in his life. 'It was
like Dickens, sitting cross-legged on a bench and padding lapels and
sewing all day – it was nice. I wasn't there for the money because the
money wasn't very good anyway – I did it for the experience. You have
a master tailor, his name was Cornelius O'Callaghan from County Cork
in Ireland, and he taught me how to cut a jacket. You never met the
customers. We had people down on the shop floor that did that – you
was just a little mouse upstairs working away.'

An oft-told story is that he once wrote 'I'm a cunt' inside the lining
of a jacket destined for the Prince of Wales. Actually, he says, he wrote
all sorts of things. 'When you first start you're there for three months
solid just padding lapels. So you get bored and then you do a bit of
scribbling inside the jacket, and you might scrawl an obscenity – like
a sixteen-year-old does when he's bored. But it was just a passing phase.
If I'd known it was going to be brought up so many times I don't think
I would ever have mentioned it.'

After two years at Anderson & Sheppard making jackets, he spent
a year at Gieves & Hawkes learning to cut trousers. I tried to track
down anyone who remembered him in Savile Row but Cornelius
O'Callaghan has suffered a stroke and a Mr Halsey I spoke to at
Anderson & Sheppard sniffed, 'A problem is that people bandy our
name about but nobody in this building remembers him. He maybe
only worked here a few weeks. There's an army expression I could use
if you weren't a lady – it goes "b******* baffles brains". You don't
know it? Well, the first syllable of the first word is "bull".'

What on earth did McQueen think about while sitting all those
months on a bench, padding jackets? 'It was a weird time for me,
because at sixteen, seventeen, eighteen, I was going through the situation
of coming to terms with my sexuality and I was surrounded by hetero-
sexuals and quite a few homophobic people and every day there would
be some sort of remark. Downstairs on the shop floor was quite gay
but upstairs was full of people from Southend and South London, just
like any other apprentice trade, full of lads being laddish. So I was

trying to keep my mouth shut most of the time because I've got quite a big mouth on me. And it happened once at Gieves & Hawkes where I had a case of homophobia and I went straight to the head of Gieves & Hawkes and said the situation had to change. And it didn't, so I left.' Mr Gieve has no recollection of this, though he remembers Lee McQueen as a 'keenly interested' apprentice.

He told his family he was gay when he was about eighteen. 'I just didn't think I was living my life the way I wanted to, so I had to change the situation. I didn't want to spend my life in Stratford getting married to a girl, and having babies, buying a house, two up, two down, and everything's hunky dory. I knew I wanted to be a fashion designer at the end of the day.' It took a while for his mother to come to terms with it, but he says the family has been quite supportive.

He took his art A-level at night school (West Ham technical college) 'which meant I ended up with housewives and people who just wanted to pass the time. So I wasn't quite where I wanted to go.' Still, the training plan he devised for himself turned out to be a good one. After learning conventional tailoring in Savile Row, he went to Berman & Nathan theatrical costumiers to learn fancy tailoring. He didn't like it much. 'I was surrounded by complete queens – and I hate the theatre anyway.' So he went to work for Kohji Tatsuno, who was backed at the time by Yohji Yamamoto, because he saw an article about him and found his work exciting. What did he wear for the interview? 'I used to have tapered trousers with a leather jacket and a piece of satin tied round my neck in an unusual way.' Nice? 'I looked a complete freak.'

When Tatsuno lost his backer, McQueen went to Italy and got himself a job as Romeo Gigli's pattern-cutter, then applied to St Martin's College of Art to teach – not study – pattern-cutting. They said they didn't have a job, but they offered him a place on their postgraduate course even though he was not a graduate. His aunt paid for him to go. In 1993, he presented his first collection, with lots of models wrapped in Clingfilm, and was hailed by the *Telegraph* as 'hopelessly inexperienced, worryingly quixotic but shockingly talented'. At that point he started using his second name Alexander, because he was still using his first name, Lee, to sign on for the dole. His March 1995 collection, Highland Rape (featuring tampon strings and bumster trousers) established him as a star. (His mother recalls that before the show, 'There were all these beautiful blue lace dresses and he was hacking at them with his shears and I was crying, "No, don't spoil them."') Since then, his reputation has grown with every collection – I saw the last one this autumn, and it was by miles the most exciting event in London Fashion Week, though pretty kinky, with women wearing horrible manacles and surgical frames. Does he really expect women to wear that stuff? 'No! Where would you wear it?' But people who knew about fashion, he said, could recognize the beautiful clothes underneath the outrageous styling.

He only started making money about a year and a half ago, but since then it's been gushing – his turnover last season was more than £1 million. And he was paid a useful £15,000 for making an Australian lager commercial and is doing a similar job for Smirnoff. The first thing he bought with his newfound wealth was a television – 'nothing too plush. Sometimes I do go a bit overboard and buy something silly like a house! No – I've only just bought a house and it's the house I've been waiting for all my life, in Islington.' Would he like to buy his parents a house one day? 'No. I'm quite generous, but it's hard to let money be a ruler of a situation. I'd help them out, but who knows? I've never seen my life as stable as a fashion designer; I don't think fashion is a very stable career. You can't count on it for years. You can be as quickly dropped as you're quickly picked up.'

Meanwhile, all the time his success has been growing, he has been looking for love – he is monogamous by nature. And for the past five months, he thinks he's found it: he has a live-in partner called Murray Arthur, who used to manage the Donna Karan shop, and now works for McQueen, paying the wages and doing the accounts. McQueen describes him as 'very intelligent and analytical' and hopes they will be together for life.

His family have invited Murray for Christmas, which is a major breakthrough – McQueen has never taken any boyfriend home before. There is a sense of bridges being mended. His father has recently had cancer – which McQueen says explains why he never came to the shows, but used to drop off Mrs McQueen in his taxi, then drive away again. But 'he shows me great respect now. I love my father dearly, and my mother. But I just wish I'd had that support in the beginning.

George,' he says, 'No, I'm his mother.' When he was in Culture Club he couldn't leave his house without being mobbed, but his attitude was different then. 'I was much more paranoid and I'm not paranoid any more. I used to be really worried about people seeing me without my make-up on but now I don't care. When I'm not working, I just slob around.' He still lives in the big Gothic horror house in Hampstead, but the knot of Boy George clones who used to wait outside in all weathers has disappeared – grown up presumably. Whereas he used to have a cook, he now cooks for himself, does his own Hoovering, and shops at Sainsbury's. 'I like being *out*, you know.'

The first thing that strikes you, and continues to strike you, is his extraordinary likeableness. I can't imagine anyone not succumbing to it. It is very different to charm. Charm is something people do to you; this is something that he *has*. I think it derives from his total confidence that you *will* like him and therefore he has nothing to fear, and also that he seems – though more on this 'seems' later – completely honest, open and self-revealing. He is like the cat that greets you by rolling belly-up. By offering himself so defencelessly he invites your protection and love.

His aim is to plug his autobiography, *Take It Like a Man*, and for once I am happy to plug away. His life story is so rich you can't say thirty-three is too young to write it – I wish he'd written more. The book is good-humoured and often very funny, even about the most harrowing days of his drug addiction – he didn't want it to be 'like Michael Barrymore tells of his living hell'. He was supposed to deliver the book four years ago, but he kept rewriting and rewriting. 'If I had my way I'd probably still be doing it. It's the most academic thing I've ever done, so I'm proud of actually finishing it.'

The book should be a social history text apart from anything else – it's a vivid spotlight on some murky corners of the British class system. He comes from the sort of family that schoolteachers go white at the sight of – five brothers and a sister, all warring at home but united against the world. When kids at school in Eltham would taunt George with 'poof' or 'shirtlifter' he'd warn them, 'Touch me, and I'll get me brothers on to ya.' His father, Gerry O'Dowd, an Irish builder and former boxer with a taste for betting, was a 'people-collector', always picking up strays, but violent and domineering at home. Mother Dinah was sometimes tearful in private but tough as nails outside –

when one of her sons was banned from a school outing she stood in front of the coach saying if Gerald didn't go no one went. They were Roman Catholics and had a picture of the Pope next to one of Muhammad Ali in the hall. The family was 'close' because they were crammed into a council house in Shooters Hill (George shared a bedroom with three of his brothers), but psychologically George was miles out of it. 'Being one of six kids and queer, I soon learned it was a solitary existence.'

It was a noisy, turbulent household, which he remembers as 'furniture flying, tears flowing, suburban psychosis'. Everyone called him a poof but never explained what it meant; sex was so unspoken-of they blushed at Carry On films. George longed for his father's attention but seldom got it; the affection was there but not often shown. Finally George concluded, 'If that's how a man acts I don't want to be one.' But through all the ups and downs of his career, he never lost touch with his parents, who seem to have been unusually tolerant – his father even gave him the money for his first pair of Vivienne Westwood bondage trousers. When George broke the news that he was gay (which can't have come as a total surprise) they assured him that they loved him whatever he was.

At fifteen, Boy George abandoned school and Eltham to find the big outside world. He lived in West End squats and went clubbing with his new gender-bender friends, Sue Catwoman, Petal the Pimp, Stephanie Suspense, Slag Sue, and Queenie who ran a Soho torture chamber. He worked as a shelf-stacker at Tesco's, as an office messenger, and as a cloakroom attendant at the Blitz Club, where he augmented his wages by going through the pockets – 'A certain amount of thieving was essential.' This was his high-camp phase when his role models were David Bowie and Quentin Crisp, his best friends were mainly drag queens, and the greatest essential in life was hairspray. One day when he was working as an office messenger, an Italian man picked him up on the Tube and took him to dinner with Anton Dolin, John Gilpin, Alicia Markova and Lindsay Kemp. Another night he found himself in Pinner making love with a male nurse, while the nurse's patient slept in the next room. It was all swings and roundabouts and Boy George says, rather wistfully, that he enjoyed writing about that period most of all.

At nineteen he was just a wannabe, like most of his friends, but in 1982 Malcolm McLaren asked him to join a Bow Wow Wow gig and that gave him the confidence to form Culture Club, who were quickly signed to a six-year contract by Virgin. Their first two singles did nothing much but in September 1982 they released 'Do You Really Want to Hurt Me?' which went to number one in eighteen countries, including the States. At that time, Boy George had never left England, never owned a passport or had a bank account – soon he was flying Concorde to New York, winning Grammys, and appearing on the cover of *Newsweek*. The glory years were 1983 and 1984, when everything Culture Club did turned to gold. Their second album, *Colour by Numbers*, sold 6 million and 'Karma Chameleon' was number one around the world. George bought his mum an $8,000 fur coat with 'To Mum, with love' embroidered in the lining. She said, 'Where am I going to wear that? Safeways?'

But at the height of Culture Club's fame, George was never happy. He was madly in love with drummer Jon Moss, but they quarrelled constantly, mainly because of George's possessiveness. He had a pattern of falling for 'straight' boys who were uneasy about loving him back. Moreover, he could never just relax and enjoy their success. He was too busy running around issuing orders, telling the other band members what to say, what to do. what to wear, banning their wives and girlfriends, fretting over publicity, telling Jon Moss's parents that no, they were not allowed to send a stripagram girl for Jon's birthday and generally 'being a drama queen, being a control freak, being a bore. I wish I'd let myself enjoy it more, instead of turning it into a big drama. And also deluding myself that because I screamed and ranted I was in control. I should have just jumped up and down on the bed and enjoyed it.'

While the other band members were partying, he'd be sitting in his hotel room, sipping English breakfast tea and plaiting his wigs, terrified to go out. Everyone knew his stance on drugs – he disapproved – so nobody invited him to any room-wrecking mayhem. But when Culture Club's star began to wane, with their third album, he emerged from his long purdah and started hitting the clubs again. In January 1985 someone casually handed him his first Ecstasy tab and he casually swallowed it. Just three months later, on a trip to Paris for the fashion collections, he took his first hit of heroin and within a year had a full-scale three-gram-a-day habit. Sweet George increasingly turned sour. He started turning up late for press conferences, being rude to promoters and screaming 'Fuck off, you little bastards' at his fans. He had fights with Jon Moss in public, and refused to keep up the pretence that they were just good friends.

At his twenty-fourth birthday party in New York, he had a bad asthma attack from all the drugs he had ingested, then went on morning radio to do an interview when he could barely talk. He began taking insane risks – carrying smack in his underpants on a flight to Israel, flying to New York with three grams of cocaine up his bottom. Inevitably rumours began to reach the press and, after he'd nodded off on the *Aspel* show, the *Evening Standard* ran the headline 'Worried about the Boy'. Richard Branson warned him that Fleet Street was offering £50,000 for proof that he took drugs. But by this stage he was beyond caring – he was having convulsions, vomiting constantly and buying heroin in broad daylight at Gospel Oak station.

In June 1986 the *Daily Mirror* ran a story, 'Drugs and Boy George', in which a photographer claimed George had sold him cocaine – George responded by phoning the photographer and telling him, 'You're gonna be dead' – the next day's headline. He foolishly appeared at an anti-apartheid rally at Clapham Common wearing a face pack, shouting, 'I'm a drag addict, not a drug addict.' His father came to his house to try to talk to him. George locked himself in the bathroom. His father started a bonfire in the sitting room to get him out ('Dad always liked dramatic gestures') and the police were called but refused to intervene. Finally, on 3 July 1986 his brother David went to the *Sun* to declare melodramatically, 'Junkie George Has Eight Weeks to Live.' Richard Branson whisked Boy George off to his home while the police raided all his known dealers – two of them went to prison for four years. He was convicted of prior possession and fined £250 – a small fine, but it meant he was banned from the US and Japan. It was the end of Culture Club.

He planned to make a solo album and invited a musician friend, Michael Rudetsky, over from New York to help him write it. Rudetsky arrived looking fit, having just been in a detox clinic. After two nights in London he looked less fit and went to sleep on George's sofa in

Hampstead while George went back to his old flat in St John's Wood for the night. The next morning George's brother Kevin found Rudetsky dead – the autopsy revealed heroin poisoning. Boy George had no idea where he got the drugs. But it was the death of another friend, Mark Golding, that finally convinced George to clean up. At the end of 1986, with the help of his parents, a doctor and two male nurses, he finally kicked heroin, though he still 'couldn't cross the road without taking a sleeping pill'. He staggered through the next year on methadone and valium. Only in 1988 did he manage to come off pills as well and start seeking psychiatric help, but by then his career was shot.

His crash, when it came, was cataclysmic; he disappeared so completely that it was a shock to hear his voice again on 'The Crying Game'. Luckily he had a good manager, Tony Gordon, who managed to salvage the house in Hampstead and eventually get him some work. He had always described himself as 'a musical odd-job man', so it was the odd jobs he returned to when the stardom stopped – producing other singers on his own dance label, More Protein, singing backing vocals, and dee-jaying in northern clubs. He calls it 'eating humble pie' and he ate it with good grace. Nowadays he is noticeably more polite about other musicians, even George Michael: the only one he can be relied on to slag off is Marti Pellow of Wet Wet Wet. He says he's more serious about his music now and 'that matters more than having my picture in the paper or turning up at the right party. Maybe that's to do with having had it all too easy.'

Even now, he says, he wakes up some mornings and thinks 'Why bother?', but generally he just gets on with it. He recites his post-Culture Club achievements with a weary, defensive air, defying you to sneer. 'I've had records out in other countries and I've toured all over the world – Istanbul, Argentina, Chile. I've toured more since I left Culture Club than I ever did with them. And I've put out three albums in the past five years and they've had a kind of relative success. People think if you're not doing well in England your career is over, but England's a very small dot. For instance, "Bow Down Mister", my Krishna song, was number five in Germany for sixteen weeks and Germany is the fourth biggest market in the world.'

Number five in Germany! It's a long way from number one in eighteen countries. He has a new album out now, *Cheapness and Beauty*, but he doesn't expect it to be number one. 'I just want to carry on making records, so I need a certain amount of record sales in order to be able to hold on to my contract. I mean, it's great to be winning on any level, but there are different levels of winning. If I look back to six years ago, I'm winning now, in the sense that I'm working. Six years ago the price for me to do a performance was a lot lower, now it's higher – that's the way it goes.' What was his price at the lowest point? 'Two thousand a night – not bad. But £15,000 is better, and £20,000 is better still.' And although the bookings are rather random – a trip to Sydney to open the Gay and Lesbian Mardi Gras, followed by a sprint to Blackpool to do the Lily Savage show – they keep on coming. The day I met him he'd been offered $20,000 a week to do *Jesus Christ Superstar* in Los Angeles, but he told his agent (singing to the tune of 'Jesus Christ Superstar') 'NO-no. NO. NO-no-No.' He would love to do stage work, or film work, but only if he could do it well. 'I don't want to make a fool of myself unnecessarily.'

When the bookings dry up, he says he'll be happy to work in a shop. 'I'll always have a life outside of being Boy George, and that is really sacred to me. If I never sell another record, if I have to go and work in Tesco's, I'd do it well, I'd do it with a smile on my face.' He might even welcome it because he enjoys meeting people – the reclusiveness of stardom was never his style. But for the moment, he says, 'I'm very lucky because I earn a good living. I have a great life, I travel all over the world, I eat great food, I stay in good hotels and people pay the bill – what have I got to complain about? I mean, I went to Australia for three weeks and spent only £500 – everyone was taking me out to dinner. People are incredibly nice to me. It's not like being famous is too much of a burden.'

This quite unusual realism is the result of all the psychotherapy he has done in recent years. After dabbling with Hare Krishna and Buddhism he got on to Turning Point, which runs very intense weekend groups where participants are encouraged to shout at each other and 'face up to their own bull'. He says Turning Point has taught him not to blame other people, but to take responsibility for his own life. He has done all the courses up to 'Point of Mastery' and also persuaded his parents to go. His father now works as a lay helper on the courses – though the main effect on his parents, interestingly, has been to turn them back to their original Catholicism – his father now goes to church almost every day. I wouldn't be surprised if George doesn't return to the fold eventually. He says he always lights candles when he visits a church or temple because 'I'm very attracted to the ritual of thanking the Giver, and I do believe that there is something, definitely, to be grateful for.'

And his love life is happier now. For the past six years he has lived with an Irish boy, Michael Dunne, and says they have a 'mother-son relationship with a bit of incest thrown in' – he being the mother. He helped Dunne come off drugs and 'for the past year, I've really wanted to be with Michael always and make it work. I've been trying not to be selfish and to think about what he needs and understanding his problems.'

Oddly, he says, many people still don't believe he is gay, and ask his brothers, 'He's not really, is he?' In his Culture Club days he shrouded the question in enough mystery and irony to keep audiences guessing. His doll-like, asexual image was brilliantly designed to make him seem harmless, so that even mums and dads were quite happy buying his records for their children. Boy George was a 'nice' pop star, such a relief after those horrible Sex Pistols.

Yet, as he says, 'I did a lot more than most militant homosexuals ever did in terms of freeing up people's attitudes to sexuality. I get letters constantly to this day saying, "You helped me come out." Sometimes image can be very political. To me, gay politics isn't about Actup T-shirts and blue jeans, it's about drag queens – that's really putting your head on the block. So for a lot of people I was kind of the benchmark homosexual, with my ribbons and bows. I mean, if anyone thought I was straight, that's their problem.'

Where it all gets very irritating is when he claims he is bisexual and justifies it by saying, 'Everyone is.' This is casuistry and anyway he gave the game away when I asked if his father had been gay and he yelped, 'No!' Seeing my gleam of triumph, he started saying, 'Well, yeah, possibly – he was gorgeous when he was younger' but then panicked and said he was only joking. Clearly the Real Man could never be accused of such a thing. In fact, when he says bisexual he simply means that everyone has masculine and feminine components. Pin him down to the real question which is 'Could he contemplate sleeping with a woman?' and the answer is no.

He has always had woman friends – as a teenager he had more girlfriends than his brothers – but, 'I'm very aware now, through doing therapy, that women actually intimidate me. Sexually, not as friends. I'm very uncomfortable with the idea of vaginas. They bother me in the way that spiders bother some people. But I do see that as an extreme form of ignorance on my part. There are certain types of women I find very attractive, but mostly they're very masculine, tough ball-breaker types. I think one of the things I resented my mother for when I was a child was not being stronger. Now I realize she was tough to have survived all that. But I do acknowledge now that women intimidate me and I could never have done that five years ago.'

He is lucky in that his family has always stood by him, though his fame inevitably disrupted their lives. Two of his brothers took to drugs; Gerald gave up a promising career as a boxer because he was so fed up with being introduced as Boy George's brother; his parents started giving interviews to the press. Only Richard, the eldest (actually a half-brother), refused to join the Boy George circus, and still keeps his distance. It took a long time to heal the rift with David for shopping him to the *Sun*, but now they are on such good terms that George is godfather to David's new baby.

People in clubs still offer him drugs and won't believe him when he says he's not interested. 'It isn't high-handed – it's just I don't want it. I've been there, done it, it didn't work. Basically, I overkilled it. It's not like I'm deeply moralistic about it.' He admits he's confused about what an ex-junkie is supposed to do. He is always being asked to stand up as an anti-drugs spokesman but he believes that would be hypocrisy. In the book, after pussyfooting around the subject for a while, he finally does come out in capital letters. 'I HATE DRUGS. DRUGS ARE A CON.'

He is eagerly looking forward to his friends' reactions to the book – 'How upset they get and what they say to the press.' He has high hopes of Marilyn, the outrageously rude drag queen who was his sidekick for many years, selling his all to the *News of the World*. Marilyn, who was never his lover but his 'sister', emerges as one of the great lovable monsters of literature, in fact he almost steals the book – Boy George seems far fonder of him than any of his lovers, past or present. I wondered if Marilyn might sue for libel but Boy George laughed.

Anyway, he said, if anyone sues, 'I'll just sell more books, won't I?' –
not a line that ever goes down well with judges.

Boy George seems open, honest and self-revealing, both in his book
and in person. It therefore comes as a shock, reading the book and his
press cuttings, to clock how many whoppers he has told. Even his
most quoted remark, 'Sex? I'd rather have a cup of tea', was a bare-faced
lie. For years, he denied that he and Jon Moss were lovers, for years
he denied that he had ever taken drugs. In fact, far from being honest,
he has often been a plausible liar.

Is his likeableness, then, a complete sham? I don't think so – it's
more complicated than that. He is naturally friendly, polite and outgoing;
he likes people and wants to be liked by them. He knows that his
likeability is a gift as secure as perfect pitch, and he enjoys exercising
it. This came out when he was talking about Marilyn and said that
although the media always portrayed them as nice Boy George and
nasty Marilyn, they were actually sisters under the skin – 'I just hide it
better.' He said when he was rude to people they took it as a joke, but
when Marilyn did it, it wasn't funny. And he thought the reason was
because, ultimately, he cared about people and Marilyn didn't. But you
occasionally sense that *he* resents being as likeable as he is. He explains,
'I kind of drift between wanting to be loved and wanting to say fuck
off, in and out of it minute by minute. It's a kind of schizophrenia.'

'But you've always been careful not to say that to the media?'

'Oh, I have, in different ways. I'll say it now, then – fuck off.'

But then he laughs disarmingly, 'Oo, that was a relief' – and I can't
help liking him again.

Michael Winner

24 May 1998

Damn damn damn. Lunch with Michael Winner and no tantrums to report. There was a highly promising moment as we approached
the restaurant of the Halcyon hotel and the man walking in front of
us failed to hold the door open. Winner turned a lively shade of puce
and started emitting steam. Ooh goodie, I thought, as Winner barked,
'Is that man a member of your staff?' at the manager. 'No,' said the
manager, 'he's a customer.' Oh. Winner deflated into quiet grumbling,
and that was the nearest we ever got to an explosion. Sorry. I should
have insisted on taking him to Mash. The Halcyon is his local, and
they obviously know him well – the chef, the sommelier, the maître d'
all came up at various times to say how delighted they were to see
him. He prefers his familiar haunts: for a restaurant reviewer, he is
wonderfully unadventurous. I think he has a great fear of *not* being
recognized, of being just an ordinary punter, and also a slight chip on
his shoulder about class. He asked me very early on what my father
did for a living, presumably to 'place' me socially – the only other
interviewee who has ever done that was Raine Spencer.

I tried *everything* to get him to lose his temper, but he never did. He's
a hopeless old sweetie, really, and quite clever enough to see me coming
– he laughed at my attempts to needle him. Yet he can be terribly
thin-skinned. Last year, I wrote a travel piece on Barbados which
included a throwaway remark about the dangers of encountering

Michael Winner at Sandy Lane, and immediately got a hurt letter saying he was 'saddened'. Fancy bothering to write – if he picks up every passing rude remark in the media, it must be a full-time job. I apologized and he consented to be interviewed.

Before lunch, he wanted to give me a guided tour of his house. He loves showing it off; is intensely proud of it; and hopes when he dies to leave it to the nation. When he was younger and couldn't sleep, he used to get up in the middle of the night and polish the furniture and dust the tops of the doors – nowadays he has five domestic staff cleaning full-time. Sometimes he doesn't leave the house for days on end: 'I mean, sometimes I go and walk round the block, because I actually haven't been out for a week.' In his newspaper columns, he likes to portray himself as a great partygoer, but he says he hates parties, and hates mingling. 'Why should I mingle? Mostly these parties are full of – as we say in Yiddish – *nebbishes*. I don't need to see them!' It sounds arrogant, but *really*, for all his bluster, he says he's terribly shy, a sensitive shrinking violet, and I am half-inclined to believe him. I certainly believe him when he says, 'I'm a very lonely person.'

His house is one of the great Victorian artists' studios in Melbury Road, Kensington, but now so modernized and manicured it feels like a hotel. His father leased it after the war and turned it into flats and Winner gradually bought out the other tenants and restored it. His bedroom, the original studio, is bigger than many houses, with a wall of north-facing windows probably 40ft high. He proudly showed me the remote-control electronic blinds, and then got agitated when one of them stuck. 'Do you actually sleep here?' I asked, thinking it must be like sleeping in an aircraft hangar. He said he did – but I noticed that through the bathroom was another much smaller, more lived-in bedroom, with a battered teddy bear on the bed.

When he talks about the house, he uses the pronoun 'we' – does he mean himself and his girlfriend, Vanessa Perry? 'Oh no, no. She's only come in recently. She obviously *partakes* of the house but she has her own flat.' So who is this 'we' then? 'Me, dear – the royal we.' Oddly enough, Edward Heath uses the same 'we' in talking about *his* house: is it something that happens to elderly bachelors? Do they start mentally cloning themselves? At all events, I wouldn't advise any woman to marry a man who thought of himself as 'we'.

The basement of the house is a giant screening room, lined with signed photographs of all the stars he's worked with: Marlon Brando, Burt Lancaster, Robert Mitchum. You always sort of forget he's a film director – he has made more than thirty films, but if you ask most people to name them, they rarely get past *Death Wish*. In America, he is taken seriously and is on the directors' judging panel of the Academy Awards. He started as a director of 'wacky' 1960s comedies – *The Jokers*, *I'll Never Forget What's 'is Name*, *The System* – but then got into action films in the 1970s. The film he is most proud of is *The Nightcomers*, with Marlon Brando. He is known as a swift, efficient film-maker who often writes, produces, directs and edits himself. Until recently, he averaged a film a year, but his new film, *Parting Shots* (which comes out in the autumn), is his first for five years. It stars Chris Rea and a host of old friends – Felicity Kendal, John Cleese, Bob Hoskins, Joanna Lumley, Oliver Reed, Diana Rigg. He tells me that it is not what the British public think of as a Michael Winner film – 'It's a totally nice, feelgood, witty film.'

As a lonely boy who didn't fit in either with his progressive arts and crafts boarding school or 'the rather sleek Jewish community' his parents belonged to, he took refuge in the cinema. At fourteen, he managed to get a commission to write a regular film column for the *Kensington Post*, and went round interviewing stars and writing about them. After Cambridge, he had a brief sortie into journalism, but was soon directing films. He thinks he has probably made more films than any other living English director.

Until about ten years ago, he was known *only* as a hardworking film director – Michael Winner the media confection who has rows in restaurants only started in the 1990s. Now, of course, he's ubiquitous: he does ads on television – 'It's a Winner!'; he writes frequent letters to the press; he is chairman and founder of the Police Memorial Trust; and writes weekly columns in the *News of the World* and *Sunday Times*. He claims he spends only half an hour on these columns, and when I say I don't believe him, he laughs, 'My dear, Alan Ayckbourn writes a play in two days!' So, in theory, he could earn a good living from journalism alone. 'Not the way I live, darling!'

On the quiet, he's a bit of an aesthete: he is very proud of his collection of children's book illustrations, by Arthur Rackham, Edmund

Dulac, Kay Nielsen and E. H. Shepard (of *Winnie the Pooh*), and plans
to leave it, like his house, to the nation. It seems an odd taste for a
childless bachelor, but these are the pictures he loved as a boy. He
started buying them in 1968 when they were dirt cheap – now, he says,
they go for £60,000 and £70,000 and 'whether I could afford it or not,
I couldn't bring myself to spend that amount of money'. But he likes
going to salerooms and following prices. His father was a serious art
collector – he paid the world-record price for a Jan van Os flower
painting and had a museum-quality collection of jade. 'He had a very
good eye, and he would sort of put his hand on my shoulder and say,
"One day all this will be yours." Well, of course, it wasn't, it went to
the Cannes casino. And when my mother eventually died and these
thirty-five crates came back that we'd paid a fortune to insure and
store, we thought: "There must be *something* in here, somewhere we'll
find a gem." But it was all six toilet rolls or a dozen 60-watt lightbulbs
– *nothing* worth anything.'

Enter Mumsy! I wondered when Helen Winner would make an
appearance, and she took no time at all. She died in 1984, but Winner
still thinks about her every day, and says he is 'haunted' by her. She
was a compulsive gambler who played poker at his bar mitzvah and
virtually moved into the Cannes casino when her husband died. Winner
says fervently, 'People don't realize, unless they've lived with a congenital
gambler, what a very serious psychological problem it is. She was a
good gambler, but you can't win if you're playing every night. She was
taking valuable paintings off the walls into the backs of taxis to get
enough money to continue her habit – the fact that they were mine is
irrelevant.' She spent the last ten years of her life suing her son and it
was this lawsuit, he believes, that brought on his first blocked artery
in 1974 (he had another in 1993). When she proposed visiting him in
hospital, the doctor said, 'The one person he mustn't see is you, Mrs
Winner – you're the one who put him there.'

Winner is disposed to forgive, though not forget. He thinks she was
unbalanced by the 'deeply harrowing' scenes of anti-Semitism she
witnessed as a child in Poland. 'It's very easy for us who have lived in
a civilized society all our lives to look on irregularities of behaviour as
something not nice, but there was a period of suffering there that was
just intense.' And, of course, he enjoyed her ferocity when he was not

on the receiving end. He recalls seeing her walk into a room full of expensive lawyers, this nice little old lady, and reduce them to oilslicks. 'She had an acidity, she had a daring, and when she decided to have a go, they were wiped out. I admired that greatly, I might add. Patronizing arseholes, they deserved it.'

He says all his girlfriends tell him that the reason he's a complete mess is because of his mother. When Janet Street-Porter suggested that deep down he was frightened of women, he agreed: 'Well, this may be Mumsy! This could be the mad mother, you know!' He gets his own back in his action films – the women are always raped or murdered or tortured. Charles Bronson (who made six films with him) once said: 'Michael Winner is a very sadistic man. He loves men falling off rooftops and women jumping out of windows and landing on picket fences. Also women getting raped. He is very hard on women.' Winner is seriously hurt when I repeat this, and says, 'Oh, he's an idiot! It's such a stupid thing to say.' But then some of Winner's own remarks are hardly pro-women – the worst was when he said about O. J. Simpson (whom he directed in *Firepower*) that if he'd swindled someone out of money he would never speak to him again, but if he had 'only' murdered his wife . . . 'Well, where did I say that? I mean, I possibly said it in a moment of madness, but would you read me the exact quote?' I fished out the 1994 *Sun* cutting and read it to him, word for word. Winner's reaction was to roar with laughter: 'Well, that *is* a reckless remark! But you know, there is something about the tragedy – because he was a very nice man – of somebody who was obviously drugged out of his mind, in this emotional situation. The courts tend to be rather sympathetic if a wife does it to her husband. No, it's an incredibly sad case. It's tragic,' he says, wiping away tears of merriment.

He says he never actually *resolved* not to marry, but even when he was madly in love with someone, he couldn't envisage marrying them. Once or twice, it was at the back of his mind to propose, 'but it was always at the *back*'. Consequently, his girlfriends tend to leave after a few years, but he's stayed friendly with them all and regards them as his family. 'This may sound crummy and stupid, but I consider that I have been greatly blessed in the ladies I have been with all through my life. I totally reject the idea that they're there for money, or for films. They don't want things, they don't ask for things, they're very beautiful people. There were a couple who went to the *News of the World* I could have lived without . . .'

My favourite was one called Sandy Grizzle who kissed'n'told in 1988. He sued for libel (he always sues if he can, and gives the money to charity, so I'd better be careful what I say), but he was happy enough to talk about her: 'Sandy Grizzle is what they used to call in the old days "a party girl" – hahahahaha. She was actually a very jolly party girl. She never took money from me; she never even went out with me. She used to come round very happily, have a bit of sex, watch *Dallas* or *Dynasty*, and I would serve her dinner while she watched television, then she'd go off to Stringfellow's to carry on the good work. She never took a penny! And she only went to the *News of the World* about two years after I'd finished seeing her. Before that, I would have described her as a very nice person.'

But it sounded so boring for poor Sandy Grizzle, I said, having to watch the same lesbian video, *Debbie Does Dallas*, night after night. 'Lynn!' he roars. 'There was no lesbian video whatsoever. I said to Michael Grade, "We've got her – because there is no such video as *Debbie Does Dallas*." And he said, "What? Do you mean you haven't seen it?" [Roars of laughter.] But this is all piffle. She watched *Dallas* and *Dynasty*, that's all she ever watched on my television.'

He got annoyed when I asked why he always went out with bimbos – 'I don't accept the word bimbo and I don't think it's a word women should ever use. What is a bimbo? If it's a young girl having fun, good luck to her. These men screwing around, nobody calls them bimbos, but they're far more mindless than the girls.' Anyway, he says, no one could call Jenny Seagrove, his previous girlfriend, a bimbo – she was a well-known actress in her own right. OK, OK, forget bimbo, but why didn't he go out with someone his own size? Not literally (heaven forfend), but in status terms. Again, he bridles at the word status, but eventually I calm him down and he admits that a friend once arranged a *shidduch* (Jewish matchmaking introduction) for him to meet a nice mature PR lady, 'and she was very nice, and she ran a big PR operation, but I didn't feel sexually attracted to her. And so we didn't meet again. I mean, you have to have a certain chemistry, don't you?'

Jenny Seagrove seems to have been his longest-running girlfriend but she left him in 1993, two weeks before his heart bypass. Then he briefly had a companion called Catherine Neilson – 'She's a very nice girl. She came to see me through this difficult period and then went back to her own life. And then very shortly thereafter I met Vanessa.' Perry is an actress and dancer who was in pantomimes and toured in *42nd Street*. He describes her as 'a sweet kid'. But he has no immediate plans to marry her.

Why is he so reluctant to get married? 'I don't know. If I knew, I'd tell you. It's not a secret.' Is it the fear that a wife could ruin him financially? 'Alimony, you mean? I don't think so. And now it doesn't matter much, because I'm so old. No, I just don't know the answer, Lynn. People make these wonderful guesses – because his mother was a nutcase – but I'm not prepared to go through six years of psychiatry to hear their stupid opinions. I don't wake up in the morning thinking, "My God, I never married so I'm a failure in life."'

I can't help feeling that money comes into it – that he has a fear of someone squandering his wealth, the way his mother did. Not that he's mean – on the contrary, he loves giving – but the giving sometimes has a hint of strings attached. A typical example happened with Tony Blair, just before the election. Blair came to unveil one of his police memorials, and Winner asked if he'd put a bet on himself winning the election. Blair said 'No,' and Winner said, 'Tell you what, Tony, I'll put five grand on for you, no, no, I'll put twenty grand on and give the winnings to a charity of your choice.' So that's what he did, and won about £1,700, and Blair thanked him and asked him to give it to the NSPCC. But Blair hasn't yet invited Winner to a party at No. 10 – Cherie has, but Blair hasn't, and Winner is a tiny bit resentful.

Or take the scene when we left the Halcyon. Winner tipped the doorman some enormous note, I think £50, but asked for change. The doorman said, unfortunately he didn't have any, and Winner said, 'Oh well, it's your lucky day.' The chauffeur then drove us the few hundred yards to Winner's house and exactly the same transaction ensued – Winner produced a £50 note but asked for change and was slightly miffed when the chauffeur didn't have any. He badly needs to rethink his tipping technique: if you want to be a big spender you have to be a *careless* big spender, not one who asks for change. The whole routine seems designed to cause himself maximum grief.

But he was brought up to be 'puritanical' about money – his parents were quite poor at the time he was born and only became rich gradually. He gets annoyed when people assume he inherited his wealth: he did inherit his father's property holdings, but long after he'd become a multi-millionaire in his own right. He is reputed to be a canny investor, who pulled out of property in 1987 just before the crash (he says he could have saved himself £4 million in tax by leaving the country for a year, but didn't want to), but says now he regrets not spending more freely. 'I was always too cautious – I wish I'd spent it earlier.' He recently made the decision to travel only by private jet but, 'It was a helluva leap to say to yourself: "I'm going to spend eleven grand going to the South of France and back." There is no way you can say that it is not obscene. But what is the point of putting up with all this inconvenience and leaving an enormous amount of money?'

Absolutely – especially as he has no obvious heirs. His only relatives are some cousins he doesn't see. I asked whom he named as next of kin when he had his heart bypass but he said he didn't name anyone – the hospital didn't ask (I find this hard to believe). But he has made a will leaving some of his estate to charity, some to Vanessa and the rest to his old girlfriends, including ones he hasn't seen for thirty years.

He feels he owes them something because, 'I wasn't mean before, but I took the view – because the girls never asked for anything, that's for sure – that if I spent much on them, I was buying them, and this was against my principles. In retrospect, I think I behaved rather badly – I should have given them bigger birthday presents, I should have been more generous. I mean, they had wonderful holidays and this and that, but in actual goodies I was not generous. And in some way I prided myself on that, because I thought, "Well, they're obviously not with me for my money, because they're not getting any." Hahahaha. More recently, I have turned from that path.'

But it is as if he can't believe in emotional ties, unless they are backed by financial ones. It affects even his friendships. The friends you hear about are the famous ones – John Cleese, Michael Caine, Roger Moore, Andrew Neil – but his oldest friend is someone called John Fraser whom he has known since school and who now works in his film company. They see each other almost every day. I asked if I could meet Fraser, and Winner hooted, 'Oh, you don't want to see him, darling!' But he said I could ring him. Fraser sounded as though he was speaking from inside a filing cabinet. He is sixty-four and, like Winner, unmarried. He first met Winner when he was eleven and Winner – who was two years his junior – offered to pay him to clean his room. Fraser did, 'because I needed the money. I liked buying books, I wanted to be a history teacher' and even when the headmaster objected, he went on doing it. So this friendship going back fifty years began – again – with Winner in the sugar-daddy role.

Winner often says his one regret is not having children – 'That is the one mistake that wipes out everything I have ever done.' About twelve years ago, he discovered he was infertile. He had been trying for a baby with his then-girlfriend, but nothing happened and tests revealed he had a low sperm count. They had three tries at IVF before giving up. The sad thing is that, when he was younger, he got a couple of girlfriends pregnant 'but for some reason I was afraid' and they had abortions. He believes that now the doctors could probably whistle up a baby for him, but he is not sure he wants one. 'I am perfectly happy. I would like to have had children but then another voice in me says, "Do you really want children?" I'm very divided on these issues.' Frankly, it is impossible to imagine a child toddling round the immaculate polished surfaces of Melbury Road. It is a 48-room shrine to a man who has organized his life *exactly* how he likes it, and if loneliness is the price you pay for perfection, then Winner is happy to pay it.

Reproduced by permission of *The Observer*.

Jonathan Ross

7 December 1997

Just as tulips are rather dull when they are in peak condition and become more interesting and idiosyncratic as they wilt, so, I find, with celebs. This is not a taste much encouraged by editors – journalists are supposed to admire what's hot, not what's not – but I find something terribly samey about successful people whereas the cold breath of failure brings an interesting twist to their petals. This is by way of defiant apology for writing about Jonathan Ross, whose career is not by any means at its peak. Too bad. I have a deep affection for him, and know of only one serious stain on his character which I shall blurt out quickly with my eyes shut: his children are named Betty Kitten, Harvey and Honey Kinny. I know, I know, it's hard to forgive but we must do our best.

I can't understand why so many people seem to dislike Jonathan Ross, but they do – the usual accusation is that he is 'loud-mouthed'. In truth, he *does* talk very loudly – growing up as the third of six children, five of them boys, he probably had to shout to make himself heard. But presumably loud-mouthed in this context means cocky. Certainly, he never did the false-modesty thing you're supposed to do in showbiz, of saying he couldn't understand why he was so successful. He would say he was successful because he was good at his job. And he was always happy to talk about money, which I suppose was a mistake, and to say that he could pick up £10,000 for speaking at a business conference or £5,000 for a personal appearance. He admitted that he had two mortgages, for £230,000 and £350,000 (actually, he still does), and fatally said in 1992 that it didn't worry him because 'I'm always going to have a huge disposable income.' It must have come across as boasting, though I'd say it was commendable frankness allied to youthful naivety – interviewers asked how much he earned and he told them. Would that all interviewees could be so frank! It seems to me that he's been punished for honesty.

And punished he certainly has been. It is some years since he had a hit show, and his career now looks very rickety. The day before I met him, ITV had dropped his exclusive contract: he will still work for them, but on a freelance basis. He can't feel so confident about always having a huge disposable income – there was a moment, four years ago, when he and his wife Jane thought they might have to sell their house in Hampstead before they'd even moved in. And they couldn't sell (and still haven't sold) their old house in Kentish Town, north London – it dropped in value and was stuck in negative equity. For much of 1994, he recalls, he and Jane just lay in bed going oh-oh, worrying about whether they'd still have a roof over their heads. It looked as though Jonathan Ross was taking the Simon Dee slide from television stardom to the dole queue.

Fortunately, he's still here, because there are enough commissioning editors who like and admire him to give him a second, third, fourth and fifth chance. And Jane Goldman, his wife, a former pop journalist, produced a couple of books based on *The X Files* which stayed on the bestseller lists for almost a full year. So things are not as bad as they were. But he has had to eat terrible humble pie. Once, he was offered a show after his friend Danny Baker had already turned it down – 'So God knows how far down the fucking pecking order I was!' And the other day Dale Winton – Dale Winton! – gave him career advice, which he felt was 'untoward'.

All these people keep trying to rescue him. Chris Evans offered to produce him and he likes Chris Evans and thinks he's a talented guy, but basically Chris Evans is only Jonathan Ross six years ago. Ross remembers, with embarrassment, that when he was at the same stage as Chris Evans is now, he befriended Peter Cook and told him he would put him on television – 'As if no one else had ever thought of that! I said, "What we'll do first is, we'll make a non-broadcast pilot," and Peter said, "Really? Why not make it a non-broadcast series?"'

Anyway, it was a slightly bruised, cautious, occasionally embittered Wossy I met this time, not the gloriously confident wunderkind I interviewed in 1990. He said he used to be too obliging, and he is not so obliging now. He went into a terrible grouch when I said I wanted to come to his house – 'What is this? *Hello!* magazine?' – but when I arrived, he was happy to show me round: zebra carpets, leopard curtains, Barbie kitchen and all. Even the baby, I was distressed to notice, was wearing lipstick-pink velour flares. His study is in a different style. Hidden behind a secret door in a wall of faux bookshelves, it contains state-of-the-art computers, an impressive film reference library, and some of his vast collection of vintage comics – i.e. a rich grown-up's version of a teenage geek's bedroom. A friend told him the other day, 'You know what this says to me? Too much money!'

I found the decor surprising, but the biggest surprise was meeting his father in the kitchen. This led me to revise my whole picture of Jonathan's background – he has always described himself as a lorry-driver's son from an 'average working-class family' in Leytonstone. But there is nothing averagely working-class about the well-dressed, well-spoken, dryly witty Mr Ross I meet – these days he is a chauffeur for a limo company, and stays at Jonathan's when he has a job in town so he can see his grandchildren. He is *far* better-spoken than his son.

Anyway, they can't have been a typical working-class family – their mother worked as an extra on *EastEnders* and put them in for television commercials (Jonathan did Rice Krispies and Persil), and most of the children went to university and ended up in film or television. Jonathan went straight from university to television, following in the wake of his eldest brother, Paul, who was a producer for the *Six o'clock Show*. After five years as a Channel 4 researcher, Jonathan and his partner Alan Marke devised *The Last Resort*. They spent months trying to find a presenter. Once, Jonathan approached Jeremy Hardy in the toilet after a gig and asked him to do it, but he said fuck off. 'And how we laugh' – Jonathan says sourly – 'when we meet now!' Of course, he wanted to present it himself, but was embarrassed about admitting it.

But finally the commissioning editor said, 'Why don't you try?' and he said, 'Who me?' and shot to fame.

Now, a decade later, he is doing *The Last Resort* again – making a special one-off revival as part of Channel 4's fifteenth anniversary celebration. Preparing for the show has meant looking at old recordings. 'I watched one and it was possibly the worst TV show I've seen in my life. Of course I still make mistakes, but really! We had Bill G. Stewart on, who produced *Bless This House,* and I was asking about Sid James because I'm quite a Sid James fan. And I said, "Is it true Sid was a diamond smuggler?" and Bill said, "No, I don't think so, but I've got some fabulous stories about him being a gambler." And I said, "Really? Tell me about your new show." Fancy being offered a feed like that! I was *such* an arsehole, I just think, "How come I was allowed to do this job?" And the weird thing about the whole setup I was involved in then is that probably no one said to me afterwards, "That was crap."'

The Last Resort ran from 1986 to 1988, and by the end of that time he was famous. But his head wasn't turned at that stage, he says, because he was so green and nervous and work-obsessed, he didn't really notice. He was very puzzled the first time someone asked for his autograph. He thinks in retrospect that girls probably threw themselves at him but 'I was always so awful at recognizing when someone was flirting with me, I'm sure I missed some fantastic opportunities!' He recalls a Channel 4 commissioning editor asking him to a dinner party: 'I was sitting there and I said, "Oh this is very nice, do you do this all the time?" and he said, "No – this is an occasion." And I said, "Oh, what's the occasion?" and he said, "Well, we just launched your show!" And I thought, "Jeezus, that's fucking weird!" – I'd never been to a dinner party before so it felt weird anyway.'

The money was good but not stupendous – £500 a show – 'So it's not like you're going to charter a jet and suddenly go on holiday with Richard Harris. It was more like thinking, "Oh, I could afford to go to Paris for the weekend." But I was quite timid. I didn't really know how to do that sort of thing.' Then he acquired a sharp manager, Gary Farrow, and started doing lucrative 'spin-offs' – advertisements and business conferences and personal appearances. By now, he was also going out with Jane Goldman who, though only sixteen when he met her, was far more sophisticated than he was, having grown up in

Hampstead, and travelled with her parents. She worked as a pop journalist, so she knew the value of fame. They met (he is embarrassed to recall) at Stringfellow's, and he was shocked when she told him her age, but they started going out together and married in 1988, in Las Vegas, when she turned eighteen. Jonathan's parents started a family at eighteen, so it didn't seem too young to him.

Meanwhile, Channel 4 was saying politely, 'What do you want to do next, Jonathan?' and he made documentaries and interviewed film directors (this was some of his best work) and his bandwagon rolled along. He set up a production company called Channel X with Alan Marke, and started hiring directors and performers. They had a hit with Vic Reeves, and were ticking over very nicely with a turnover of £10 million at one stage. Jonathan would go into Channel X's groovy offices every day and park in his expensive parking space and hold meetings and discuss whether he should commute to America and become the next David Frost, or whether he should conquer prime time and become the next Wogan. He stood in for Wogan very successfully in 1990, and then did his own three-nights-a-week Channel 4 chat show, not so successfully. He wanted to go mainstream, he said, because he didn't know where else to push his career. But, of course, as soon as he went mainstream, his cult late-night audience deserted him.

By now his head was beginning to be turned by fame. 'I don't think I ever turned into a *complete* wanker, where I thought I was special because I was on TV; I've never thought that. But I think – and perhaps this happened to Chris Evans a bit – I went through a phase where, because everyone's saying you're marvellous, you do think, "Yes, I'm really good at this." Sometimes, when Chris runs around saying he's going to produce me and do this and that – it's very well-meaning, but you think, "Well your show isn't *such* a shining example of innovative television." He's very full of the joys of his own brilliance at the moment, and he *is* very talented, but I expect he's not as talented as he actually believes himself to be. It's the vanity of youth, is what it is.'

Jonathan's problem is what he calls 'a mad kind of hyper-obligingness' whereby he would say yes to almost anything – for instance, he invested heavily in a vintage comics shop just because someone asked him to. He was drinking too much, making a fool of himself at parties, and his weight increased to fifteen stone. Give the period, and the general extravagance of his lifestyle, it would be strange if cocaine didn't come into it somewhere, but my question produced a most uncharacteristic pause for thought, and the cautious answer: 'The reason I'm loath to say anything about cocaine is it's fine in the *Observer*, but anything you say then becomes front-page in the *Sun*. There were certain social nights out we had with people in showbiz which were excessive, but I don't tend to do them any more.'

Anyway, it was in 1993 that things went belly-up. It started with a programme called *Saturday Zoo* which he devised and launched for Channel 4. It was good in parts – it had Joanna Lumley and Steve Coogan – but its audience never got beyond 2 million, and the critics were hostile. And he felt Channel 4 wasn't supporting the programme as much as it should, so when he was asked if he wanted to do another series, he said no. 'I thought, "Well fucking hell, I'm technically one of the best at doing this in the country, but I still only get audiences of 2 million," and it used to annoy me when I'd see people doing these shows everyone was talking about that got huge viewing figures and that I thought were not very good. You know, I'd like some of that attention, please.'

He blamed the failure of *Saturday Zoo* on his production company. He felt he was working to feed its now enormous payroll, so he walked out, leaving all his capital behind. He thought Marke would walk out with him, but he didn't (Jane has not spoken to Marke since). 'Then I found myself alone with no back-up. And I didn't realize quite how much I'd relied on my partner.' Financially, he was in dire straits because he had no capital, no immediate income, a new baby on the way and two enormous mortgages. 'It was a pretty awful time. I worried about whether we'd be able to keep this house, because I'd suddenly got nothing on the table. Jane and I spent a lot of time in bed, going oh-oh, because I think you just retreat to the womb. We had an awful Christmas that year, the whole family.'

He dithered endlessly over whether to sign a deal with the BBC, but eventually didn't. And there was a long period when he was negotiating with different producers about different shows – 'I mean, some of the shows I did, I don't look back at with any great degree of pride, but the shows I turned down! I got offered a fortune to do a family show opposite the *Gladiators* and the big gimmick was that if the family wasn't doing well, you hoisted their granny up higher and higher! [That was the show Danny Baker had already turned down.] I had any amount of meetings, but in the end I just couldn't go through with it. The problem, I now realize, was me not quite knowing what I wanted to do, because I was very disillusioned with my own judgement which had led me down such a terrible cul-de-sac.'

In the end, he resigned himself to just being a good television hack. 'Maybe I made a decision not to do shows that I cared about quite so strongly for a while – I've had a few years of that, where you wind up doing shows you don't really want to do. But – you know, I work for a living. It's a job. I thought maybe I should coast for a while. And with the children, obviously, you want to make sure you're financially stable, so if someone says, "We've got this slot – ten shows in the summer" and it's a vast amount of money, you go OK. It's perhaps a tad soul-destroying, but at the same time it's quite a useful lesson.'

On the personal level, he says, things improved after his break with Channel X. He made a new resolve to discuss everything with Jane, and not to do daft things like taking on comics shops without consulting her. 'I think, in terms of our relationship, it probably was a good thing. Though I still occasionally don't listen or don't talk as much as I should.' He went on a diet and cut out alcohol for a year, got down to twelve and a half stone and felt terrific, and 'actually had muscles for the first time'. The only drawback was that, 'I think I probably became a bit dull, company-wise. There's a line in a Joyce Carol Oates story about a person who doesn't drink, and she says it's like watching all your friends climb on board a cruise ship and they sail away and you're left on the beach alone. You do miss out on the social side of life. So then I thought, "Well, hold on, this is silly because you live in a city where most of the social life doesn't revolve around the beach, it revolves around going out to dinner and getting pissed." So I got a bit of balance back. But I don't drink much at home. The only thing I miss – the thing I loved about that period – was that I used to read a lot more, because you find yourself going to bed stone-cold sober and you can squeeze in an hour's reading.'

His daily life centres on the family – he takes the two older children to school in the mornings, brings Jane breakfast in bed because she's still breast-feeding, plays with the children when they get back from school. 'Sometimes it gets a bit boring. You think, "Oh I don't really want to watch *Postman Pat* again", but I do find the children terribly entertaining and rewarding and pleasant to be with.' Consequently, he says, the tabloids have never really found any dirt on him because there isn't any to be found. He was never a Lothario: he had just one one-night stand in his life, and even then spent weeks on the phone to the girl afterwards, apologizing. When he interviewed Madonna and she offered to suck his toes, he refused because Jane wouldn't have liked it. He also refused to kiss the model Caprice in his recent Pizza Hut commercials because he didn't want the children to see it.

But he admits that, 'Sometimes I feel tempted now, when I look at attractive women and realize that sometimes, perhaps, fairly casual meaningless sex is available to me, and it might be fun. But I've never really had it. One of the things that stops me is I know I would just *die* if I read about it in the papers, and I would never put Jane through that – although as a mature adult I don't think, if I did want to sleep with someone, she'd be that bothered. But imagine her having to read in the papers some girl saying, "He did this and he said that" – I think that would be awful, and it shows such a lack of respect for the person you're with. So I wouldn't do that.'

In theory, he should be blissfully happy – he has Jane, he has the children, he has a nice house in Hampstead, a good income and, as he says, 'We have a lovely fun lifestyle – here I am, talking about myself for hours and that's considered *work*!' But he has lost one great love, his love of television. It somehow soured, not with failure, but with success: he was a victim of answered prayers. Even when I interviewed him in 1990, when he was still at his peak, he talked about the difficulty of keeping his self-respect. It was as if he found his own success faintly disgusting, as if the great mystery and wonder of television had turned out to be a sham. He had studied it so hard in the 1980s, watched all the old Simon Dees and Parkies and Wogans (he admired Wogan when it was very unfashionable to do so), searched hard to find new techniques, new formats, to break the mould. And then it turned out television didn't really care: it just wanted new faces, any faces, and got bored with them as soon as they were familiar.

'When we had our first child,' he recalls, 'I was still going to the office every day and I'd sit there and people would come and see me and have meetings about fatuous projects that were never going to happen – we were all so puffed-up with our fucking place in the mediaocracy – and then I thought, "What are you actually doing with your life? This is complete and utter junk." I look at TV, I look at most modern forms of entertainment, and I think, "This is all really inherently worthless." I mean it *is*. I'm sure one day people will say, "We've had enough. Can't we just go back to having local passion plays?" But of course that's what I feed off to a large extent, and when you loathe what you feed off, sometimes you can wind up not liking yourself.

'But I think I've got it in a degree of perspective now – I think, "Well, hold on, it's sort of harmless, and you enjoy doing it and it's your *job*." And even if I wanted to change jobs, I probably couldn't. But I think what's helped me is realizing its worthlessness and realizing that the important thing – really the *only* thing you can do – is try and raise your children in a nice way, and make sure you are *kind* to the rest of the world. I don't consider myself to be an *artist* or anything ludicrous like that. I feel like a talented craftsman, and you think, "Sometimes you don't make the table *you* want, you make a table that someone just wants to eat on." So, of course, no one's going to make a big fuss and say, "Wow, you're doing something new with tables!" In a way, I feel quite heartened that people do sometimes see me as working beneath myself. Sometimes people stop me in the street and say, "*Why* are you doing this?" And I think, "What's it got to do with you?" – but it's rather sweet of them really.'

Reproduced by permission of *The Observer*.

Felicity Kendal

23 February 1997

You can get quite sick – if you are a woman – reading Felicity Kendal's press cuttings. They consist of endless male journalists going all googly-eyed and using words like 'delectable' and 'cuddlesome'. Hardened hacks who never knowingly write purple prose start waxing lyrical about her gurgling giggle or her honey hair (dyed I may say). Declaring love for Felicity Kendal seems to be a necessary English male assertion of heterosexuality, meaning no more than, 'I am normal; I am English; I'm a man.' She is known to be Paddy Ashdown's favourite pin-up but she's probably John Major's and Tony Blair's too. Wives never seem to mind – she is the ultimate safe sex symbol.

She represents, in blokish breasts, some image of the eternal feminine. But 'cuddlesome' rather than sexy – the conventional cliché is that one would like to snuggle up with her under the duvet. Whether hanky-panky is then meant to transpire is left unclear. I imagine not. I imagine that bottom-smacking and the exchange of Beatrix Potter nicknames would suffice. Personally, if a man says he fancies Felicity Kendal, I take it as a sign that he is sexually defunct. But don't mind me, I'm jealous.

Anyway, this is all terribly unfair. Felicity Kendal is not to blame for her image; in fact, Felicity Kendal has nothing to do with her image. The image is entirely based on the character she played in *The Good Life* all those years ago, Richard Briers's little wifey Barbara, who was always so sweet and so supportive and so good-humoured and altogether perfect. I imagine most women watching it wondered, as I did, why she stayed with her pathetic hangdog creep of a husband, but to men that would have been precisely the appeal – he *was* a creep and yet she adored him. *The Good Life* went through eight series in the 1970s and was watched, at times, by 18 million viewers, making it one of the most popular sitcoms ever made. The weird thing is that, at the time, Felicity Kendal didn't seem to make much impact – it was Penelope Keith, as the bossy neighbour, who completely stole the show. But obviously 'Felicity Kendal' (meaning Barbara) somehow seeped into the national male consciousness as the image of the perfect helpmeet who would never be ratty. And thus the manhood of England took her into their duvets.

But this is not the real Felicity Kendal. The real Felicity Kendal is an actress, and a good one, and a tough cookie. Men see her as soft: I see her as hard – hard-working, hard-headed, hard cheese if you want x and she wants y – she always gets her own way. Thus, although I put up a little strop about how I wanted to interview her at home, I ended up interviewing her in a hotel, as she wanted. But then she was punctual and friendly and remembered that we'd met before, and in no time at all I was being charmed, and she was making me laugh, and I was thinking, 'Oh well, at least she's got a sense of humour.' Of course, she looked wonderful, wonderful skin, hair, figure – even her neck is unlined – though I was secretly gratified to notice her hands looked older than mine, hideous knotted bony claws with crimson talons.

She said she'd had a 'terrible' morning, though when I asked her to expand, she only said that her son Jake, nine, had trod in some dogshit as he was getting into the car, making her late for the school run. She had spotted the dogshit the night before and actually taken the trouble to move it, but Jake had managed to step in it anyway. So then she was late for the school run and her whole morning, she said, was ruined. Odd. Surely nine-year-old boys tread in dogshit every day. Is she one of those people with an absolute horror of dirt? Or was she really saying that she was having a terrible morning because she was meeting me? I do feel this undercurrent in Felicity Kendal – a deeply buried aggression that wants to scream 'I hate you, I hate you' but puts on a sweet face and behaves politely because that is what she has been trained to do. Her mother always taught her that you could achieve as much by asking people nicely as by screaming and shouting. Maybe you can – but at some cost, I think, to honesty.

Anyway, whether she hates it or not she is here, valiantly plugging her new play, as she always does. Other, grander actors, like Michael Gambon or Paul Scofield, can refuse to do it, but she says reasonably, 'It would be somehow pretentious if I did because I don't *mind*.' She is nothing if not a trouper. One time she gave an interview saying that her father had just had a stroke, and she longed to be at his bedside, but, of course, she did the interview rather than rushing to the hospital – the show must go on.

The plug this time is for the new Peter Hall season at the Old Vic, in which she plays the lead in *Waste*, an Edwardian melodrama, and then (the prize for her) Madame Arkadina in *The Seagull*. She is committed to the Old Vic until the end of the year and says she likes 'the security blanket' of being part of a company. And she enjoys working for Sir Peter Hall – this will be the seventh time he has directed her – because, 'He's such fun and he gives you a courage that I don't always have. And even if something doesn't work, he doesn't make you feel it's the be-all and end-all. He gives you a feeling of *balance*, that it's terribly important but it isn't brain surgery . . .'

Her last job – Peter Hall's production of Feydeau's *Mind Millie for Me* – finished six months ago, so she has had rather a long time 'resting'. She says she uses these periods to 'pay her dues' as a mother – to do the school run and sew on nametapes for Jake (she also has a 24-year-old son, Charlie, who still lives with her), but she gets rattled when she is out of work for too long. She has a large house in Chelsea to maintain, and a father in a nursing home, and although her ex-husband Michael Rudman supports their son, she still has plenty of bills to pay. In theory, she should be rich from repeats of *The Good Life* (it is still going strong in the US), but the BBC sold it outright and she got about £700. 'I know! Pain! Never mind.'

This 'never mind' is quite a refrain in her conversation. She uses it again when talking of her father Geoffrey Kendal, who has been lying paralysed in a nursing home for almost four years, after a series of strokes. 'He is alive, and not alive. There is a clinical term for it, PVS [permanent vegetative state], which sounds like a plastic tablecloth, and he's not far off it. He's on a tube that feeds him, he can neither move nor speak nor communicate – my family aren't very good at dying.' Her mother died in 1992 and then her father amazed everyone by having an affair with her nurse when he was eighty-four. Felicity found this disconcerting at the time, but now, 'There's a bit of you looking at him lying there that thinks I can't stand this, and then you think, never mind, he had a wonderful life.'

If you have seen the early Merchant-Ivory film *Shakespeare-Wallah* you know all about the Kendals, but in case you haven't – her father was one of the actor-managers who ran concert parties for ENSA during the war, and then just went on, taking a touring company round India, playing the classics. He and his wife Laura played the leads and their daughters Jennifer and Felicity did backstage chores when they weren't needed on stage. Consequently, Felicity had almost no schooling and came to England aged seventeen, unqualified to do anything but act. Her sister Jennifer, who was twelve years older, went on touring with her parents until she married the Indian film star Shashi Kapoor. She died of cancer in 1984 at the age of forty-nine.

Felicity turned fifty last September, and says the only thing she disliked was remembering that her sister didn't reach that age. 'I found it very shocking to suddenly be older than her. There's so much to say and do and see and read and good times to have, and I hate to think that this age is where she stopped.' But she says her sister 'seemed older than I am now. She looked 102, to be honest. I think it was a lot to do with illness.' They were very different in temperament as well as looks – Jennifer took after their father, Felicity their mother. And whereas Jennifer seemed to age prematurely, Felicity's looks have steadily improved with age – photographs of her in her twenties show a terribly bun-faced woman, all cheeks, no eyes.

I told her that, even at fifty, she seems to be a femme fatale who can have any man she wants, and she did a silvery laugh and would have tapped me with her fan if she had happened to have had one. 'Really! Now Lynn! Come on!' Well, I persisted, she does seem to have taken men when she's wanted them. 'Maybe they've taken *me* when they wanted!' OK, I said, fed up with all this Restoration archness: specifically, Tom Stoppard . . . 'I don't talk about Tom Stoppard, you know, Lynn. We have a pact never to talk about each other. We *can't*. It's an agreement.'

She goes on: 'I've been married twice and I've been divorced twice, and I think actually, to be quite honest, it's because I *don't* talk about it that it's interesting. I'm very old-fashioned in that I have a tremendous need to protect a certain area: my slightly Victorian upbringing comes into play and I bring down the blind. It's a very comfortable blind, but I suppose that probably leads ... Everything is pretend, and if you don't know about something sometimes, you can imagine something much more interesting than the bare bones of reality. But on the other hand, I don't intend to tell you the bare bones of reality either!'

Damn. I shall have to sketch them as best I can. To say she has been married twice and divorced twice is a gross over-simplification. She married her first husband, the actor Drewe Henley, in 1968, and had a son, Charlie, by him. She left him for Robert Bolt, then returned, before divorcing in 1979. She is supposed to have had an affair with Tom Courtenay around this time. She married the Texan theatre director Michael Rudman in 1983, and had a son by him, Jacob (Jake), in 1988. But soon afterwards the marriage seemed to go sour and in September 1990 she moved out and began being seen around town with Tom Stoppard. On Christmas Eve 1990, he officially separated from his wife of eighteen years, Dr Miriam Stoppard.

The tabloids were quite excited by these goings-on, and Kendal was doorstepped, with cameramen camped outside her house. Most people react with horror to this experience, but she found it 'quite interesting. It was nothing serious, just four or five people and then it dribbled down to one, sitting in his car with a cup of tea, rather sweet, really. It only lasted three or four days and then something more interesting happened and they moved on – it's a slightly depressing thought that it depends on how boring the news is that you get that much coverage.'

For most of 1991 she and Stoppard appeared at parties and premières together and everyone expected them to marry when their respective divorces came through. But it didn't happen. Nevertheless, he went on writing plays for her – *Arcadia* in 1994 and *Indian Ink* in 1995, the latter clearly inspired by her own Indian background. But even friends didn't seem to know if they were still together. One told Nigel Dempster, 'They have what you might call an interesting arrangement; basically, they can't live with each other, but they don't want to live without each other.'

So who broke up whose marriage and why? The rumour at the time was that Felicity Kendal left Michael Rudman when she received anonymous letters telling her that he was having an affair, and that Stoppard 'consoled' her in her distress. But what always puzzled me was why, if she was going to fall for Tom Stoppard or vice versa, they didn't do it years earlier. After all, they had known each other from at least 1981, when she worked with him in *On the Razzle* and, significantly, in 1982, he wrote a play called *The Real Thing* in which an actress leaves her marriage to go off with a tall, dark playwright. But the very next year, she married Rudman, before working with Stoppard again on *Jumpers* in 1985 and *Hapgood* in 1988.

The latter might have marked the beginning of the end of her marriage, because Rudman didn't like her going back to work immediately after their baby was born. She admits, 'It was too soon. But you know, you do it and it's done.' She says it happened by accident. She was all set to start rehearsals for *Hapgood* when she fell pregnant, and Stoppard agreed to postpone the opening until after the baby. She allowed herself six weeks before starting rehearsals but the baby was late, so she went back to work when Jake was less than a month old. Was that why her marriage broke up? 'No, not at all. Outside forces, I think, very rarely have anything to do with what goes on in a marriage. People say, you know, "Oh, if only you hadn't done this, or that, he wouldn't have left you" – but, in fact, he probably would have done. I mean, that's the sort of way I *have* to look at it, otherwise ...' Otherwise, presumably, she would have to blame herself. Never mind.

There were reports that Rudman was very bitter about their break-up, and cut Felicity's face out of all the family photographs. He was also dismissed from his job as artistic director of Chichester Festival in 1991, amid rumours that he was 'ill'. But by the end of 1993, she was on good terms with him again and saying, 'He's wonderful, Michael. We always spend Christmas together, always. We spend every weekend together, more or less. We have a very, very close relationship.' At the time, she also said she was still close to Tom Stoppard, but they have not been seen together for some time, whereas she and Rudman have been spotted out on the town, even at synagogue. Kendal converted to Judaism before Jacob was born and is, she says, still Jewish – 'You can't not be. I'm not Orthodox, but certainly Jacob will have a bar mitzvah.' Jacob sees his father 'all the time'. So might she and Rudman get back together? 'I don't know – that's behind the blinds, that one.'

She has always said that she has only lived with two men in her life (her husbands) and when I ask if this is still true, she laughs. 'Yes. Shocking isn't it?' She points out that Elizabeth Taylor operates by the same rule, but you would think it might have occurred to her by now that Elizabeth Taylor is not a good marital role model. Wouldn't it be quite a good idea to try living with the next Mr Right before marriage? 'I've never said I won't. But I haven't – I just don't. I do have a rather exaggerated sense of responsibility to my children – I've probably got it out of proportion, but I like it out of proportion. I'm going back now to my hot youth. It's totally irrelevant because I'm far too old to be in that world. I mean I'm *not* too old – people can do it till their eighties, as my father proved – but I am in my head. I remember, when I first left Charlie's father, I was living by myself and my mother would babysit, and when you're – however old I was, twenty-five maybe, twenty-eight – you're still very young – but I could never, ever, whoever I was dating, bridge the gap. And it wasn't because I thought it was wrong, I just didn't feel comfortable with it. Bear in mind I was brought up in India in a very, very strict environment and I arrived in the 1960s and it was Wow! What is going on here? I couldn't believe it.'

I think this is perhaps the key to her character. She refers often to her 'Victorian' upbringing and no doubt her parents taught her that a woman mustn't 'cheapen herself' by living with a man without securing a wedding ring. There was nothing unusual about being brought up with this attitude in the 1950s. What is unusual is retaining it in the 1990s, as though feminism never happened. It is almost quaint. But Kendal strikes me as someone who is so inflexible (she calls herself 'pig-headed') that, having decided on something, she will stick with it against all reason.

I can't see her as a *grande horizontale* because I think she is probably too conventional, and too brisk. But, of course, I could be wrong about that – she has certainly pulled some very dishy men in her time. She claims to be 'a conformist' and 'a tremendous believer in codes of behaviour and moral laws'. She can often sound quite reactionary – she went into a great lecture to me about how *The Good Life* was really about loyalty and how everyone is so disloyal nowadays. I think she sees herself as a moralist in an immoral world. But it sometimes seems that she is paying lip service to conventional pieties rather than actually living them – for all her 'exaggerated sense of responsibility to her children', she *did* go back to work when her baby was less than a month old. And I was quite shocked by her saying that she waited until she was out of work to 'pay her dues' as a mother – it smacks of the American 'quality time' idea that you can slot in a bit of parent duty when you happen to find a gap in your diary.

In the past, she has often said she would hate to live alone and that her idea of hell was 'being totally independent without a man'. But she also says, 'I don't suit marriage. I'm just difficult to be with, I'm always absolutely sure I'm right.' This is quite an impasse. So what is she to do? 'I'm happy with my independence at that moment, and I live with my two boys *exactly* how I want. I'm a great one for making the best of things and being quite happy.'

The obvious thing to do in her situation is to take a toy boy, but when I asked if she would contemplate it, she laughed. 'You know, I don't think that's something you could contemplate unless you *were* contemplating it! You don't set out thinking "I must look through Yellow Pages!"'

'But don't men your own age seem a bit old?'

'What *for*, Lynn? It depends what you want them for.'

'I always think men of fifty seem so stick-in-the-mud.'

'I don't think they do. I don't know any stick-in-the-muds. One of the attractive things about being older in the make-believe world of the theatre is that everybody's acting ten years younger anyway, and you don't get to the point where you wind down or retire, so nobody goes through a change. We are all like rather old children.'

So no toy boy, then. I wonder who she *is* going out with? She went into a sudden riff apropos of nothing about how exciting it must be to be a newspaper editor, which made me do a quick mental tour of newspaper editors. As far as I know, they're all married apart from Andrew Neil . . . Perish the thought.

Tom Stoppard called her 'a bossy blonde', and that seems accurate. I think of her as pragmatic, efficient, practical, brisk, well-organized, probably quite good at money, shrewd about people, above all *realistic*, not self-deluding as actors tend to be. A century ago, she would have made a very good district commissioner's wife, but it is strange to find this sort of personality in an actress. I suppose the explanation is that she is merely following in her parents' footsteps, so it is yet another manifestation of her conventionality.

As an actress, her only ambition now is to keep working – 'That's an ambition in itself and a very strong one.' Any Hollywood hopes she might have harboured died a long time ago, when she was auditioned for Miss Moneypenny in the Bond films and blew it. Her television career took a knock in 1994 when she starred in the sitcom *Honey for Tea* and was clobbered by the critics. She still feels sore about that, and points out that many successful television series got off to a bad start, but the BBC pulled the plug after six episodes. On the other hand, her theatrical reputation has gone from strength to strength and, if she can pull off Madame Arkadina this year, she will be getting into the Diana Rigg league. She might just do it: she has a habit of surprising people. But she will have to shed all her caution and her sugar coating. We await our surprise.

Reproduced by permission of *The Observer*.

Redmond O'Hanlon

13 October 1996

A couple of weeks ago Dr Redmond O'Hanlon had a nasty experience in a hotel restaurant in Rotterdam. He was dining with his Dutch publisher, and 'Emile got me drunk, or I got myself drunk', and he realized, at the end of the meal, that he had lost his fetish. This disgusting object, made of monkey fur and supposedly containing a child's finger, was given to him by a Congolese witch-doctor six years before. 'I like to think I kept calm about it,' says O'Hanlon – his face blanching even as he speaks – but he was distraught enough to persuade the hotel manager to put six members of staff on combing through the hotel dustbins. 'I think they realized that losing a fetish was like losing your blue blanket,' he explains, though the fact that he had just been on Dutch television may have helped. Anyway, they found the fetish and O'Hanlon was saved. But phew!

O'Hanlon is still mourning the loss of his manuscript, *Congo Journey*. He went to the Congo for five months in 1989 and has been writing about it for six years since – he only stopped on 30 July when his editor came in and snatched the manuscript away. 'He thought I was becoming obsessed. I *was* obsessed. Still am a bit actually – it becomes far more real as the years go by.' He was £30,000 in debt and getting deeper by the day; he hadn't seen any friends for two years because he'd decided he could only write at night, but he just couldn't bear to stop.

Congo Journey is very different to O'Hanlon's two previous travel books, *Into the Heart of Borneo* and *In Trouble Again*. It is (alas!) not nearly so funny but altogether darker, more soul-searching, more ambitious. It is his *Heart of Darkness* – a perilous journey into the uncharted jungle of his brain, a meditation on reality and religion, a memoir of his childhood. In his previous books, he often seemed 'mad' but in a jovial, eccentric we're-all-mad-here sort of way – this time he *really* seems mad and loses all sense of narrative control. It is not so much a flawed as a cracked masterpiece. Readers probably think of him as a jokey, light writer, but he is actually aiming far higher than that. When I asked who he thought he was competing against (expecting names like Bruce Chatwin or Jonathan Raban), he said, well, Tolstoy or Gogol, basically. It is this hugeness of ambition that makes him so interesting. *Congo Journey* is not his *Dead Souls*, but one lives in hope that the next one might be. If he doesn't go completely barking first.

His house is madness visible – a smallish Oxfordshire cottage jumbled to the rafters with the terrifying lumber of O'Hanlon's brain. Everything he has ever valued is stacked up around him – stuffed animals he made at school, skulls, prints and posters from university, a giant pelican, a mummified frog, hundreds of photographs of pygmies and Yanomami indians, and thousands of books arranged according to some O'Hanlonesque notion of the evolution of ideas – all piled against the walls as bulwarks against reality. He says that Belinda, his wife, made him tidy up yesterday because I was coming. 'Really? Where?' 'I made that path across the floor.'

He looks older than forty-nine. He has thickets of white hair sprouting in unusual, nineteenth-century, places. He is wearing his trousers tucked into two pairs of socks, as a precaution against chiggers and leeches and those deadly Cotswold cobras. Belinda hovers in the background, looking like a Burne-Jones angel, though actually she is a brilliant businesswoman who founded the Oxford dress shop Annabelinda, which our mutual friend Howard Marks used as cover for his early drug-smuggling career. Their two beautiful blond children, Puffin and Galen, come to say hello and Puffin kindly shows me her pet rat. O'Hanlon has prepared a tea consisting of red wine, white wine, and whisky.

When I ask if I can smoke, he produces an enormous box of King Edward Invincible De Luxe cigars and begs me to take them. Two or three times during the conversation he leans forward and kisses me, a normal O'Hanlon *politesse*. We knew each other slightly at Oxford and in fact, he tells me, I was at the party in his room at Merton where he first met Belinda. He is one of the few people on earth who has read my book *The Heyday of Natural History* so he fondly imagines that we are going to spend the afternoon discussing pre-Darwinian naturalists.

The great tragedy of O'Hanlon's life is that he was born in the wrong century – he should have been there when *On the Origin of Species* was published. He had all the right qualifications to be an eminent Victorian naturalist – his father was a vicar who believed in natural theology, and encouraged his boyhood interest in bird-watching and entomology. But because of the tiresome twentieth-century insistence on maths, O'Hanlon couldn't do science at university (though he came from a good science school, Marlborough) and had to read English at Oxford. He was thrown out in his first year for writing a pornographic novel but he managed to get back and do a PhD, which he later published as 'The influence of scientific thought on Conrad's fiction'. He was briefly an Oxford don, but sacked for teaching his students the wrong century. He was also a research fellow at St Anthony's where he saw his job as bringing famous people to dinner at high table – his greatest coup was getting Terry Wogan – but that finished when he ran out of celebs. He was, until last year, an editor on the *Times Literary Supplement* but Belinda made him give it up after demonstrating that he was only earning about 7p an hour, what with his train fare to London and heavy lunches. Cruel Belinda!

His travel writing career started almost casually in 1983 when his friend James Fenton, the poet and journalist, suggested a holiday expedition to Borneo. 'But for James, I think I'd still be under the table, in a black depression.' The original idea was that Fenton would write and O'Hanlon take photographs, but in the end O'Hanlon did the book, *Into the Heart of Borneo*, as a light-hearted squib. It took him just a year and was an international bestseller.

Unfortunately, when O'Hanlon suggested another expedition, to the Amazon, Fenton replied: 'I would not go with you to High Wycombe.' So O'Hanlon found Simon Stockton, casino operator, ladykiller, and one of the great characters of twentieth-century literature, for *In Trouble Again*. But Simon, like Fenton, said never, never again, so this time

O'Hanlon took another friend, Professor Lary Shaffer, an American zoologist and all-round good egg. O'Hanlon was a little disconcerted when Lary admitted, just as they were setting out, that he had multiple sclerosis, but he survived. In fact it was O'Hanlon who almost died, in Brazzaville, from malaria.

Belinda made the great mistake of ringing him and was horrified when she heard his voice. 'Normally I don't worry about him because he's big and strong and charming and everybody loves him so I just always assume he's fine. But this last time he sent quite a lot of letters, saying bizarre things like "The Congo is the best-run country I've ever been to", so I eventually twigged that he must want me to ring. When Redmond came to the phone, he could hardly speak. And then I was really worried and it made me very miserable, so I'm never going to ring or contact him again, because it's too upsetting.'

O'Hanlon always maintains that he becomes a different character when travelling – fit, energetic, positive, with no time to be depressed. I rang Lary Shaffer in the States and he confirmed it. 'Of course there's a veneer of chaos – socks everywhere – if you've been to his house, then you'll know – but the organization is down to the last dotted i and crossed t. He's got all the permits, fixed all the government officials, got all the equipment – probably far too much – and of course done massive research.' And does he seem sane? 'Yes, perfectly sane – a perfectly sane nineteenth-century explorer. He's nothing if not consistent. He's always lived in this great fluffy ball of bits of paper and empty bottles and unspeakable dead things, like a bower bird's nest. He doesn't change.'

O'Hanlon is already planning his next journey, to New Guinea, though he thinks he might 'cheat' this time and go with a film crew to help him through the most perilous part – getting all the equipment out of the airport and into the jungle without having it stolen. The *National Geographic* wants to make a documentary about cannibalism and O'Hanlon has promised to find them someone who has eaten somebody. But then he will proceed on a 'proper' expedition with one friend – if he can find anyone willing.

Why does he do it? He is almost fifty and not, by any stretch of the imagination, fit. Fenton accuses him in Borneo of trying to prove his manhood and obviously there is an element of that – he worries a great deal about his penis. But he is not driven by the usual explorer motive of wanting to escape the wife and have sexual adventures – he adores his wife (they have been married twenty-nine years) and chickens out of any sexual adventures. To some extent, he goes simply in order to acquire material to write about. But he also deludes himself that his journeys are serving some scientific purpose: he boasts that every bird or insect sighting is accurate to within a hundred yards. 'You can't just have a morpho butterfly whizzing past because you need it for a break in conversation. I feel a moral duty.' O'Hanlon was terribly shocked when one German critic said that he skipped all the natural history observations: to him, they are the justification, or at least the excuse, for his travels.

But he admits that really the aim is 'to rediscover childhood. It is an amazing moment when you genuinely don't know whether the thing that suddenly flies across in front of you is a bird or a butterfly or a bat. I think that's why I like jungles so much – the unexpectedness. And there's that childhood pleasure when sometimes it matches the picture in the book. Plus the feeling of intense strangeness and newness – because all the bodily sensations are different – and the fact the competent people with you, the pygmies, are treating you more or less as a child. So, consciously or not, you return to childhood, and that's the most extraordinary feeling. The world looks all washed, wonderful.'

He had been very religious as a boy – 'You have to be to survive being brought up in a vicarage' – but he became, on discovering Darwin at fourteen, not merely an agnostic, but a militant atheist, much to his father's distress. They still don't talk about it. His mother, he says, is also very religious but in an emotional way: 'She believes that in heaven she will be reunited with every spaniel she has ever owned.' While O'Hanlon was away in Africa, his older brother, a book rep, took Belinda and the children to communion. O'Hanlon was shocked, but 'I decided not to be angry about it. A real atheist, you see, is not exercised about it.'

In Africa, however, something happened. He didn't revert to Christianity, but he did come to accept the power of spiritual belief. He saw tribesmen pining away and dying because the witch-doctor had put the hex on them. And he was given his own fetish, which of *course* he doesn't 'believe in' but, still, there was that shaky moment in Rotterdam. In the Congo, he admits: 'I discovered – uncomfortably – that the religious impulse is really deep and basic, and we all need it. It protects you from the terrors of the ungovernable, and the fear of death. I hadn't realized that. I thought it was some kind of decadent nonsense really, but now I don't.'

And in Africa, he found that science, which he had invested with a quasi-religious power, just wasn't enough. He still believes that the story of evolution is the greatest story ever told, 'But if you're a bit depressed on a grey day, it doesn't quite . . .' Cheer you up? 'Yes. You have to be feeling very well and active to be deeply excited by bacteria building colonies four and a half billion years ago. Because it's arduous, science. It doesn't have instant, nice, calming myths. You can take it either way – the empty and infinite space up there can relieve you of your petty anxieties or depress you so that you slit your throat. The great thing Christianity did was to make it possible to think that every individual really was valuable in some absolute way, and biology can't really help you on that.'

Depression is always hovering – in the past, he has sometimes had to go to bed for weeks on end, and he still sleeps at odd times in the day to avoid the pressures of reality. The only way he could get his book done, finally, was to write at night and not see anyone ('not even Fenton') or answer the phone for two years. Envy is a problem too – it is perhaps unfortunate that his best friends are James Fenton, Julian Barnes, Martin Amis, Ian McEwan, Galen Strawson – 'all the boys, really'. He says that, when writing, 'You must never ever think of your contemporaries – you must let all that superficial stuff go. But if you're connected to the mistle thrush on the vicarage lawn, then you know it's going to be all right, that somehow the prose is cleansed of all jealousies.'

Does he worry about going mad? 'Well yes, I've always been terrified of that. I'm desperate to be normal. I really would like to have a routine and live a normal life.' But Belinda says he can't do it: if he starts to establish a routine, he deliberately disrupts it after a few days. Instead, he relishes his peculiar 'coping mechanism' – the bower bird's nest of objects which, despite their apparent chaos, somehow serve to keep madness at bay. That is why tidying up is so deeply traumatic.

He said that yesterday, when Belinda made him clear a path to the tea table, it brought on a terrible anxiety attack. 'It makes you more vulnerable because then someone can come in and find something that matters to you and *get* it. And I think perhaps that goes back to being a student and my mama coming along . . . Pa took me out to a meal in a hotel and my mother took everything out of my digs and burned it.' Why? 'Because it was immodest and indelicate. I can understand now from their point of view – they thought it was semi-criminal, these appalling books about surrealism and frightening pictures by Bosch. So there was a bonfire. It was the last evangelical Christian clean-out.' So since then he has clung on to everything? 'Yes. Because the mess kind of stops them in the doorway. That's when you feel completely safe.'

Isn't it the school locker syndrome, the terrible legacy of prep school? 'Oh yes, yes! That gave me a frisson! You're absolutely right. Seven years old, looking out of the window, and this little bundle of possessions is all you've got. What a horrible thought!'

If anyone was ever crying out for psychoanalysis, it's O'Hanlon, but: 'Oh no. That would be weakness, that would be self-indulgent.' Whereas trekking into the jungle . . . ? '. . . is perfectly straightforward, yes. And the bit you hang on to is the birds. Because that locks into childhood so it must be healthy. But I am sort of vaguely aware that it's not.'

Before I leave, as a great mark of honour, he takes me to his fetish house. It looks, from the outside, like a large windowless garden shed. Going in, though, you immediately enter a sinister world, especially as you have to step into pitch darkness before you can turn on the light. The main fetish – the fetish *d'honneur* – is a Maxwell House jar containing part of a man's charred foot. He was a friend from school, Douglas Winchester, who committed suicide by setting fire to himself in Holland Park. O'Hanlon went to the site and managed to retrieve part of his charred foot. It is his most precious fetish, the one he could not live without.

'What it's really saying is: there are things that are worth it in life; there's no point killing yourself. In the morning, when you wake up, it's very difficult to have lofty thoughts like that, and you have to motivate yourself.' So does he visit the fetish house every morning?

'Oh no. Mustn't look in there too often or it loses its wop. The mind can do it.'

So when does he go? 'Whenever I need . . . when I can't think what point there could possibly be in carrying on with this paragraph . . .'

Reproduced by permission of *The Observer*.

Stephen Fry

10 May 1998

Where do we stand on Stephen Fry? There seems to be a full gamut of views ranging from 'He was never funny', to 'He was once funny, but no longer', to 'Total genius in everything he touches'. His enemies include the predictable homophobes who hate him for being a public school poofter, and the show-must-go-on luvvies who believe he 'let the whole profession down' when he walked out of Simon Gray's play *Cell Mates* in the West End. There is a Jewish angle I can't quite get the hang of that seems to claim he is anti-Semitic (although, or perhaps because, he is half-Jewish). There are those who maintain he is 'too clever by half' and others who think he is not as clever as *he* thinks he is. But his novels have brought him a whole new adoring audience, who seem to regard him as the Robert Robinson version of a towering polymath. Personally, I can't stand his novels, but I like him because he makes me laugh and was once very sweet to my daughters at a party.

Still, I wouldn't want to go into the jungle with him. He is, to put it mildly, a tricky character. When he first became famous, he was always quite frank about his delinquent past – he was a kleptomaniac at school and went on the run with stolen credit cards, ending up in Pucklechurch remand centre – but it was easy to think of that as a former life, a troubled adolescence now safely behind him. Then in February 1995, he went completely off the rails again – no stolen credit cards this time (he doesn't need them: he is a millionaire), but a sudden disappearance, followed by a flurry of contradictory explanations.

Fry says he has always tried to 'demystify' himself in interviews – a wonderfully condescending way of putting it. But then he resents it terribly if journalists claim to understand him – the demystification is not meant to go *that* far. I suspect he spins these glittering cathedrals of words not to elucidate, but to daze and confuse. This makes an odd basis for an interview. I will ask him questions but distrust his answers! But when I interviewed him in 1990, I felt afterwards that I had been somewhat suckered by his charm. He *is* charming and I was charmed again this time. But somehow you feel that whatever he says doesn't *mean* anything.

We met at the Groucho Club, his home from home, and I was struck immediately by the change in him. He has shed many of his mannerisms, his Jeevesian flourishes, and seems, at forty, both younger and more grown-up. And *bien dans sa peau*, which he never seemed before. I told him he seemed different, and he asked how. There were several polite (and true) things I could have said – slimmer, fitter, more relaxed – but instead I said what I actually meant: 'You seem less brilliant.' He took it well. 'Yes, or less concerned to be. Less approving of myself. You know, that cliché about engaging in life in every second, living it fully, is *true* – but you don't live life fully by *examining* every second you live.'

Of course, he is in love; that is the huge difference. After fifteen years of saying he hated sex and couldn't stand the idea of relationships, he now rabbits on dotingly about the joys of sharing his bed and having someone to make his flat a home. He has been with the boyfriend (I am only allowed to call him the boyfriend; he is ten years younger than Fry, and not in showbiz) for almost exactly two years and is still totally besotted. He says all his friends like him – 'Probably more than they like me! And they all tell me how much better it has made me – which always makes me wonder, what was wrong with me before? But I think what they mean is that they find me less intense.'

He definitely seems less 'driven'. He still works incredibly hard but not in the frantic God-will-strike-me-dead-if-I'm-idle way he did before. Recently, he came home from filming in America to find almost a roomful of letters waiting for him, all personal ones that his P A couldn't answer. In the past, he said, he would have taken seven Benzedrine and a pot of black coffee and stayed awake for four days if necessary, until he'd answered them all. But this time, he was philosophical and said, 'Well, some of them will have to wait and if they're offended, that's their problem.'

So obviously some of his despised psychotherapy has had an effect. He isn't so desperate to please or to impress; he has learned to say no and, most importantly, he has committed himself to a relationship. Full marks to the Santa Barbara shrink he picked out of the Yellow Pages. And tentatively, warily, he is mending some of the bridges he burned over *Cell Mates*. The most important is that this month he returns to British television having been off it for three years. He plays the controller of Radio 2 in a new B B C 2 serial called *In the Red*, which starts on 26 May. But what makes *In the Red* particularly significant is that Rik Mayall is also in it. Mayall, you will remember, was his co-star in *Cell Mates* and must have been particularly upset by Fry's defection, since it was Fry who had persuaded him to do it in the first place. He had to go on night after night to dwindling audiences, and reportedly came off stage in tears when he found himself playing to forty punters; soon afterwards he 'ran amok' in Covent Garden and started firing a cap pistol at American tourists. Mayall and Fry have not met since. Fry claims this was merely a coincidence (ha!), but he took the precaution of phoning Mayall before they started making *In the Red* and Rik was 'wonderful, so wonderful, because he's a terribly sweet man'.

Fry admits he has a problem in talking about *Cell Mates*. 'Because, you know, one of the awful things about the whole business is that it's so easy to start talking about it in a trivial way, but I would hate people like Rik or any of the other actors to read me being incredibly frivolous about it. So you have to tread this delicate balance between being over-serious and . . .'

Quite. His own inclination is to downplay the whole episode – 'my little wobble', 'my trip to Bruges' – though he says the generally approved expression seems to be 'débâcle'. He looks surprised when I call it his nervous breakdown: he never uses that term himself. It probably seems too banal to him – he will talk about 'despair' but not depression – and also too *pathetic*. But this is where he runs into difficulties, because there are other people who suffered from his defection. Not only Rik Mayall, but the other actors in the company, the friends who were so alarmed on his behalf, Simon Gray who felt his play was killed at birth and the producer Duncan Weldon, who lost half a million pounds on the aborted run. (Simon Gray wrote his account of the episode, *Fat Chance*, within weeks of it happening. He claims Fry was never fully involved in the production – he demanded a two-week break at Christmas and turned up late for rehearsals – and that as an actor he was somehow never 'there' for his colleagues. Fry claims not to have read the book, and he certainly would not enjoy it if he did.)

The play opened on a Tuesday to mixed reviews – one, from the *Financial Times*, was particularly vitriolic. On the Sunday, Gray rang Fry at home and found a sinister message on his answering machine saying, 'I'm sorry. I'm so very sorry.' But when he rang later in the day it was a different one, saying only that Fry was out.

It was on Monday that the roof fell in. Fry's agent, Lorraine Hamilton, found a message telling her to collect some letters from his flat – one for her; one for Simon Gray; one for Rik Mayall; one for his sister, Jo; one for Hugh Laurie. The letters were difficult to interpret, but made it clear that he had left *Cell Mates* and was never coming back. Gray describes his as an 'ambiguous suicide letter'. In it, Fry talked about 'the lumpen, superior "act" that bored an audience every time he opened his mouth', which was almost a word-for-word quote from the *FT* review. That night, the theatre manager announced that Stephen Fry was 'indisposed' and the understudy went on.

It took a day or two for the press to get wind of the crisis, but by Thursday, the tabloids were trumpeting 'Fears grow for Stephen Fry' and talking about possible suicide. At this point, some members of the public came forward to say they'd seen him on the cross-Channel ferry earlier in the week, indeed that he had signed autographs for them, and also that he had been spotted lunching in Bruges wearing a black beret. Soon afterwards, Fry contacted his family to say he was all right and his father picked him up in Amsterdam.

Was suicide ever a serious possibility? Fry told *Woman* magazine that it certainly was: 'I was sitting in my car with a duvet round the door so the exhaust fumes would be kept in. The only thing that stopped me turning on the ignition was the thought of what my parents would go through.' But Rik Mayall told Simon Gray at the time: 'He hasn't killed himself. Not Stephen. I *know* Stephen. He'd never do it.' In any case, Stephen's sister, Jo, who acted as his PA, revealed that he had instructed her to ensure his Barclaycard was in credit, and his bank manager said he had spent a lot of money on whisky, cigarettes and books – not a normal preparation for suicide.

So what was he doing? It seems that he was just doing a bunk, running out of *Cell Mates* because he couldn't face the sense of failure. For someone who relied so much on being liked, and who had had almost uninterrupted success since Cambridge, the shock of bad reviews was obviously severe. At that stage, he probably never thought for a moment about the financial implications or the publicity. He never dreamt it would be front-page news. And if he just wanted to get out of the play, his flight can be seen as a smart move. By making it so dramatic, by disappearing without explanation, by raising fears of suicide, he made sure that everyone was relieved when he returned, rather than furious that he had gone. But that makes it all sound too calculating. I think it was probably more like his stolen credit-card spree when he was seventeen – something that started on impulse and escalated beyond his control.

After four days of wandering round the continent, he turned up at Hanover station and saw the British newspapers. He was appalled by the headlines and decided to let his friends know he was all right. But, typically, he wouldn't phone – he spent three hours tracking down a piece of cabling so he could connect his laptop to the German phone system and send a fax. 'I was not in a state where I could trust my voice to carry my meaning without it cracking or failing or succumbing to pressure. I felt an urgent need to get across a message which neither revealed my whereabouts nor forced me to speak in real time.' But when he switched on his laptop he found a huge number of e-mails from friends, family and strangers, all expressing their concern. Months later, he wrote an article in the *Telegraph* to thank these Internet correspondents: 'Alone and fretful in a hotel room overlooking the Alster, I could read them slowly, without the need for an instant response. A few hours later, I swallowed my pride and a *bockwurst*, pointed the car towards Holland and drove home to family, friends and help.'

(Don't you hate that *bockwurst*? So cheap, so flip. He claims to loathe his own flipness, but then why doesn't he edit it out? Probably because he writes so fast, he doesn't re-read his copy. And he has a fear of being boring. Actually, he couldn't be boring if he tried, but he gets bored with *himself*, and thinks he has to make a joke to jolly things along.)

Anyway, I asked what happened next – the period he has never talked about. He remembers the next few weeks as 'absolute tumult'. His father and family doctor met him in Amsterdam and admitted him to the psychiatric ward of the Cromwell hospital in London. 'I write a diary and because I was stuck in this loony bin, I was writing twelve pages a day, and I remember reading it about six months ago, and I was shocked by my *fury* with the nurses and psychiatrists – perfectly decent people whose job is to come and sit on your bed and talk to you and try and get you to join in these therapy groups – and I just couldn't *bear* this whole cheesy kind of world. Then I got absolutely terrified because the Marquesa [de Varela – of *Hello!* magazine] was on the female floor and sent a note saying she'd like to interview me.'

But what *really* upset him was that the psychiatrist diagnosed him as cyclothymic (manic-depressive), and put him on lithium. Fry hated that diagnosis. 'He may have been right about certain things but at the risk of sounding Hitlerian – which you always do when you mention the poor man's name – I do think a touch of Nietzsche would do the world a bit of good these days; just the belief that we have such a thing as a *will*. And yes, I have all the trends of the mania side of manic depression – shopping and hyperactivity and intensity and all that – and I do get Churchillian black dogs as well, but I don't have them to the extent of people who really do need to be controlled with drugs. I remember a doctor wrote telling me off because I'd said I was "an asthmatic" and he said "Nobody is 'an' anything, medically. You may have episodes of asthma but you are not *an* asthmatic, and if you call yourself that, it almost becomes a self-fulfilling prophecy." So it was just the labelling – the idea that I was "a" manic-depressive. I mean, I was occasionally subject to these mood swings, but I didn't want to feel I was going to live the rest of my life sort of distrusting myself and my ability to control . . . I wanted to be true to *myself*, more than I wanted not to be sued by Duncan Weldon and have to sell my house or whatever.'

Simon Gray claims that Fry flatly refused to let the insurers' doctor examine him, but in the end a settlement was hammered out whereby the insurers paid Duncan Weldon £235,000, and Fry paid £20,000, presumably in acknowledgement that he carried some blame for the loss. But the fact that the insurers paid at all means they must have been convinced he was mentally ill.

Once Fry escaped from hospital, he went off to Santa Barbara to stay in a borrowed house by the sea for three months. He was alone, and lonely, and rather confused about what to do – his instinct would have been to start writing but he had been told to get rid of the idea that everything should be work all the time. So he decided to compromise by working on his body, and went to a gym every day and developed pectorals and put Sun-In in his hair to make it blonder which, as he says, was quite brave of him because it meant admitting he was *trying* to look good and risking failure. And even more bravely, he went to a shrink three times a week for three months – he simply chose the one in Yellow Pages with the most New York-sounding Jewish name – and 'he was actually a terribly nice chap, and wore a suit'.

Obviously the time in Santa Barbara did him a lot of good. First, by toning his body, he got rid of the physical self-loathing that had kept him celibate for fifteen years. And second, he realized one of his problems was that he was lonely. 'Although I was sociable, I suddenly thought I never use the first person plural much, in the way that other people say "We saw that film", and it almost made me weep because I thought, all these elegant defences, these attacks on sex or whatever – I was just lonely.'

Of course, it took him a while to find a boyfriend, and he was still very hesitant: 'I still felt deeply insecure and I felt that for fifteen years I'd been away from the game of relationships and that I wouldn't know the first way to set about it, and that I would look like a hopeless clumsy amateur in every department, not necessarily just in bed. But of course, I hadn't realized that every time anyone starts on a new relationship, it's as if they'd never had one before. And oh, it's just miraculous really, isn't it? I did skip about, like a teenager. It was as if I had spent my whole life never being alone – it was the oddest thing, it really was.'

With his boyfriend, he has established a living pattern he is happy with – quiet writing periods in Norfolk interspersed with sociable acting periods in Hollywood or London. (He has just returned from making a Hollywood courtroom drama with John Travolta, whom he found charming.) I always assumed that Fry regarded writing as something to fall back on between acting jobs but not at all. He says he regards himself primarily as a writer and that he has 'a more compulsive *need* to write than to act'. In that case, why doesn't he spend longer on his books and make them better? He knocks them out in a few months.

Last year he published his autobiography, *Moab is My Washpot*, which should have borne the fruits of his psychotherapy, but seemed like a complete cop-out. He blethered on about Uppingham, his public school, for chapter after chapter, and then brushed aside a teenage suicide attempt in a couple of sentences. Worse, he still seemed to blame his father for everything. He presents Alan Fry as a less cuddly version of Darth Vader: all brain, no heart. (Incidentally, his father's engineering firm is called Alan Fry Controls – and what a rich Freudian seam *that* opens up!) I asked if he thought he'd been too hard on his father in *Moab* and it produced the rarest of all things in a Stephen Fry conversation – a long, long silence. Finally, he said, 'No. I think most people who read it could see that it was an incredibly troubled relationship, but I don't think anyone felt that he came out of it badly. I was incredibly hard on him when I was young – well, I was terrified of him so I wasn't hard on him literally, but I thought *evil* thoughts about him, I mean I hated him, certainly absolutely hated him, was also deeply proud of him in some ways, and admired him: which I still do, and I'm very fond of him, adore him.'

He has no plans to write another volume of autobiography, or at least not for twenty years, because he says he would have to address questions like 'What is Rowan Atkinson really like?', and 'Either I'm going to be greasily charming – which is very easy to be because he's a wonderful fellow – or I might write about some of his foibles, perfectly forgivable foibles, and he might regard it as a betrayal. And I know that Hugh [Laurie] would *loathe* to be written about – by me or anybody else. It's just not my right.' And also, of course, the next volume might have to explain what happened in *Cell Mates*.

What *did* happen in *Cell Mates*? Why did he crack up *then*? Doesn't his diary provide any clues? 'Yes. I can see lacunae, that's what's very interesting. Almost to the day – I think the first day of rehearsals got a diary entry and then I don't do any more. And that in itself is very revealing. I can remember getting home after rehearsals and thinking, "Oh fuck it, I'll write an entry when I've got more of a sense of what's going on."' Was there something about the play, or the part, that was particularly upsetting? 'Mmm, you know, that never occurred to me before. It was about a deeply manipulative, secretive man, rather a dull man, whining and self-justifying – exactly like me, really. He used people, lied to them and got his own way.'

Is that really like Stephen Fry? Surely not. He is deeply loved by his friends, especially his old Cambridge friends, and by most people who meet him. But he thinks of himself as an impostor who cleverly cons people into liking him. He believes that if people saw his real self, they would loathe and despise him. Hence his need to keep control at all times. Even when drunk, he never loosens up – he says his friends are always telling him they'd love to see him get shit-faced, but he never does, however much he drinks.

Was he drinking or using cocaine a lot during *Cell Mates*? 'No, not a lot. I've always only used either recreationally – terrible word – but it was always to get something more … I am, as you know, an exceptionally dull person and I'm particularly dull in the evenings. And the great thing about recreational drugs like alcohol or cocaine is they kind of give me an extra three hours of being awake and involved with people. But this is an *awful* minefield to get into – I just cannot *bear* the British attitude towards drugs, it's a no-win situation.'

Anyway, stimulants had nothing to do with it. He thinks it was more 'a sort of crisis of identity – I just didn't know who I was any more. I felt almost as if my self had gone out of me and gone into the public domain, that everyone else knew who I was better than I did. It's a terrible feeling when someone you haven't even met writes: "Stephen Fry is always trying to …" And how do they know? But then you think, well maybe they do know me better than I know myself …'

Yes, maybe they do – because he doesn't seem to know himself very well. All the more reason to carry on with psychotherapy. But he absolutely won't. He sees it as self-indulgent, navel-gazing, 'bolstering people's vanity'. This man, who is so intelligent and sophisticated in other ways, suddenly starts talking like Prince Philip: 'I've never met anybody, no matter how many years of therapy they've had, who has any better insight into the way they behave than anybody else. It may sound pompous but I think you can gain far more insight into human motives by listening to a Beethoven symphony or reading a good poem than you can from hearing someone talk about denial. And, you know, we can all do it *ourselves*, we don't need the mechanistic, functional fallacy of psychotherapy. It's like bad films – you see a murderer and then a flashback of him watching his mother being raped or something – it's just *nonsensical*.'

Really? No wonder he doesn't like to hear people talking about denial. He prefers the Uppingham spirit, stiff upper lip, moral fibre, backbone, self-discipline, Nietzschean will – Stephen Fry Controls. But given that the control system has already broken down at least twice, isn't he frightened that it will happen again? 'Yes, but I'm far more frightened of being a boy in a plastic bubble, and being so scared of it happening again that you don't actually do anything at all. I would like to be happy, so I'm not *ashamed* of having gone to a therapist. But I don't think that self-interest, self-absorption is the path to self-esteem. I'm too vain to be that vain, if that doesn't sound too tricksy . . . I'm sure it does.' It does, Stephen, it does.

Reproduced by permission of *The Observer*.

Lord Deedes

12 October 1997

Several of my dearest friends are currently sitting on my back, twisting my arm in a half-nelson and hissing, 'If you dare, *if you dare for one minute*, to say anything nasty about Lord Deedes, you are *dead meat.*' These are people who would happily let me slag off Mother Teresa, but somehow Lord Deedes – Golden Deedes – provokes a fierce protective devotion in anyone who has ever worked with him. However, I have Lord Deedes's farewell ringing in my ears. 'Do your worst!' he cried.

He is eighty-four – a fact you won't find mentioned in his new autobiography, *Dear Bill – W.F. Deedes Reports*, because he believes, or claims to, that if his *Telegraph* editor ever notices how old he is, he will be forced to retire. This is, of course, nonsense: he is an outstandingly good reporter whom any newspaper would be glad to employ. Thanks to his contacts in the international aid agencies, he often manages to get into war zones or emergency situations that are generally closed to the media. It was typical that he should turn up escorting Princess Diana to Angola and Bosnia in her final months' campaign against landmines. The rat pack could only gnash their teeth at being so comprehensively scooped, but he had earned his place at the Princess's side – he had been campaigning against landmines for five years.

We met for lunch at his usual Italian restaurant. From reading *Private Eye*'s 'Dear Bill', I was expecting to pour quarts of gin down him, but he lunched very frugally on two starters and half a bottle of house white, saying he had to keep a clear head for the afternoon's leader conference. He still goes in to work at the *Telegraph* every day, travelling to Canary Wharf by public transport – no mean feat at any age, let alone eighty-four.

Those who saw him recently on *Alan Clark's History of the Tory Party* will already be familiar with his amazing range of physical tics and grimaces. Apart from his famous lisp (inspiration for *Private Eye*'s 'Shome mishtake shurely?'), he does things you've heard of but never seen performed – he furrows his brow, gives you a nod and a wink, puts his tongue in his cheek – all while waving his arms like a sea anemone. But when I mentioned an *Evening Standard* story that he was writing a book about Princess Diana he went into the full Peter O'Toole-as-Macbeth mode, tearing his hair, gnashing his teeth, rolling his eyes. 'No! It is very important that you correct that story. I am writing the introduction to a book called *Diana Remembered* which the *Telegraph* is publishing and all the profits are going to the landmine fund. Full stop. I am moderately laid-back, I don't take offence at things, but when I read that story in the *Evening Standard*, comparing *me* to Andrew Morton, I *must say* the blood began to tingle!'

He has always said, for years, that he wouldn't write an autobiography, so how come he has written *Dear Bill*? He claims it is not an auto-biography but a series of essays about aspects of his life, a somewhat casuistical distinction. Anyway, he did it because his long-term friend Anne Allport, a fellow director of Care, offered to help put it together, and suggested the money could be put into a trust fund to support his favourite charities after his death. But it was a point of honour, he said, that he should only do it in his spare time, so he did it at weekends, which cut grievously into his golf. 'I mean, a lot of people take six months off, but I didn't think that was a good idea – because, you know, I'm lucky to be employed by anyone at my age.'

Ya, ya. I'm never sure how to react to his outrageous, ostentatious, flamboyant modesty. There was a striking moment when I said that really everything he'd done had turned out well, and he semaphored his arms and shrieked, 'What do you mean it's turned out well? I began life on the *Morning Post* – and the *Morning Post* went down, right? While I was on it! The war . . . well, we did win the war so that's fine. Then

I became a Cabinet minister. Well! That ditched the government. It did! I was supposed to present the government in a good light and they lost. Anyway, it was a ridiculous job. Then I edited the *Daily Telegraph* under Lord Hartwell, whom I was devoted to – and what happened to that? Went straight into the sandbank, rescued by Conrad Black. So, all right, you tot up the successes out of that! There are only two things I think I was reasonably good at: being a soldier and being a reporter.'

This idea that newspaper dynasties founder, that governments collapse at his approach – the curse of Deedes – is not so much modest as insanely solipsistic. Obviously there is genuine modesty – when he says, for instance, that he was 'reasonably good' at being a soldier, this is Deedes-speak for having won the Military Cross. But he also has a subtle way of wrapping boasts in modesty. For instance, he told me he was always so embarrassed when Margaret Thatcher introduced him to people as 'the only man who has been both a Cabinet minister and a newspaper editor'. It is as if he assumes (modestly) that you will take him for a complete duffer unless he (immodestly) arms you with a few facts to the contrary.

His autobiography has the same push-pull between egotism and self-disparagement. He never bares his heart. The most amazing thing about it is the short shrift he gives his wife – she gets a couple of name checks but doesn't even appear in the index – whereas he devotes many adulatory paragraphs to his various handmaidens – 'the women who have been kind enough to assist me' – such as Mary Ann Sieghart, Anne Allport and his *Telegraph* assistant (now church affairs correspondent) Victoria Combe. When I told him I found the omission of his wife and children surprising, he said, musingly, 'Yes, the publisher said the same. But once you enter into family, you've got to keep track of them all the time, you've got to say they went to school or wherever.' But couldn't he at least have said all thanks to my wonderful supportive wife? 'Yes, I suppose I should have said that. You're probably right, I've probably dropped a clanger.'

He came from 'a county family' in Kent and spent his early childhood in Saltwood Castle, where Alan Clark now lives, and at Harrow. But his father went bust in the Wall Street crash and he had to leave school at sixteen and get a job. He is fond of dwelling on his lack of academic qualifications – he never progressed beyond School Certificate (A-levels). 'I often think I've been luckier than my qualifications deserved. I mean I was, mistakenly, once, in the Cabinet. I am lucky! I am lucky! ... There were times up to the war when the county families were thought to be ideal governors of the country. And funnily enough, it went along quite well. But then a time came in the late fifties, early sixties, when the class thing didn't count for nearly so much. Sir William Haley [editor of *The Times*] once looked at me very pointedly and said, "The future lies with a meritocracy." And this knocked me sideways. I thought, "Where do I stand in a meritocracy?" I thought it was a disaster for me!'

Actually, of course, he has done very well in a meritocracy, though he started by nepotism – an uncle found him a job on the *Morning Post*. It was a 'true Blue' newspaper, he recalls, with a failing circulation, where he soon made his mark as a feature writer.

In 1935 the paper sent him to cover the war in Abyssinia, where he shared digs with the *Mail*'s correspondent, Evelyn Waugh. Everyone has assumed ever since that William Boot, the hapless reporter in *Scoop*, is based on Deedes, but Deedes seems oddly unenthusiastic about the identification, perhaps because it impugns his journalistic skills. He is always quite happy to admit that he was 'Dear Bill', the recipient of the spoof Denis Thatcher letters in *Private Eye*, but he won't thank you for calling him Boot. Did he read *Scoop* when it first came out? 'Course I did, but when it first came out it was just a funny novel about journalists. And because I was with them in Abyssinia, I can recognize the other characters – except for William. I mean, I didn't offer to go in a boat.' But then why have people always assumed he was Boot? 'Oh, that was because of the luggage. The *Morning Post* didn't really expect to see me again – which is possibly why they sent me – so they sent me out with a quarter of a ton of luggage. Evelyn, who travelled with a suitcase – he was a wonderful African traveller – thought this was hilarious. And I have to admit, I was twenty-two, moderately naive about what one did as a war correspondent – he saw me coming. I don't mind that.'

In 1937 the *Morning Post* reached its long-expected demise and was taken over by the *Telegraph*, which appointed him political correspondent at £15 a week – he says he has never felt so rich since. Then came the war, in which he ended up a major and won the Military Cross. He returned to the *Telegraph* to write its Peterborough diary. In 1950, when his local MP retired, he thought it would be 'rather a lark' to stand as candidate and beat Ted Heath to the job. He remained the Tory MP for Ashford until 1974, and moved quite far up the greasy pole, culminating in two years, 1962 to 1964, when he was Minister without Portfolio in charge of information – a sort of Jurassic Mandelson – in Macmillan's Cabinet.

In this capacity, he drafted Profumo's famous statement to the House in which he said he had never slept with Christine Keeler. Deedes's excuse for accepting Profumo's lie is that teams of senior ministers, lawyers and whips had already grilled Profumo at length and supposedly established the facts, and all he had to do was compose the statement. But surely, as a reporter – and also as someone who had been at school with Profumo and knew him well – he must have had *some* opinion. Did he think it was inconceivable that he had slept with a callgirl? 'Not necessarily. But my job was to ensure that the government could face the House at eleven the next morning with a statement, and now we were at 2 a.m., and Peter Rawlinson and I typed it out on my typewriter. Now of course with hindsight, yes, we were all daft, yes yes.

'Looking back on it, I do feel I might have done a bit more. Because, after all, what was I in the Cabinet for? I was supposed to be Minister of Information, I was supposed to be close to the newspapers – which I was. I had many friends in newspapers and if I had listened more sensitively to what they had to tell me, I could have possibly – only possibly – contributed to averting the ultimate disaster.'

This was his last Cabinet post, though he was an industrious backbencher. But in 1974 there was a vacancy at the *Telegraph*, so he resigned as MP and offered his services to Lord Hartwell, the proprietor. He claims he never meant to be editor – he thought Hartwell would make him deputy editor, at best – but anyway editor is what he became, and what he remained until, in 1986, the Hartwell ship went down and Conrad Black moved in and appointed Max Hastings in his place. Deedes gracefully reverted to being a reporter – albeit a reporter who played golf with Denis Thatcher and was regularly invited to private suppers at No. 10, and had been given a baronetcy by Mrs Thatcher in return for the *Torygraph*'s loyalty.

It is difficult to find anyone who thinks Deedes was a brilliant editor of the *Telegraph*, and he is happy to agree: '*Anything* but brilliant, anything but. Lord Hartwell was editor-in-chief, and I learned in the army to do, broadly speaking, what the colonel wants. But we were prisoners of war to the printers. And in the end I rather lost heart. But I'm not excusing it – no, I was a grey editor, definitely.' He was happy to preside over this sinking ship – he says in the book that 'a sinking ship is my spiritual home' – but of course it was frustrating for his staff, three of whom eventually defected to found the *Independent*. Stephen Glover, one of the three, wrote in the *Spectator* that Deedes seemed to suffer from a deep pessimism, that made him almost relish the *Telegraph*'s decline. Deedes agrees: 'Yes, it's true. I'm a natural pessimist, but this was reinforced in me during the war. I always found if you expect the worst, and something else happens, you're better off.'

Stephen Glover suggested his pessimism stemmed from his father going bust but Deedes is not happy with this idea: 'I never know about these childhood things. I had a rather . . . dramatic childhood, with my father being monetarily mercurial, but I don't know that it had all that much effect. I don't believe in this new fashionable idea, which is to blame your parents for everything.'

Along with his pessimism and modesty goes a deep unwillingness to have rows. He says that 'the women who are kind enough to assist me' complain that he will put up with anything. He won't even complain when a waiter brings him a different cup of coffee to the one he's ordered. 'I think it's very wrong to tick off servants. But I think you're on to a good point: when it comes to a row, I tend to be wet, yes. I am not aggressive by nature. I'm emollient.' Perhaps that means he had a bad experience of rows in his early childhood? 'Could be. Could be. Yes. We did have rows in the family, yes. I never saw the virtue of it. Yep. Yep. I am a reluctant row-maker.'

So what he needs, I tell him, is a course in assertiveness training. He sputters and hoots and waves his limbs delightedly. 'All right!' he says. 'If you say so!'

There are parts of Lord Deedes one doesn't like to probe too deeply – his views on ethnic minorities or homosexuals are not *quite* in line with modern thinking. He believes that the decline in educational standards has been caused by immigrants and he told me solemnly that there has been a mistaken desire 'to make the homosexual appear to be totally on all fours with the heterosexual!' However, he wisely protects himself from his worst buffer instincts by consulting 'the women who are kind enough to help me' and says: 'I've stopped laying down the law at my age, I listen to what the younger generation say – you realize that at eighty your opinions are unreliable.'

He is still game for anything. He starts each morning by hitting 100 golf balls into a net and he is now 'catching up' on his golf, having neglected it while he was writing his autobiography. Alas, his long-time partner Sir Denis Thatcher no longer plays, because he has a back problem. When I asked which of the two was the better player, Deedes gave a huge, delighted wink, threw modesty to the winds and shouted 'Me!'

A few years ago, Deedes collapsed when stung by a bee and was warned that the next bee or wasp sting could kill him. He is supposed to carry adrenalin with him at all times but of course he doesn't. 'Well, I mean, everything's chance. I'm hoping to go to Laos soon and it's no good going to these places and expecting to find yourself always safe. I'm not sure Piccadilly's all that safe now!' And then he looks at his watch and squawks, 'I say! Is that the time? I'm going to get the sack if I don't leave now!' and the Great Survivor whirls out into the traffic.

Reproduced by permission of *The Observer*.

Dale Winton

25 August 1996

Your feelings about Dale Winton entirely depend on what you do at 9.35 on weekday mornings. If you've never gone wild in the aisles – if you've never watched *Supermarket Sweep* – then you probably have no feelings about him at all and frankly we might as well part company right now. Dale Winton is a mildly camp, mildly funny 41-year-old game show host, and either you love him or you don't. He is particularly loved by students, and several colleges have complained that it is now impossible to get anyone to attend 9.30 a.m. lectures because they're all watching *Sweep*.

You might have seen him in *Trainspotting*, but that was a pink lamé parody of himself, too clever by half. Your real Dale is an innocent naif, vaguely Californian in his airhead sunniness, who prattles away and confides, 'I don't *think*, Lynn. No, I *do* think, but I don't think when I'm speaking – do you know what I mean?' Yes, Dale dear, of course we do. His appearances on *National Lottery Live* (which he has been presenting this month) or *Pets Win Prizes* are enjoyable but not so *ur*Dale as *Sweep*. *Pets*, of course, is a more brilliantly kitsch show but Dale inherited it from Danny Baker, and then he was made to adopt a slightly fake Larry Grayson persona with scripted bits of camp innuendo ('I'm not very good with birds . . .') which he knows don't really suit him. He says he will drop them in the next series and just 'be himself'.

Being himself is his glorious, unique talent and he is most completely himself on *Sweep*, which is entirely ad-libbed. I watched him taping a couple of shows at the Carlton Studios in Nottingham, and the transition from Dale on camera to Dale off was seamless. Normally with television presenters, there is a revealing moment when the camera stops rolling and they sag slightly, show their tiredness or irritability and revert to being their real, somewhat less charming, selves. But no such moment ever occurs with Dale. Before the show, between takes, at lunch in the canteen and burbling away in his dressing-room, he is the same sunny soul, even though recording seventy-five shows in three weeks is an incredible marathon. I concluded that maybe he had a rule of being 'on' all the time he was on television premises, so I arranged to see him at his home in Hampstead where I thought I might find a different Dale.

I don't know whether to be glad or sad to report that there is *no* different Dale. Journalistically it's a bummer, but as a *Sweep* fan I find it heartening. The only difference is his clothes – none of the snazzy Mr Eddie suits he wears on the box, but tracksuit and trainers, amazingly butch. He welcomes me into his smart new mews townhouse, apologizing for the non-existent mess. There is an elegant beige and cream sitting room, but of course he prefers to sit in the kitchen where the table offers a delicious spread of coffee, Danish pastries, three packs of cigarettes, two lighters, four asthma inhalers (he last had asthma when he was seven) and countless overflowing ashtrays. 'Have a pastry, darling, go for it. Ooh no – you're like me, you want a fag!'

We are soulmates immediately; I want him for my best friend. But Dale has that effect on everyone. His real best female friend is Lisa Tarbuck, Jimmy's daughter, who comes along later to take him out to lunch and rescue him from me, otherwise I think I would still be sitting at his kitchen table, telling him *my* life story. (Someone in television should have the wit to sign him up immediately as an interviewer: I believe he could be as good as Russell Harty, who was the best.)

One of the standing jokes on *Supermarket Sweep* is that contestants always use his name. When asked, say, to name a hot red spice used in cooking, they say 'paprikaDale'. One always hopes they'll be asked to name a soft, crumbly Yorkshire cheese so they can say 'Wensleydale Dale'. Nowadays, the producers tell contestants not to do it, but they still do it anyway – especially the students. How could they not when Dale himself punctuates almost every sentence with either his name or yours? – 'I'll tell you Lynn, I always say to myself, "Now Dale . . ."' It's a habit he presumably acquired originally from watching television. While other kids were going out to play football, he was staying in to watch *Family Fortunes*. It is additionally delicious to think that he was named after Dale Robertson, an American TV actor who starred in *Wells Fargo* in the 1950s and made a comeback on *Dynasty*.

Dale was born to give away fridges; he was anointed by his fairy godmother to preside over canine karaoke. I have never interviewed anyone who has so totally achieved his life's ambition – he could die tomorrow a happy man because he has presented *National Lottery Live*. 'I can't understand why Anthea gave it up. It was madness, Lynn: it's the biggest show in television.' While he describes *Sweep* as 'my *Vortex*' (the play that made Noël Coward a star), his only remaining ambition is to have 'my own *Blind Date*, my own *Noel's House Party*'. He means his own star vehicle, and at the rate he's going, he could achieve it next year. He says he has already done a *wonderful* pilot for the BBC which is 'basically a Saturday night-type relationship game show', though ultimately he would like to do 'something like a Des O'Connor chat show with music'. Bogglingly repulsive though both these ideas sound, they will no doubt be redeemed by having Dale Winton do them.

It is quite . . . mm . . . an unusual ambition to want to present *Supermarket Sweep*, but I can see how it happened. He grew up watching television with the added excitement of sometimes seeing his mother Sheree Winton on it. She had complained that her husband Gary, a furniture salesman, was always glued to the box and he replied that the people on it were so much cleverer than her. So, according to Dale, 'The next day she went to a theatrical agent and at the end of the following week she was Box 13 on *Take Your Pick* in a mink bikini.'

Consequently, he grew up in a mildly showbiz atmosphere. He met Sid James and Margaret Rutherford and even the Beatles because his mother had a bit part in *A Hard Day's Night*. 'I had an autograph book to die for, Lynn!' Nowadays, when he meets people like Bruce Forsyth and Bob Monkhouse, they tell him: 'Oh, your mum was *so* lovely!'

At fifteen, he auditioned for a game show – Hughie Green's *The Sky's the Limit*. But a woman in the waiting room told him she'd been on all the game shows, and the important thing was not to get all the answers right. 'They don't like a clever dick.' But he, being a clever dick, thought she was just trying to ruin his chances and answered all the questions correctly. So he didn't get chosen. Perhaps that was the last occasion on which Dale Winton let his intelligence show; these days he is very happy to be taken for an idiot.

Like most overnight successes, he was actually slogging away at what he calls The Career for years. He left his north London school at the age of seventeen with five O-levels and worked for a while in an HMV record store, then got little jobs deejaying at local clubs and parties. By 1978 he was a full-time professional DJ on Radio Trent in Nottingham, and did that for eight years. But he was never really in love with radio, he says; 'I just liked playing records and showing off.'

In 1985 Radio Trent suddenly decided not to renew his contract. He wasn't very worried because he'd had other job offers. But unfortunately he gave an interview in which he said Radio Trent was forced to make cutbacks – implying some financial malaise – and the company responded by saying Dale was a troublemaker. Dale sued for libel and, although he eventually won a handsome apology, was tied up in litigation for two years and other radio stations were frightened off. So he got deeper and deeper in debt – and, simultaneously, fatter and fatter until he weighed 18 stone. By 1987 he was £40,000 in debt and the bank was threatening to repossess his house. Luckily, a buyer turned up in the nick of time and he sold the Nottingham house, paid off his debts and moved to Beacon Radio in Wolverhampton in 1988.

'I was actually on a high again, living in Bridgnorth, working in Wolverhampton. I had my idyllic cottage – but I'm not a country dweller, and within two days of going there I was thinking "Why am I doing this?" I'd drive to work down these country lanes every day and Lynn, may I never see another bloody tractor as long as I live! I moved there in July, and by August I was driving to work and thinking, "I don't want to do this." I'd got myself out of debt, I'd got a regular job again; but I was playing Elkie Brooks on the way to work and thought, "I don't like this record. I don't like this singer. I don't want to be here." So I walked into the MD's office and said, "What's the earliest I can leave?"'

So, three months after buying it, he put his cottage up for sale and made £20,000 profit. With this nest egg, he set out for a new life in London. He put his possessions in storage, drove to an estate agent's in Harrow (he had grown up around Harrow) and said he wanted to rent a flat that day. He had decided to break into television. Unfortunately, living in London was twice as expensive as living in the Midlands, so the £20,000 soon ran out. Meanwhile he had a nose job and started dieting frantically because the first time he saw himself on telly he almost died of shame. It has been a long, hard slog to get down to his present 13 stone – he still thinks of himself as a fat man inside a temporarily emaciated body. He did any work he could – selling timeshares, presenting shopping programmes on cable, hosting semi-pornographic game shows in which topless girls had to pick up bananas with their breasts. Then he had what seemed like a breakthrough, doing the *Bobby Davro Show*, but the show was a disaster and everyone involved thought 'this is our *Heaven's Gate*'. Meanwhile, the debts were mounting again. He kept the bank manager at bay by showing him a pilot he'd made and telling him, 'This is going to make me a star' – but actually it never happened. Then, in 1993, *Supermarket Sweep* came along.

His friends all fell about when he said he was presenting a show called *Supermarket Sweep* because he has been a shopping addict all his life. 'I'm never happy without a couple of Tesco carrier bags. It's sad, isn't it? I'm very suburban in that respect.' He knew *Sweep* would be a success as soon as he saw the set – he felt at home immediately. But actually the first series didn't make him a star. It got good ratings (and bad reviews, which were expected), but audience research suggested viewers were doubtful about Dale himself. 'You have what is called an A1 factor, which is audience appreciation – mine was neither positive nor negative. It was, "Well, we think we quite like him, but we're not sure who he is."' He had followed the producer's orders to 'think butch' and so was striding around looking manly, being not at all the Dale we now know and love. It was touch-and-go whether he would be signed for a second series, and a very very scary wait because 'You do one series and you're gone. The attitude is "Well, we tried him with his own show and it didn't work."' Luckily, they signed him again – and allowed him to be himself.

Dale was paid £500 a show for the first two series of *Sweep*, but wouldn't tell me how much he is paid now – he says people have silly ideas about television fees. But he reckons that by next year he should be earning £300,000. And he must be doing quite well because he has just bought a new mews house in Hampstead and the 'Princess Di car' (an Audi convertible) he always wanted – and he turned down £50,000 to do the Dime bar ad, naked with a chocolate bar covering the strategic bits. 'When my agent rang, he said: "Of course you can always use a body double. I'd advise you to." Cheeky bastard!'

As the morning rattles on – 'Have another pastry, darling, go for it' – he shows me his model car collection, the contents of his fridge and the Lo-fat Caesar Salad Dressing he found in Harvey Nicks ('Isn't that *brilliant*? Would you like a bottle?'). But we both know that, sooner or later, he will have to start talking about his mother.

Before he does, though, there is a flurry of displacement activity while he shows me endless photographs and a video someone has compiled of all her surviving TV appearances. Of course, not many do survive, but there are about half a dozen clips adding up to ten minutes of tape. I find it deeply unsettling to sit at the kitchen table watching a son watching his dead mother performing dross on tele-vision, and I can't think of anything to say – but Dale happily provides a running commentary: 'That's her at the blackboard, but it's only a tiny sketch. Wait till she turns round . . . There! Beautiful, isn't she?' The sketch consists of a classroom with a teacher in a mortarboard and gown writing on a blackboard – the 'joke' is that, when she turns round, we see she is a stunning blonde with enormous boobs.

Most of Sheree Winton's television appearances seem to be of this order, playing a starlet, or a bathing beauty, or a Jayne Mansfield clone in small, unfunny sketches. There is always the big hair, the big smile, the big cleavage. Her career high points, apart from these television sketches, were playing a Bond girl and being tested for (but not getting) Purdey in *The New Avengers*. But she worked fairly regularly – Dale shows me a list of all her BBC contracts: the *Benny Hill Show*, the *Ted Ray Show*, *Michael Bentine*, *Braden's Beat*, *Christmas Night With The Stars*. 'She always did well. She was a very canny woman. Her problem was that, because she was a blonde bombshell, people never used to take her as seriously as she would have liked.'

She married Dale's father, Gary, a furniture salesman, when she was eighteen and he forty. Dale was their only child. I asked Dale to show me a photograph of his father, but though he riffled through dozens of his mother, there was no trace of his other parent. 'I used to have *nightmares* about my father and I can't tell you why, because he never used to beat me or anything. But I was always afraid of him. I never felt a warmth from him. He was very macho, very strict. I remember coming down to breakfast one day when I was about six, and playing with my toy cars on the breakfast table, and him saying "Do your three times table" and I couldn't do it, and he lost his temper and threw the cars across the floor. It was like an act of *violence*. He never hit me, but I always thought I had to be a bit careful. And yet, for the early part of my parents' marriage, my mother was very happy with him. Their problem was that she became more successful, and because of that he was insanely jealous.'

Dale's parents divorced when he was nine, and his father died four years later. 'I remember at the funeral I wasn't upset, I wasn't moved at all. It was very odd.' There was a brief stepfather, Norman, when Dale was fifteen. His mother put him in a boarding school for six weeks while she went on honeymoon, and he comfort-ate his way through the entire tuck shop. He had always been a chubby child, but now he was seriously overweight, and she whisked him off to a health farm on her return. Once the stepfather was out of the way, it was just Dale and Sheree, and they had what he calls 'a brother and sister relationship – she would always say, "I am your best friend as well as your mother".'

She would also tell him about her boyfriends, though not the 'intricacies'. 'What she would say to me would be, "Well, I tried going out with so-and-so. He was very nice but you know, dear, he didn't open the door for me." That sort of thing. Or, "When he followed me to the petrol station, he left me there to fill the car up – and really I'd have liked him to see that I was all right there on my own." She was quite a genteel lady, and her philosophy was always Dignity At All Times. She would say to me, "Dale, whatever you do, be dignified" – I can't imagine what she'd think of what I do for a living! Actually, she'd be very proud. But I think she'd find today's world uncomfortable – she was from a different era.'

She made her first suicide attempt when Dale left school at seventeen. She had always suffered from depression – Dale now thinks it was

PMT and could have been cured with hormones or Prozac, but in those days they just gave her tranquillizers. There were four or five more suicide attempts, and Dale would rush her to hospital. 'She was always very sorry afterwards. I remember once she'd done it and had her stomach pumped – which sounds revolting, to talk about it like this – but I remember her being in bed recuperating and I got very emotional and I was crying, because we were very close and I adored her, and she was upset that I was upset, and she said "I promise I'll never do it again." But there is that moment with someone who is suicidal, and they can't control it – they just want peace of mind . . .'

On 28 May 1976 he came home to Hatch End from deejaying at a local club and saw the Do Not Disturb sign on his mother's bedroom door. This was not unusual, so he went to bed. Next morning he found her dead – she had overdosed on barbiturates. She was forty, he was just twenty-one – but a very young twenty-one, he thinks. A psychiatrist came to see him and asked him lots of weird questions, including whether he had ever slept with his mother. Dale was outraged and has distrusted psychiatrists ever since.

Three or four months after his mother's death, he got engaged to a girl she had known and of whom she had approved. (He had had other girlfriends of whom she didn't approve – she particularly didn't approve of any who looked at all glamorous, and told him never to marry a sexpot.) But the engagement was short-lived, a symptom of his post-bereavement confusion.

I assume that he is gay. When I tell him this, he says I can assume what I like but he won't be confirming or denying anything. It might be because he thinks it will upset some of his women fans – 'You should see the letters I get, Lynn' – and professionally he thinks ambiguity is an advantage. But when I ask if he might conceivably ever get married, he says no, definitely not, 'It's not on the cards at all.'

He says he would love to be in a full-time relationship and would even give up The Career if necessary (I'm not sure I believe him on this) but he never falls for the right people. 'I've always picked the path of most resistance. Oh, I'm passionate. I wish I was of the mentality that could be cavalier about it – go to a pub, pick someone up – but I'm still looking for the romance. It's got to be the whole thing. Sex is great, don't get me wrong. I *love* sex, but I feel I did all that in my teens

– I did loads of it – and the thing about today's world is that sex is very available, like "You're up for it, let's do it." And I find that it makes me feel worse afterwards than it did before. So I'd rather wait and . . . I mean, it's difficult. I've never got it right yet.'

His fame doesn't help, because many partners are frightened off by it. 'And I also have this sort of camp approach which is sexually terribly unattractive. So, I think the right one is there: they know who they are, and I'm madly in love – but it's a disaster, it will never happen. Oh, it's driven me round the twist . . .'

This relationship has been on-again, off-again for several years. He told *OK!* magazine that the partner couldn't adjust to him being famous. 'Also,' he told me, 'it was fear of rejection on their part, and insecurity, again because of what I do – "You'll get bored with me, Dale" – and I'm thinking, "Oh, give it a try. We've all been hurt." But of course, the older you get, the more baggage people bring with them.'

In the past, he always used to think the reason he wasn't in a relationship was because he was too fat or too broke or lived in a grotty flat. But now he has nothing to blame it on and realizes it must be something more fundamental – a fear of commitment based, presumably, on that 'ultimate rejection' from his mother. 'I don't look any more. I don't look. And the one I talked about before will never happen – that time has come and gone.' But Dale, I said, you just told me you were in love. 'It's very weird that I said that. I often wonder . . . maybe it *is* true.'

But I can see that people must find him very difficult to be with because of this factor of being 'on' all the time. He said one of his old friends complained about it the other day, when they were (guess where?) in a supermarket. 'I was out shopping, thinking "Shall I buy this, shall I buy that?" and there was a woman behind me in the queue. She looked quite nice, so I said to her: "Have you ever bought this? What's it like?" and she said, "Oh, it's quite nice" – so I bought it. When I came out, my friend turned round to me and said: "Dale, *why* do you feel you have to involve everybody? We feel like we're bit players in your performance. The trouble with you, Dale," he said, "is you're never off." To me, you see, it seemed like the most natural thing. But he said, "Ever since I've known you, even before you were well known, you lived your life like that. You've always been larger than life."'

Larger, I wonder, or smaller? Being friend to all the world means being intimate to none. And his eternal sunniness makes one long, sometimes, for a patch of cloud. Is he *always* this cheerful? 'Yes. Because I lost my mother when I was twenty-one, and because the career has gone the way it has done – up and down, up and down – I feel you can throw what you like at me and I'll be happy because one doesn't know how long one's going to be here, or what's going to happen next. So I've always been a happy soul. The only thing that ever brings me down is other people – if my faith in someone is shattered, I find that totally devastating.' And having been devastated once, it won't happen again.

Reproduced by permission of *The Observer*.

Harriet Harman

31 May 1998

A few months ago, Harriet Harman said that maybe she should start a charm offensive. Maybe she should – but she's left it a bit late. And if she was aiming to start it with me, she forgot the key ingredient. Before we met, she got her new director of information, Martin Sixsmith (who used to be the BBC correspondent in Moscow), to ring and sound me out. He was very sweet and apologetic, and said that the secretary of state needed to know what sort of questions I would ask so she could prepare her brief. Oh dear God, no, *please* don't let her prepare a brief! We have all heard her speaking-clock impression. I told Sixsmith as tactfully as I could that I was hoping for something more spontaneous. He said the secretary of state hoped I would ask what she felt she'd achieved in her first year in office. Oh, all right, I sighed – it's like when you interview actors, you know you have to let them plug their latest film – so yes, I said, she could tell me what she'd achieved in her first year of office. 'What's she like, anyway?' I added. Poor Martin Sixsmith! He is, as I say, new to the job and next time he'll know to say 'Wonderful!' without even drawing breath. Instead, he said, after a pause, 'She is actually quite personable.' Oh dear!

In fact, I know what she's like because I met her once before. It was in 1995 and I was interviewing Gordon Brown at Millbank. While he was having his photograph taken, I waited outside his office, chatting to Ed Balls. Suddenly la Harman erupted from her nearby office and gave me a great lecture about how to conduct interviews, and how it was a mistake to expect politicians to be matey. Gordon Brown emerged from his office, looking matey, while she was in mid-flow, but she just ranted on, wasting valuable interview time. It was as if one of the Wimbledon ballboys had piped up to tell Pete Sampras how to serve – Gordon Brown was *quite* capable of looking after himself.

Anyway, this time she started off being friendly. I asked the question she'd requested about how she'd enjoyed her first year in office, and instead of going into a boring lecture about social security, she talked very engagingly about the joys of having civil servants. 'Because, you know, we've all watched *Yes, Minister*, so you expect everyone to be lurking, looking through the slits of the bunkers, waiting to frustrate your every move. So then, when I arrived and opened my day-one brief in its red folder, and saw "New Deal for Lone Parents; Help to the Poorest Pensioners", I thought, "It's amazing! These people think just like I do!" They'd read all my speeches, all my parliamentary questions – it wasn't just the manifesto they'd gone through line by line – and there they were in our first meeting with their pens literally poised to write down and implement what I wanted to do. Sometimes it felt almost spooky!'

Gosh. But once we moved on from the prepared question, it was downhill all the way. Sixsmith had warned me that she wouldn't talk about her private life. Normally, when people say that, it means they won't talk about their family or love life but with Harman, I discovered, it meant much more – she wouldn't talk about her *life*. I asked some very innocuous question about what she remembered as her first political thought, and she said firmly: 'Well, one of the things that, actually, I've never spent much time doing is delving into my own motivation and thinking about my own past. I'm just not a navel gazer. I mean, really, I am chronically not interested in navel gazing. I just find it a bit pompous and wearisome; when I see other people doing it, I think *oh dear!* So I don't really find it terribly easy to answer those questions. I suppose I ought to invent a script of, you know, what made me what I am, but I just don't.'

But why does she have to 'invent a script'? Why can't she just tell the truth? She doesn't, as far as I know, have any skeletons in her cupboard: her life seems boringly normal, though perhaps a bit posh for Labour tastes. She was born in 1950, grew up in St John's Wood, north London, was educated at St Paul's. Her late father was a consultant physician in Harley Street, and her mother a barrister-turned-solicitor who once stood as a Liberal candidate. Lady Longford is her aunt, Lady Antonia Pinter her cousin, her paternal grandmother was one of the first women doctors in the BMA, so it is a family with a tradition of high-achieving women. All four Harman sisters (Harriet is the third) qualified as solicitors. Sarah, the second sister, is currently leading the campaign for women whose cervical smears were misdiagnosed by Kent and Canterbury hospitals. Harriet studied politics at York University but then did law, and worked at Brent Law Centre. 'That's where I found my spiritual and political home. Some people go to university and see the world fall into place, but I saw it fall into place at Brent Law Centre. And then I went to the NCCL [National Council for Civil Liberties], which was brilliant.'

She met her husband, Jack Dromey, while she was in Brent. In those days, he was an 18-stone red-hot trades union activist known as 'Jack of all Disputes', and a leader of the Grunwick strike. Nowadays, he is the much slimmer national secretary of the TGWU. He comes from a very different background to hers – Kilburn-Irish working class, father a road digger, four kids to a bedroom – and once said, rather touchingly, that he never expected to have a daughter who played the piano. When he met Harriet, he was better known than her – nowadays he refers to himself jokingly as 'Mr Harman, né Dromey'. They married in 1982, when she was pregnant with their first child, and now have two boys, aged fifteen and thirteen, and a girl of eleven. The children used to have names but now don't, thanks to a High Court injunction. We know that the eldest is at an opted-out London school; the second son is at a grammar school; the daughter, for all we know, might be at Roedean.

Harman became MP for Peckham in a by-election in 1982 when the sitting MP died. It was good timing – Labour desperately needed more women to promote. Having three babies in her first five years in Parliament might once have counted against her, but in the 'having it all' 1980s, when every other women's magazine article was about juggling career and motherhood, she was just the ticket. In those days – unlike now – she was quite happy to sit on Anne Diamond's sofa with a baby on her lap and chatter about her domestic life. Meanwhile, she whizzed up the fast track from Social Services to Health to Treasury affairs to Employment.

In the 1980s and early 1990s, she was such a bright, shiny New Labour star. She was best friends with Blair and Brown, approved by feminists and loved by the media for her photogenic looks. So what happened? Why does everyone now loathe her? Why is every single political commentator convinced that she will definitely be demoted, or even sacked, in the next Cabinet reshuffle? Basically – to use her favourite word – she has run out of friends. Old Labour always disliked her as a middle-class do-gooder, but went ballistic when she revealed in January 1996 that she was sending one of her sons to grammar school. John Prescott is supposed to have exploded before an ITN interview, 'I am not going to defend any fucking hypocrites,' and Gerry Steinberg, the chairman of Labour's back-bench education committee, resigned in disgust. It was a gift for the Tories: John Major scored a gleeful soundbite telling Blair to be 'tough on hypocrisy, and tough on the causes of hypocrisy'. But Blair supported her – in fact, he really stuck his neck out to defend her. She is often accused of being insufficiently grateful, so – was she grateful? 'He did what he thought was right,' she says sourly. 'And there was a big row.'

But it was the cut in benefits to lone mothers that really ditched her. This was a cut foretold in Labour's manifesto, and largely repaired by the Budget, but it came as a shock to feminists and, of course, to lone mothers. Her own attempts to explain it were completely inept – John Humphrys asked her four times on the *Today* programme whether the cut in benefits was designed to force single mothers into work and she simply recited the same non-answer. From having once been a media asset to the party, she was now a liability. And then, in February this year, she lost her oldest, staunchest ally, Gordon Brown, when she gave an interview to Polly Toynbee in which she appeared to leak Budget details. She was reportedly 'torn limb from limb' in Cabinet and Alastair Campbell was so angry he had to be scraped off the ceiling. He wrote an apoplectic fax telling her to 'enter a period of pre-Budget purdah'. This might be the first time she has been let out since then.

She knows she has a problem with interviews. She thinks it is because she is 'prickly' but a better epithet might be snotty. She can't really see why anyone has the right to ask, let alone know, any more than she chooses to tell them. And she believes (wrongly, in my view) that people ask her questions they would never dream of asking a man. For instance, I asked how she and her husband spent their joint income of £122,000 and she duly freaked. 'It's really, frankly . . . [sputter, sputter] . . . If you go over to Tony and ask him and Cherie what *they* do with their money, and he answers, then I'll answer you. It's just that I'm fed up with not answering these questions on my own behalf, because I feel it's making me look kind of secretive. But perhaps you *would* ask Tony how he spends his money?' 'Yes, of course I would.' 'Anyway, I'm not answering that question.'

Obviously she doesn't have to tell anyone how she spends her money (not on clothes, judging from the outfit she was wearing), but she shouldn't find it amazing to be asked, any more than Tony Blair should. But she has the sort of damn-you-for-your-impudence attitude one expects more from Tories than New Labour. Moreover, she believes that the media have conspired to misrepresent her: 'Some of the descriptions of me I just can't recognize. Thick. Docile. Acquiescing. Walking out. I mean there's a whole load of things that people use to describe me which might be a suitable description to describe *something* but they're not describing *me*.'

Really? 'Thick. Docile. Acquiescing. Walking Out.' Let's start with thick. I asked what degree she got and she said 'Politics'. Once we'd established that she got a 2:1 at York University, I asked why she thought people said she was thick. 'Well, I mean, people do write lots of . . . things. But I've never kind of felt the lack of . . . I mean, I just think it's ridiculous, absolutely ridiculous. I mean, absolutely bizarre. And actually, you know, there's lots of people in politics they say are very clever but there's no evidence of their brains. I mean, at one time I was shadowing William Waldegrave and everyone used to say he was terribly clever, a Fellow of All Souls, but actually I used to look really hard and think, "Where is the evidence of any brain? What is clever about him?" And actually, you know, clever is as clever does. I have never ever had an intellectual inferiority complex.'

Of course, not having an intellectual inferiority complex is not exactly proof that you are clever. But let's continue. What about walking out? This accusation presumably started in February when she, er, removed herself from a *Woman's Hour* interview mid-question. Jenni Murray asked if she was going to be sacked, and she said, 'Must go now. Must, must, must. Bye-ee.' The innocent listener might well have imagined she was walking out – unless, of course, she was running. But, 'I don't walk out. I never walk out. I mean, bombs drop on my head and I carry on, so I never walked out. I could easily have stayed there and just not answered the question. That's my way of avoiding the difficulty and it's not a very good thing to be doing, but I didn't walk out, that's just wrong.' She claims that she told Murray beforehand she could only stay for five minutes, because she had promised to help her son with his GCSEs, and when the five minutes was up, she departed. 'But basically I was in trouble and being criticized, and so I was fair game. And it was a great irony that it was *Woman's Hour*, don't you think?'

Duh? Does she seriously mean that, because she is a woman, *Woman's Hour* is not allowed to attack her? Perhaps we should file this example under Thick. She evinced a similar attitude when we talked about the public reaction to her cuts to lone mothers' benefits. Didn't she anticipate trouble? Evidently not – but it is her explanation for why not that is so amazing. 'For many years I was the sole voice in Parliament speaking up for lone mothers. And therefore I didn't think that people would think that I'd got into government to do down lone parents. But the timing of the machinery of government meant that I was standing there with what looked like a very anti-lone-parents proposal, and I actually thought that people might realize that we had a longer-term view and that there would be a whole range of measures, not all of which we could announce at once. I thought that people would actually recognize that I hadn't turned into somebody different when I came into government. I actually thought that my track record would count for something.'

Trust me, I'm Harriet Harman? It was at this point that I completely lost whatever sympathy I might have had for her. The idea of single mothers sitting around in their council flats saying, 'Well, the money's less, but I know I'll be all right because Harriet Harman is in charge,' is frankly bizarre. I think what she actually means is that she never thought about public reaction at all, and couldn't imagine it if she did. Imagination is not her strong point, and she has lived almost her entire adult life among Labour activists.

But it is accusations of her being 'docile' or 'acquiescent' that seem to annoy her most. Perhaps she realizes – too late – that in being a totally obedient Blairite, she has entirely lost any popularity or personal credibility she might once have had. Time and again, she told me that she was never docile, never acquiescent. And yet, she also told me: 'You know, in the old days in Opposition, the worst thing you could do in a way was to say something that then made a story run. I'll never forget – I was doing a series of local radio interviews, where you sit in a darkened studio, and do lots of different radio stations and we got to Radio Cumbria, and suddenly, at the end, the interviewer asked me something about Sellafield. Now, I kind of knew about it, but I didn't know what the line was – I wasn't doing Environment at the time, or Energy – and I actually thought, "If I say something which creates a frenzy among the environmentalists, or the people working in Sellafield, this will be a real problem." So I kind of felt myself choosing to just sound completely ignorant. Because the people listening might think, "Bloody hell! What an airhead!" but actually it wouldn't go anywhere, it wouldn't cause problems for my colleagues . . . But I think problem-avoidance has meant that sometimes I've created a situation where I look as if I've got a problem myself!'

This must surely be the purest exposition we have ever heard of Mandelsonian politics. You have to know 'the line'. If you don't know the line, you are not allowed to speak. You are not allowed to have views, or even knowledge, of anything outside your brief. Better to fall on your sword and say that you have never *heard* of Sellafield than to express a non-line view about it. It is a remarkable tribute to her docility – though not perhaps to her common sense – that she went along with it so wholeheartedly. And now she complains that she is seen as an automaton.

She thinks all would have been well if she had spent more time 'mingling' with journalists. She thinks it is all a matter of buying them a few drinks. 'You know, there are some people who after work go to the pub, and there are others who just get on with the job and go home. And by and large the people who go to the pub are the ones people think are friendly and nice, and the ones who go home, they just think they're snooty. So – I think I was a bit too utilitarian. Because it is part of the job to be friendly with everybody all around and I never did those edges in a way. I'm not against being clubbable – I just somehow never found that I was doing it. I was doing work and family basically, whereas actually clubbability is part of work.'

Suddenly one has this vision of her civil servants grimly flicking through the diary saying, 'Find twenty minutes for clubbability' and dispatching researchers to find suitable pubs and suitable hacks for her to be clubbable with. In her constituency, she is known as 'Two-Minute Harman' because she is only ever willing to 'look in' at social events for two minutes. She always says in interviews that she is 'utilitarian' and I always assumed this was her being thick and misusing the word the way people misuse simplistic for simple. But actually she was using it absolutely correctly: she can't see the point of anything outside work. When she was forced to take time off with pneumonia in 1989, she said afterwards that it was wonderful because she learned how to use a word processor and 'my output doubled'. She can do 'clubbability' as long as she thinks it's part of her job, but the idea of doing it for pleasure is beyond her ken. As for whether she has any hinterland, any interests outside work and family – oh, why even ask? There are none on record, and I would be amazed if anyone could find any.

Finally, I asked the *Woman's Hour* question – did she expect to be fired? – and she didn't walk out. 'Well, I think there is a kind of fashion of reporting it. But I remember during the school crisis, there was not a single person that didn't write that I was going to get the sack. I never thought I was going to get the sack, but I couldn't help noticing that they were all writing it. There was a *complete* homogeneity of view. And it was wrong. And then, before the election, everybody said that I wouldn't get a job in government, that I was being phased out, being sidelined in the election campaign. And I thought, "That's curious, I don't feel sidelined at all. I feel absolutely worn out going up and down the country and speaking at press conferences." So I think that what's written in the papers doesn't necessarily turn into reality.'

Well, all my political colleagues are 100 per cent convinced that she *will* be sacked in the next reshuffle. Some say that she is already negotiating her move – a face-saving position somewhere out of harm's way. But she has survived before; she *could* survive again. If I were Tony Blair, I would keep her as a tasty morsel to throw to the lions much nearer the next election. It is quite useful for a prime minister to have the odd thick, docile, acquiescent minister to do the unpopular work of government. Oh sorry – she's not thick, docile, acquiescent, she told me so – I forgot.

Reproduced by permission of *The Observer*.

Richard E. Grant

9 November 1997

This article originally began 'I have lost my heart to an actor!' I'd spent two hours with Richard E. Grant at a Soho club, liked him enormously and decided that, despite my habitual misgivings about actors, he was a thoroughly good egg. I already admired him as a writer (from his *With Nails* film diaries) and, after what seemed a very enjoyable and frank conversation, I liked him as a person. This sunny state lasted all of three days. Then his PR rang to say that Richard had so much hated being interviewed by me, he had refused to do any more interviews. *What?* The bastard, the creep, the treacherous two-faced slimeball! How could he smile and laugh and be so friendly and then turn round and say he hated me? Because he's an actor, dummy. How could I have forgotten?

A flurry of phone calls and faxes ensued. Officially, his complaint was that I hadn't asked enough about the film he was meant to be plugging, *Keep the Aspidistra Flying* (from the George Orwell novel), which opens the London Film Festival this week. I'd asked him two questions – quite enough in my view. I asked if he liked George Orwell – he said not much, but he thought Alan Plater's screenplay improved on the novel which he found 'relentlessly nihilistic'. I asked if he'd enjoyed making the film and he laughed and said, 'I did! Yes! . . . Have you ever met an actor who said, "No, I hated every minute"?' He also said he'd seen the film a couple of days before and found it 'gruesome' but he quickly explained that he meant not the film, but his own performance – he claims he always hates seeing himself acting and can't even bear to watch *Withnail and I*. He said he'd gone into a 'big old droop' afterwards, till his wife got impatient with him. Perhaps this should have been a warning of his mood swings.

What he was *really* upset about was that I asked him about a *News of the World* interview with his brother, which we shall get on to later. Almost anyone who has been a star for a decade, as he has, can expect to attract the odd heel-biting from the tabloids. Very often it's some disaffected relative or discarded lover coming out of the woodwork to give their version of events. It doesn't mean it's gospel. But it means that it's there, on the record, and can't be ignored.

But let's forget the aftermath for the time being and go back to that enjoyable morning in Soho when he was so friendly and likeable. And handsome, of course – he turned forty this year, but still looks much the same Withnail. We did the photographs first – Harry Borden made him swap trousers because he thought his own black ones would be better than Richard's blue jeans – anyone who wanted to be starry and difficult could well have thrown a fit at that point but Richard was fine. While doing the photographs, we chatted about Twickenham, where he lives and I grew up.

He told me he is writing a novel set in Hollywood and had just spent a fortnight staying with his friend Steve Martin (they correspond daily by e-mail – Martin's nickname for him is Relentless), doing background research. He has written three chapters so far and has to finish it by next spring. He is also writing a screenplay about his native Swaziland which, ideally, he would like to direct but not act in. And then there is his *Spice Girls Diary* about the making of the Spice Girls film in which he plays their manager. He says he has never been so much in demand – *everyone* wants to buy the diary and his agent (the fearsome Andrew Wylie) is going to hold an auction. I reminded him that it was the *Observer*'s arts editor, Jane Ferguson, who launched his literary career – she commissioned him to write a diary about the making of *Prêt-à-Porter*, which had publishers falling over themselves to sign him up. He said he was eternally grateful to *The Observer* – but alas didn't offer to do a special cheap deal on the *Spice Girls Diary*. (Who cares about the crummy old Spice Girls anyway!)

Even now I gnash my teeth at the mention of his name, I still think that Richard E. Grant is a brilliant writer. He writes well about himself, of course, but he is also very observant – the portrait of Sandra Bernhard is his *With Nails* diary is really fine. And there is an energy in his writing that any professional writer would envy, with barely a slack sentence anywhere. It is easy to dismiss *With Nails* as the rantings of a self-obsessed lunatic luvvie, but I can't think of anyone who has conveyed the mindset of the lunatic luvvie better.

I told him sincerely, but perhaps not very tactfully, that I wished he would concentrate on writing, not because I don't think he's a good actor (though in truth I'm not sure – he seems a bit mannered to me but I'm a lousy judge) but I *am* sure that he's an unusually gifted natural writer. 'Oh thank you!' he said. 'You've just basted me with a big buttery compliment!' (See what I mean? Alpha metaphor.) And he said, promisingly, that he found writing his novel 'one hundred times more satisfying than anything I've done on screen'. But alas, he is hooked on acting – he loves the intense, intimate contact with other actors and dislikes the loneliness of writing. As a child in Swaziland, he made his own cardboard theatre and wrote a play at the age of eight, then progressed to having a proper marionette theatre in the garage.

He joined an amateur dramatic society while in his teens, went on to read drama at university, started his own (multi-racial) theatre troupe, and finally came to England to tread the boards in 1982. Joel Silver once asked him why he wanted to act and he said, 'Revenge! To prove to all those little fuckers who said, "You can't, you'll never make it," that I could.'

His first film, *Withnail and I*, made him a star in 1986 – the trouble is that he has never really surpassed it. He had a wonderful cameo in Robert Altman's *The Player*, as a desperate scriptwriter pitching a script, but then he committed the Hollywood crime of being in a mega-turkey, *Hudson Hawk*. He admits he did it for the money – normally he doesn't care about money – and has paid the price since. He was also in the disappointing *Prêt-à-Porter*, and the even more disappointing Jane Campion film, *Portrait of a Lady*. Since then, his film career has looked pretty patchy and Hollywood is not exactly clamouring. But he has four films in the pipeline – *Aspidistra*, *The Serpent's Kiss* with Ewan McGregor and Greta Scacchi, which is an official selection for next year's Cannes Film Festival, a Robert Louis Stevenson swashbuckler with Miranda Richardson, and *Spice: The Movie*, out on Boxing Day. So one or other of them should revive his fortunes.

Let's go back to the very beginning: his childhood in Swaziland. In his diary, and in interviews over the years, he has painted a truly idyllic picture of the country, 'the Switzerland of Africa', and his beautiful home overlooking the Ezulweni valley, which the Swazis call 'Valley of Heaven'. His father was the minister for education under the British and so popular with the Swazis that they asked him to stay on after independence in 1968. The family enjoyed a comfortable, old-fashioned lifestyle, with three indoor and three outdoor servants, and lots of entertaining. Richard's mother Leonie Hogan remembers it as 'terribly colonial and slightly decadent'. Richard is still deeply attached to Swaziland, revisits it often, has many friends there and wears two watches, one set to Swazi time. His set piece for auditions, when asked to sing, used to be a stunning rendition of the Swazi national anthem.

The first hiccup in what had so far been a pleasant conversation came when I asked Richard about his name. In early interviews, he always said that he simply inserted an E in his name because there was another Richard Grant in Equity. But last year his brother revealed that their real surname was Esterhuysen. I asked if it was an Afrikaner name (their father's forenames were Hendrik Abraham) but Richard said no, the Afrikaner or Dutch spelling was Esterhuizen, and his father told him it was Hungarian originally. He changed his name at university because, 'They said: "If you don't speak Afrikaans" – which I didn't – "you ought to use your second name because otherwise people might expect you to be bilingual."' Still, it seemed an oddly touchy subject. When I remarked casually that he didn't look very English, he snapped, 'I don't know. You tell me. So I've been fraudulently playing all these English people all these years?'

Stuart Esterhuysen's *News of the World* interview revealed a lot more than just their surname – mainly his extraordinary difference from Richard. He is two years younger than his brother, works as an accountant and specializes in liquidations, is newly married and lives in Johannesburg. He emerges as Mr Conventional: 'I think anyone who goes to see hippie films like *Withnail and I* must be dodgy,' he opines. As a child, he said, 'I would call him [Richard] a pansy for playing with puppets and he'd shout at me for wandering around in rugby shorts.' He says that, 'Richard was more like an estranged sister to me than a brother. We were never, ever close.'

They went to different schools – Richard to Swaziland's equivalent of Bedales and Stuart to Durban – and to different universities – Richard to the University of Cape Town to do drama, Stuart to Pietermaritzburg to do accountancy. The last time they saw each other was at their father's funeral in 1981 when, Stuart claims, 'He had the nerve to arrive at this sober, dignified funeral with bright orange hair. As far as I'm concerned, that was just downright disrespectful.' Stuart has never met Richard's wife but he nevertheless told the *News of the World*, 'From what I've seen, she's a complete dog.'

Richard confirms that they were never close – 'My father always said we were chalk and cheese' – and that even though he visits his mother in Johannesburg, she never suggests a meeting with his brother. 'She doesn't ever talk about him, to be honest. Oh, she did tell me that he'd got married. Whether she tells *him* about me, I couldn't tell you.' Would he quite like to see his brother? 'No.'

It occurred to me that his brother was probably more typical of the boys they grew up with and that perhaps playing with puppets did make you a 'pansy' in Swaziland. 'Yes,' Richard laughs, 'having a marionette theatre was a terrible indictment of your manhood! But I wasn't bullied or tormented for doing so. I suppose the most taunting thing was if somebody said, "Why do you have puppets? Are they doll substitutes?" But as soon as they discovered that I was earning *money* out of doing puppet shows, then that explained everything.'

Seriously, though, did he or anyone worry that he might be gay? 'God, I've never been asked that question before. I was involved in this amateur theatre club that was thriving when I was living there, and most of the English people in the club were either civil servants or electricians or UN workers, apart from a hairdresser called Paul who had purple hair and seemed a thousand years old – he was the only person I can remember, in all my growing up years, who was identifiably different, and that people said, "Oh, he's a bit of a pansy!" I suppose Swaziland, when I was growing up, was in a time warp, at least ten or fifteen years behind the rest of the world. Put it this way – there were so many people with very distinct idiosyncrasies, there were lots of them who were very, very odd. Everybody knew everybody, it was a very small, gossip-ridden society, like Hollywood, so I suppose people were accepted for who and what and how they were. Much more important was the social pecking order, of where you lived, and where your position was in the hierarchy. And the amount of shagging that went on! Paul-the-hairdresser's life was completely celibate, so if I think of somebody being a role model . . . !'

Anyway, this Happy Valley idyll was shattered when he was eleven and his mother ran off to South Africa with a mining engineer, leaving her two sons behind. It was a huge scandal in Swaziland: 'Everyone had affairs, but they didn't get divorced. Being the only person in the class with divorced parents was *such* a stigma, and because of my father's social position, it was really compounded.' To make matters worse, the mining engineer and his wife were friends of the family, and Richard and Stuart played with their children. His mother disappeared almost literally overnight. 'She did tell us she was leaving, but she told me at six o'clock in the morning – "I'm off, today" – without any prewarning. It seemed so brutal at the time, but how *do* you tell someone, how do you prepare someone? I mean, is it better to say, "I'm leaving in three weeks' time?" I don't know.' His father, who was deeply in love with her, 'fell apart . . . I was forced almost to parent my parent.' His father got custody of the children and thereafter Richard only saw his mother once a month and in alternate school holidays.

It is very striking in *With Nails* that, while he often talks lovingly about his father (who died of cancer in 1981), he never mentions his mother. In fact, they are now on good terms – she came over for his fortieth birthday – but he admits that for years he felt bitter resentment. 'I've come to terms with all that because nothing is ever so cut and dried. And I know, being married, that it's cause and effect. So – if she was unhappy in her marriage, then to have stuck with it is torture that you shouldn't endure, and I think her logic was that it would be more upheaving to take the children away from everything they knew than if she just left. But I couldn't see that for *years* and years, and certainly there was a time when I found it very, very difficult.'

The mining engineer soon went back to his wife, but Richard's mother stayed on in South Africa; she married someone else five years later. His father also remarried, six months after the divorce, and Richard got on well with his stepmother. 'So I think that – God, it sounds so reasoned and mature to say all this! – but I do see that it hasn't been all disaster, doom and gloom. Although ideally I would have preferred that my parents hadn't split up.'

He says in *With Nails* that his parents' divorce made such a profound impression that he resolved never to marry himself. I wondered what he planned to do – was he going to be a great philanderer? 'I hadn't really thought that through. I knew what I *wasn't* going to do but I hadn't thought what I was. I had never fallen in love with anyone, really. I'd had mad passions about people, fixations on them, but I know that I'd never really fallen in love. And because that hadn't happened, I thought it was something that filled up three-minute hot spots, I thought it was a cheesy thing that happened in romantic films, that didn't really exist in real life.'

And then, a few months after arriving in England in 1982, he met Joan Washington. She was an actors' dialect coach, eight years older than him, unhappily married with a seven-year-old son, Tom, when he first went to one of her classes at the Actors' Centre. Later, he asked her to teach him a Belfast accent, and she asked him to record some Zulu 'with all the clicks' to help another actor. And suddenly they were in love. I asked if the fact that she was older and already had a child somehow made it easier for him to take the risk of marriage? 'No, it put me off. It put me off completely. If we could have been the same age and she could have never been married before, that would have been so much easier, because then there would be no complication. According to the plan that I had in my head, she was the *last* person that was suitable. But then – love truly is blind!'

He says the age gap was never a problem – he only ever thinks about it when asked in interviews – except when it came to having babies. Joan had three miscarriages, and then a daughter who was born prematurely and lived less than an hour. The gynaecologist advised her not to attempt pregnancy again, because the risks were increasing sharply every year. Richard's attitude was, 'Oh well, that's it, somebody's saying, literally, Biological Clock Time.' He told Joan, 'You have a child by your first marriage, it's really not something that I feel that strongly about.' But she was very determined. 'And we went through the exact same horror show again because at exactly the same point, at seven months, she was rushed into hospital and it was sort of touch and go for weeks – absolutely terrible. You think, what did you put yourself through all this for? But, as soon as you have a child and it's normal, then you forget all that stuff.' Their daughter, Olivia, is now eight, and he says he barely remembers his life before he had a child: 'It seems like a previous existence.'

I wondered whether he really thought of himself as having two children, one who died, or whether the child who lives sort of subsumes the one who died? 'It does, because . . . I heard my first child cry but then she died after half an hour . . . But every day I drive past the cemetery where she is buried and I never drive by and don't think of that. It's not morbid or self-pitying, it's just something that you don't forget. But I think I would feel differently if I didn't have the daughter that I do have. And she knows that. We haven't dwelt on it but she is aware of what her sister's name was and how old she would have been: every now and then, she asks: "How old would she have been now?" And she says, "Oh, it would be nice to have a big sister."'

He is a devoted father, who makes it a rule never to spend more than four weeks away from home. In *With Nails*, he recounts how, after a long stint filming in Los Angeles, he flew home, collected Olivia and took her to Swaziland to revisit his childhood. I'm sure that his childhood is the key to everything, but I can't quite unlock it. I tracked down someone who knew him in Swaziland, but Richard forbade her to speak to me. Like many actors, he is self-invented, right down to his name. His brother told the *News of the World*, 'I really don't know who the real Richard is. He's been playing different roles his whole life . . . He knows I see through the posh accent and the acting.'

I *thought* I knew him after the interview, but then came that phone call from his PR and it all went belly-up. Perhaps I should have been more attentive to the hints he dropped – I realized when I listened to the tape again that there were some signs that he was having *doubts*. He said at one point that people have different agendas and, 'If I had to write down my experience of being here with you this morning, it's not going to be the same as what *you* would write down.' And I noticed belatedly that whenever I asked him a question he didn't like, his invariable response was, 'Oh, I've never been asked that before.'

Unfortunately it was far too polite a reproach to make any impression at the time.

One problem throughout the interview was that he kept asking *me* questions: 'Are you divorced?' (No.) 'Are your parents divorced?' (No.) 'How would you describe yourself if you were going on a blind date?' (Duh.) I was quite amused and flattered at first, but then got irritated because it was wasting so much time, and finally told him not to do it. But apparently he always asks questions – he said when he edited his diary for publication, he realized there was a constant refrain of people telling him, 'You ask too many questions.' I don't understand why he does it. Is it meant to be disarming, 'bonding'? But I always suspect with actors that the only question they're really interested in is, 'What do you think of *me*?'

So what do I conclude about Richard E. Grant? Just . . . bafflement. Perhaps I hit him at a bad moment when he felt insecure about his performance in *Aspidistra*. I must admit I didn't rave to him about the film as polite interviewers are supposed to do.

But at the time, at the time, all my better instincts told me we were getting on swimmingly. I found him completely delightful while I was with him, and I'm sure so would you, and you, and you – but when he's alone in a room . . . Who knows?

Reproduced by permission of *The Observer*.